ORTEOUS

DANIEL

old
Test
ament
lib
rary

NORMAN PORTEOUS

DANIEL

A Commentary

SECOND, REVISED, EDITION

SCM PRESS LTD

In grateful memory of
Adam C. Welch
and
Godfrey R. Driver

334 00292 3

First published 1965
by SCM Press Ltd
58 Bloomsbury Street, London, WC1
Reprinted 1972, 1974
Second, revised edition 1979

Printed in Great Britain by
Redwood Burn Limited
Trowbridge and Esher

CONTENTS

PREFACE TO THE SECOND EDITION

THIS COMMENTARY on the Book of Daniel originally appeared in 1962 as Volume 23 of the German series of commentaries *Das Alte Testament Deutsch* (ATD) and in 1965 in English in the the Old Testament Library series. The decision of the German publishers to issue a third edition has given the author the opportunity to make a number of corrections and brief additions to the text. Since the book was first published, however, a number of outstanding commentaries have appeared, especially those of Plöger, Delcor and Lacocque and, unfortunately published too late to be used, the Anchor Bible commentary of Hartman and di Lella. Further, the historical period to which the Book of Daniel belongs has been splendidly illuminated by the work of Martin Hengel. As an alternative to the rewriting of the commentary the addition of a substantial Supplement has made it possible for the author to take some account of important new developments and to indicate his positive or negative reaction to them. He is glad in this way to acknowledge his indebtedness to colleagues who have enriched his own knowledge and stimulated him to further thought.

The author would like also to recall how much he owes to the late Professor Dr A. Weiser, former Joint Editor of the ATD series, to Professor Dr W. Beyerlin who made the original translation into German with the help of Dr R. Walz and, for the second edition, of Professor K. Seybold. To Professor Dr O. Kaiser, one of the new editors, he would express a quite special word of thanks for his skilful and ungrudging help and generous encouragement. His warm thanks are also due to the Editor of the SCM Press for so willingly making possible a new English edition.

Owing to the special character of this commentary with its theological slant it is assumed that students of the Book of Daniel will turn to other commentaries for much of the linguistic, textual, historical and religious-historical information which could not find a place here. The English reader is particularly well served in this respect. The author is deeply indebted to the various well-known writings of

7

H. H. Rowley, to the philological suggestions of G. R. Driver and, in a quite special way, to A. C. Welch's *Visions of the End* (1922, reprinted 1958), a book distinguished by a rare spiritual insight.

NORMAN W. PORTEOUS

Edinburgh, August 1978

ABBREVIATIONS

ANET	*Ancient Near Eastern Texts*[2], 1955
BASOR	*Bulletin of the American Schools of Oriental Research*
BJRL	*Bulletin of the John Rylands Library*
BZAW	Beihefte zur *ZAW*
Camb. B.	Cambridge Bible for Schools and Colleges
Cent. B.	Century Bible
EB	*Expositor's Bible*
HAT	Handkommentar zum Alten Testament
HUCA	*Hebrew Union College Annual*
IB	*Interpreter's Bible*
ICC	International Critical Commentary
JBL	*Journal of Biblical Literature*
JTS	*Journal of Theological Studies*
KHAT	Kurzer Handkommentar zum Alten Testament
OS	*Oudtestamentische Studien*
RB	*Revue Biblique*
SBT	Studies in Biblical Theology
ThR	*Theologische Rundschau*
ThSK	*Theologische Studien und Kritiken*
ThZ	*Theologische Zeitschrift* (Basel)
TLZ	*Theologische Literaturzeitung*
VT	*Vetus Testamentum*
VTS	*Vetus Testamentum* Supplements
ZAW	*Zeitschrift für die Alttestamentliche Wissenschaft*

BIBLIOGRAPHY

COMMENTARIES

A. A. Bevan, 1892; G. Behrmann (HAT), 1894; F. W. Farrar (*EB*), 1895; J. D. Prince, 1899; S. R. Driver (Camb. B.), 1900; K. Marti (KHAT), 1901; W. Baumgartner, 1926; J. A. Montgomery (ICC), 1927; R. H. Charles, 1929 (and Cent. B.); A. Bentzen (Handbuch zum AT), 1952; E. W. Heaton (Torch Comm.), 1956; A. Jeffery (*IB*), 1956; J. Barr in *Peake's Commentary on the Bible*, 1962

OTHER LITERATURE

W. Baumgartner, 'Ein Vierteljahrhundert Danielforschung', *ThR* 11, 1939, pp. 59–83, 125–44, 201–28; 'Zu den vier Reichen von Daniel 2', *ThZ* 1945, pp. 17–22

A. Bentzen, *Messias-Moses redivivus-Menschensohn*, 1948 (Engl. transl.: *King and Messiah*, 1955); *Introduction to the Old Testament²*, 1952

E. R. Bevan, *The House of Seleucus*, 2 vols., 1902; *A History of Egypt under the Ptolemaic Dynasty*, 1927; *Jerusalem under the High Priests*, 1904

E. Bickermann, *Der Gott der Makkabäer*, 1937

W. Bousset-H. Gressmann, *Die Religion des Judentums im Späthellenistischen Zeitalter*, 1926

M. Burrows, *More Light on the Dead Sea Scrolls*, 1958

F. L. Cross, *The Ancient Library of Qumrân and Modern Biblical Studies*, 1958

R. P. Dougherty, *Nabonidus and Belshazzar*, 1929

S. R. Driver, *Introduction to the Literature of the Old Testament*, ⁹1913

O. Eissfeldt, *Einleitung in das Alte Testament²*, 1956; ³1964 (Engl. transl.: *Introduction to the Old Testament*, 1965); 'Die Menetekel-Inschrift und ihre Deutung', *ZAW* 63, 1951, pp. 105–14

J. A. Emerton, 'The Origin of the Son of Man Imagery', *JTS* New Series IX/2, 1958, pp. 225–42

D. N. Freedman, 'The Prayer of Nabonidus', *BASOR* 145, Feb. 1957, pp. 31–32

S. B. Frost, *Old Testament Apocalyptic*, 1952

A. von Gall, *ΒΑΣΙΛΕΙΑ ΤΟΥ ΘΕΟΥ*, 1926

G. L. Ginsberg, *Studies in the Book of Daniel*, 1948

H. Hölscher, 'Die Entstehung des Buches Daniel', *ThSK* 92, 1919, pp. 113ff.

C. Kuhl, *Die drei Männer im Feuer*, BZAW 55, 1930; *Die Entstehung des Alten Testaments*, 1953 (Engl. transl.: *The Old Testament: its origins and composition*, 1961)

A. Lods, *Histoire de la Littérature Hebraique et Juive*, 1950

W. Lüthi, *Die kommende Kirche: die Botschaft des Propheten Daniel*[3], 1937 (Engl. transl.: *The Church to Come*, 1939)

T. W. Manson, 'The Son of Man in Daniel, Enoch and the Gospels', *BJRL* 32, 1950, pp. 171–93

G. F. Moore, *Judaism*, I–III, 1927–30

S. Mowinckel, *Han som kommer*, 1951 (Engl. transl.: *He that cometh* 1956)

M. Noth, 'Zur Komposition des Buches Daniel', *ThSK* 98-99, 1926, pp. 143ff.; *Geschichte Israels*[2], 1960 (Engl. transl.[2], 1960); 'The Understanding of History in Old Testament Apocalyptic' and 'The Holy Ones of the Most High' in *The Laws in the Pentateuch and Other Studies*, Engl. transl. 1966, pp. 194–214 and 215–28

G. von Rad, *Old Testament Theology* II, Engl. transl. 1965

H. H. Rowley, *Darius the Mede and the Four World Empires in the Book of Daniel*, 1935; *The Aramaic of the Old Testament*, 1929; 'The Bilingual Problem in Daniel', *ZAW* 9, 1932, pp. 256–68 (for other literature on the linguistic problem of Daniel see Bentzen's Commentary, pp. 12–13); *The Relevance of Apocalyptic*[2], 1947; *The Unity of the Book of Daniel* (*HUCA* Anniversary Publications, 1950–51, pp. 233–79), republished in *The Servant of the Lord and Other Essays on the Old Testament*, 1952; 'The Composition of the Book of Daniel', *VT* V/3, 1955, pp. 272–6

D. S. Russell, *Between the Testaments*, 1960; *The Method and Message of Jewish Apocalyptic*, 1964

E. Schürer, *Geschichte des jüdischen Volkes im Zeitalter Jesu Christi*[4] 1901–9

E. K. T. Sjöberg, *Der Menschensohn im Äthiopischen Henochbuch*, 1946

P. Volz, *Die Eschatologie der jüdischen Gemeinde im Neutestamentlichen Zeitalter*, 1934

A. Weiser, *Einleitung in das Alte Testament*[2], 1956, [5]1963 (Engl. transl.: *Introduction to the Old Testament*, 1961)

A. C. Welch, *Visions of the End: a study in Daniel and Revelation*, 1922

ADDITIONS TO BIBLIOGRAPHY

COMMENTARIES

O. Plöger (Kommentar zum Alten Testament), 1965; M. Delcor (Sources Bibliques), 1971; A. Lacocque (Commentaire de l'Ancien Testament), 1976

OTHER LITERATURE

M. Black, 'The Son of Man Problem in Recent Research and Debate *BJRL* 45, 1963, 305–18; *An Aramaic Approach to the Gospels and Acts*, with Appendix by G. Vermes, ³1967

C. H. W. Brekelmans, 'The Saints of the Most High and their Kingdom', *OS*, Deel XIV, 1965, 305–29

J. J. Collins, *The Apocalyptic Vision of the Book of Daniel*, Harvard Semitic Monographs 16, 1977

J. Coppens, *Miscellanées bibliques* XXVIII–XXXI, *Analecta Lovaniensia Biblica et Orientialia*, Ser. iv, Fasc. 8

G. R. Driver, 'Sacred Numbers and Round Figures' in *Promise and Fulfilment* (Essays presented to S. H. Hooke), 1963, 62–90

O. Eissfeldt, 'Daniels und seiner drei Gefährten Laufbahn im babylonischen medischen und persischen Dienst', *ZAW* 72, 1960, 134–48

A. Feuillet, 'Le Fils de l'Homme de Daniel et la tradition biblique', *RB* 60, 1953, 170–202, 321–46

G. L. Ginsberg, 'The Oldest Interpretation of the Suffering Servant', *VT* III/4, 1953, 400–4

M. Hengel, *Judentum und Hellenismus*, ²1973 (Engl. trans.: *Judaism and Hellenism* I-II, 1974)

K. Koch, *Ratlos vor der Apokalyptik*, 1970 (Engl. trans.: *The Rediscovery of Apocalyptic*, SBT 2.22, 1972)

O. Plöger, *Theokratie und Eschatologie* ²1962 (Engl. trans.: *Theocracy and Eschatology*, 1964)

D. Rössler, *Gesetz und Geschichte*, 1960

A. Szörényi, 'Das Buch Daniel, ein kanonisierter Pescher?' *VTS* 15, 1966, 278–94

INTRODUCTION

THE BOOK OF DANIEL contains twelve chapters, the first six containing stories about a Jewish captive, Daniel, and his three young compatriots at the court of Nebuchadnezzar and his successors Babylonian, Median and Persian, and the last six containing a series of visions which came to Daniel and were interpreted to him by angelic agency. The first of the visions (ch. 7) has its parallel in Nebuchadnezzar's dream (ch. 2) and links the two parts together. Another feature of the book is that ch. 2.4a–ch. 7 is in a late (not earlier than third century BC, perhaps second century) dialect of Aramaic, while the rest of the book is in late Hebrew. The linguistic evidence and the fact that the visions reveal a vague knowledge of the Babylonian and Persian periods and an increasingly accurate knowledge of the Greek period up to and including the reign of Antiochus Epiphanes, with the exception of the closing events of that reign, suggest a date for the book shortly before 164 BC. The only element of genuine prophecy relates to the anticipated death of Antiochus and the expected intervention of God in the establishment of his kingdom. Everything else that is 'revealed' to Daniel is history viewed in retrospect either in symbol or as interpreted to Daniel or, in one case, by Daniel to a heathen king.

The status of the Book of Daniel was variously assessed in ancient times. The Palestinian Jewish Canon placed it among the Writings (*Kethubhim*, Hagiographa), i.e. in the third division of the Old Testament books, and not among the Latter Prophets as in the Greek Canon, which, whether or not Kahle is right as to its origin, was determinative for the early Christian view of the book. A clue to this is given in Matt. 24.15 where Daniel is referred to as a prophet who foretells something that is still future in the time of Christ. The so-called 'abomination of desolation', of which Daniel spoke, when set up in the holy place, will be one of the signs of the end. Josephus, however, makes it clear by implication (*Antiq.* XII.7.6) that the reference in the Book of Daniel was to something that happened during the reign of Antiochus IV Epiphanes in the second century BC. Both in Matthew and in Daniel, on the other hand, an individual

living in Babylon during the exile is represented as prophesying
events hundreds of years ahead and, so long as that was accepted as
historical fact, there would seem to be no compelling reason why the
book should not be classified among the Prophets. Josephus, indeed,
maintained that Daniel actually surpassed the other prophets by not
only prophesying of future events, but also determining the time of
their accomplishment (*Antiq.* X.11.7). For reasons which we can only
guess at Rabbinic Judaism, while not denying the inspiration and
value of the Book of Daniel, did not include it in the prophetic
Canon. It may have suffered from its resemblance to the other
apocalyptic books which were excluded from the Palestinian Canon
and, with the exception of II Esd., also from the Greek Canon. What
saved it from sharing their fate may have been its emphasis upon
Daniel's loyalty to the precepts of the Jewish Law. But, though it
was retained, there may have been some tradition among the Rabbis
that the book had appeared as late as the second century and that
would offset its claim to be regarded as prophetic. In the third
century AD the neo-Platonist Porphyry, as we know from Jerome,
maintained the modern critical view that the Book of Daniel was
Maccabaean.

In accordance with the form-critical method of approach, there
has been much discussion as to the proper classification of the book.
The most obvious line to take is to regard it as a sample of the class
apocalypse (from Greek ἀποκάλυψις, revelation) and group it with
books like Enoch, the Testaments of the Twelve Patriarchs, Baruch,
the Assumption of Moses, II Esdras and even Christian apocalypses
like the Ascension of Isaiah and the Book of Revelation (this
last-named book, however, breaking with the habit of pseudonymity). There are sundry elements in these books, however, which
either do not or scarcely appear in the Book of Daniel and a writer
as wise and discerning as A. C. Welch (*Visions of the End*, p. 129) has
uttered the caution that in certain respects 'it may be wiser . . . to
interpret Daniel from his predecessors rather than from his successors.' It is true that certain sections of the prophetic literature show
characteristics which link them with the later apocalyptic literature
(e.g. Ezek. 38–39; Zech., especially the visions in 1–8, and Deutero-
Zech.; Joel 3; Isa. 24–27) in some of its more bizarre features. The
Book of Daniel reveals these traits only in part, but, what is much
more important, it shares with the oracles of the great eighth- and
seventh- and sixth-century prophets the view that history has an end

which will be brought about by God and that, when that consummation comes, there will be a judgment which will make manifest who
are on God's side and who are at enmity with God. Certain of the
alleged differences between the Book of Daniel and the great prophets
of Israel are actually developments of the prophetic teaching adapted
to a later time. If the early prophets pronounced doom upon Israel
for its sin, whereas the Book of Daniel is concerned with the doom that
is about to overwhelm the nations, it should not be forgotten that the
saints of the Most High, to whom the sovereignty is to be given, are
not Israel as a whole, but those who, in the crisis which was initiated,
not by Antiochus Epiphanes, but by the hellenizing Jews who invited
his intervention (I Macc. 1.11ff.), stood their ground bravely and
refused to compromise.

S. B. Frost (*Old Testament Apocalyptic*, especially ch. 3) has argued
that apocalyptic came into existence as a result of the blending of
myth and eschatology and that this took place from the time of the
exile onwards. But, while it is true that Frost places his finger on one
of the important features of apocalyptic, the blend of which he speaks
began much earlier than he supposes and his tendency to relegate to
the post-exilic period passages in the pre-exilic prophets which do not
fit his theory must be carefully scrutinized.

Another attempt at the classification of the book is that of A.
Bentzen (in *Daniel*, Handbuch z. A.T., Erste Reihe 19) and elaborated by E. W. Heaton (in Torch Commentary on Daniel) who is
anxious to avoid limiting the author of the Book of Daniel to the
prophetic apocalyptic tradition, which we have been examining, and
tries to represent him as standing in the main stream of normal
Judaism. The author is represented as a scribe, a man of learning,
belonging to the sect of the Ḥasidim who were opposed to any compromise with Hellenism and adhered to the Maccabaean resistance
movement until they became convinced of its essentially secular
character. He is compared and contrasted with Jesus ben Sira, the
author of Ecclesiasticus, and it is suggested that Ecclus 39.1–5 might
almost be regarded as furnishing the hints which were elaborated into
the stories of the Book of Daniel. On the other hand it is admitted that
the author of the Book of Daniel wrote in a period of crisis, whereas the author of Ecclesiasticus did not. Yet, in spite of this contrast, it is
argued, the Book of Daniel can most properly be classified as a
wisdom book, Daniel himself being an example of a man who,
through his obedience to God and his reliance upon him, has the

divine wisdom put at his disposal and so has no difficulty in defeating
the wise men of Babylon on their own ground.

Yet, however much the Book of Daniel draws upon wisdom
material, easy as it is to enumerate ways in which the Book of Daniel
differs from the later apocalypses and cannot be regarded as a typical
specimen of apocalyptic literature (see Welch, *op. cit.*, pp. 101f.),
Heaton's contention that to accept the book uncritically as apocalyptic is 'to divert our attention from the particular historical crisis which
called it forth', really turns against himself. The Wisdom literature
concerns itself with general problems of human concern, whereas the
apocalyptic form of writing relates itself more easily to particular
historical crises. It is certainly possible and even helpful to take the
stories contained in Dan. 1–6 and compare them with stories like
Tobit, the tale of the three youths in I Esd. 3.1–4.42, Esther and
Judith and the apocryphal additions to Daniel, viz. the history of
Susanna, the double story of Bel and the Dragon, and also the
international romance of Aḥiḳar. It is also possible and for certain
purposes legitimate to set the parables of Jesus alongside the stories
in the Haggada and point out parallels. Something vital, however,
is missed if we overlook the urgency that is communicated to stories
by their being brought into connection with the imminent kingdom
of God. It may or may not be (good arguments can be adduced on
both sides of the debate) that the stories in Daniel came into existence
and circulated perhaps as early as the third century B C illustrating
frequently recurring situations in the Diaspora. As we now have these
stories, however, they are intended by the author of the book to
illustrate the qualities of loyalty and endurance which the crisis of the
second century B C called for. They can indeed help us to realize the
urgency of the challenge which comes to us all, but they do so because they speak to us out of the urgency of a particular historical
situation.

Perhaps the wisest course is to take the Book of Daniel as a distinc-
tive piece of literature with a clearly defined witness of its own, and
to take note of the various ways in which it borrows from and is
coloured by the earlier prophetic literature, the Wisdom literature
and the Psalms and has its successors in the apocalypses, though these
often exhibit an extravagance and a fantastic imagination which is
less prominent in the Book of Daniel. It is quite true that in the
ancient world the different types of literature were traditional and
developed easily distinguishable characteristics which tended to limit

an author's liberty of invention. As time went on, however, and particularly after the exile the lines of division became blurred and mixed forms became commoner. When one remembers too that the scribes and wise men must have had much to do with the instruction of the people, it is not surprising that a book like the Book of Daniel reveals indebtedness to the Wisdom literature and indeed makes a point of the superiority of Israel's wisdom since it has a divine origin. There is truth in Heaton's assertion (*op. cit.*, p. 44): 'It is evident that by the time of Ben Sira (*c.* 180 B C), the sages had become the students, guardians and teachers of the *whole* Jewish tradition and that *all* Hebrew literature was now by adoption and interpretation the wisdom of the scribe.' At the same time, in spite of all resemblances, it is important to recognize that the difference between the Book of Daniel and, let us say, the Book of Ecclesiasticus is a difference of kind. In the Book of Daniel something of the old prophetic inspiration is present again confronting the challenge of a new day. It may have incorporated wisdom material, that is to say stories which might have been used to illustrate general truths about life, but, as we have them, the accent of the impending crisis rests upon them. It is this accent of urgency which must not be lost in interpretation.

One of the marks of Jewish Apocalyptic is pseudonymity and the Book of Daniel is no exception to this rule. It is usually argued that, since the age of prophecy was believed to have come to an end, the authority of a great name from the past was claimed for writings which would otherwise have had no claim upon men's attention and might even have brought trouble upon their authors. It is difficult, however, to see how the name 'Daniel' could have served to give the book named after him the desired authority, since, apart from the book itself, we know nothing about this Daniel whom it describes as living in Babylon during the exile. It is true that Ezekiel speaks twice of a righteous man, Daniel, whom significantly he couples with Noah and Job (14.14, 20), and once of a wise man, Daniel (28.3), whom he compares with the prince of Tyre, but it is obvious that this Daniel referred to by Ezekiel cannot be an exilic figure, though he may have suggested a name for the latter. The discovery at Ras Shamra of the mythological poem *Aqhat* which tells of a King Danel who defended the rights of the widow and orphan has been hailed as explaining the references of Ezekiel, though it seems to have been overlooked that in the Book of Jubilees (4.20) there is mention of a Danel who is actually said to be the uncle and father-in-law of Enoch

D.–B

and who therefore would be the great-great-grandfather of Noah. There is possibly a link here on the one side with the apocalyptic literature and on the other with Ezekiel. The Danel of Ras Shamra or the Danel of Jubilees may have coloured the conception of the exilic Daniel, but it should be noted that the latter was neither a patriarch like Enoch or Noah nor a prophet like Isaiah nor the associate of a prophet like Baruch. Daniel in fact seems to have acquired whatever authority he has from the book which bears his name.

There is a great deal to be said for the brilliant suggestion of H. H. Rowley (see especially his article, 'The Bilingual problem of Daniel', *ZAW* 9, 1932, pp. 256–68) that the Maccabaean author originally issued the stories (chs. 2–6) anonymously in Aramaic, to encourage those who were suffering under the persecution of Antiochus Epiphanes, and later added chapter 7, also in Aramaic. When still later he issued the eschatological visions, which were different in character but related to the same critical situation, he wrote them in Hebrew, the sacred language (though one with which he was less familiar), because they were intended for a somewhat different audience, but attributed them to the Daniel of the stories to make clear the common authorship of both parts of the book. The Aramaic beginning of chapter 2 was replaced by the introductory chapter 1, which prepares the way for what follows, and the first few verses of chapter 2, the whole introduction being in Hebrew. The pseudonymity of the book would, therefore, actually be a kind of signature guaranteeing its unity and would not be due to any desire to deceive the reader. The pseudonymity, as opposed to anonymity, which became a characteristic of later apocalypses, may have been due to a misunderstanding of the pseudonymity of Daniel. Yet, even if Rowley were wrong in this explanation and if it could be shown that the author of the Book of Daniel intended to deceive his readers and to claim for his book an authority to which it was not entitled, while we would rightly deprecate the deception, we would have in fairness to recognize that the real authority of the book would remain unimpaired, *viz.* the divinely imparted conviction that God is sovereign over history and is guiding it towards an end determined by himself. It is much more likely, however, that no deception was intended and that intelligent readers would recognize, and were intended to recognize, the literacy device of *vaticinium post eventum*. When, of course, the genuine attempt at prophecy (Dan. 12.40ff.) was not fulfilled, it is understandable that later apocalyptists like the authors of Baruch and II (4) Esd. writing in the first century AD, should have supposed that the fourth kingdom of Daniel must have been Rome and not Greece. The Habakkuk Scroll from Cave I at Qumran shows us how scripture was reinterpreted to make it relevant to new situations.

The Book of Daniel, chs. 1–6, is rightly compared with the stories in Genesis about Joseph as illustrating the pride of the Jew that members of his race were able to play an important part at foreign courts and even win recognition for their religion from pagan potentates. It should be noticed, however, that the story of Joseph is integrated into the *Heilsgeschichte*, while the story of Daniel is linked with the promise of an end to history which will imply God's triumph. The theme of God's sovereignty over history is common to both sections of Scripture.

It is a curious fact that the career of Alexander the Great, perhaps the most decisive event in world history up to the date with which we are concerned, did not make the impact upon Jewish thought that might have been expected, perhaps, it has been suggested, because no prophet arose to interpret it. It was not till the time of Antiochus Epiphanes, after the Jews had moved from the sphere of influence of the Ptolemies to that of the Seleucids, that the issue Hebraism versus Hellenism became manifest. A division among the Jews themselves regarding the right attitude to civilization had appeared as early as the time of Nehemiah in the fifth century, but it was not till the second century that the struggle between the two conceptions of life became one of life and death. We may regret that such a struggle was necessary. Yet in this strange world the good oftener than not does not survive by compromise however reasonable, but by adopting an extreme position, and it is usually the men who stick to principle even in matters which seem in the world's eyes of little moment who stand firm in the evil day when issues of ultimate consequence are involved.

It is argued that the stories of the first part of the book show a different attitude to the heathen world from that of the visions in the second part. It must be pointed out, however, that even within the stories there is a double attitude. Daniel as a civil servant is loyal to the heathen state so long as its royal master does not challenge his conscience. Yet in chapters 2 and 7 the doom awaiting the kingdoms symbolized by the beasts is proclaimed. Is it not possible that the author of our book himself shared this double attitude? It has been shown that Antiochus did not interfere with the Jews everywhere and was driven to his oppressive actions by the fact that there was a division among the Jews in Judaea and Jerusalem, many desiring hellenization with the opportunities it brought to the ambitious and many, on the other hand, preferring the old, divinely sanctioned beliefs and practices and opposing those with whom Antiochus felt he could work in the furtherance of his grandiose plans for uniting his realm. The author of the Book of Daniel may have recognized that Israel might have continued to serve the world in the midst of which it lived, if the fanaticism and megalomania of Antiochus Epiphanes, nicknamed Epimanes, the madman, had not forced the issue to a point where the ultimate choice for or against God was set and for a loyal Jew there was no alternative to resistance to the death.

It seems to have been the fact of martyrdom which led our author to break the silence of the grave and proclaim at least a modified belief in resurrection (12.2–3). Whether the apocalyptic section of the Book of Isaiah (chs. 24–27, see especially 25.8 and 26.19) has the priority or not it is impossible to determine.

The relation of chapter 7 to the chapters which precede it and to those which follow it is sufficiently discussed in the body of the commentary. In a sense it is the central chapter which binds the whole together. The attempt of those who argue for two editions of chapter 7, the second one introducing the references to Antiochus Epiphanes, is not convincing. It is more natural to suppose that the chapter first came into existence in response to the situation of crisis. The whole book, as we have it, belongs to the few years, 167–164 or possibly 169–164 BC, but it must have been completed before the re-dedication of the temple by Judas Maccabaeus and the death of Antiochus. That the book cannot have been written in the exilic age is proved by the author's vague acquaintance with the Babylonian and early Persian period and his actual inaccuracies, by the character of both the Hebrew and the Aramaic in which it is composed—there is nothing inconsistent with their being of the second century and the presence of Greek words points to an age after the conquests of Alexander— by the literary references to the book which give no support to an early date for its composition, by its position in the Canon and by the character of its theology and angelology. It is probably of real significance that the Book of Daniel seems to have been cherished by the Qumran Community which was also interested in traditions about

Nabonidus (see the Commentary). This Essene (?) sect was living in the expectation of the end and in isolation from orthodox Jewry.

In conclusion, it is theologically of the greatest importance that it should be recognized that the Book of Daniel not only links up with the *Heilsgeschichte* of earlier writers by witnessing to the final act of God when he will bring in his kingdom—the prayer in chapter 9 recalls the mighty acts of God on behalf of his people—but shows us glimpses at least of the Israel which God had created to respond in faith and action to his mighty works. There are Daniel and his friends, whose characteristics, however one-sided, would be unintelligible apart from the Israel of which they are representative. There are the saints of the Most High who (*pace* Noth) must be the faithful in Judah who will stand in the day when God tests all things. And, perhaps most significant of all, there is the prayer of chapter 9, often wrongly regarded as an interpolation, but surely a contemporary witness to the profound sense of sin, the piety and the fidelity which helped to bring the Jewish people through the fearful ordeal of persecution. God's mighty acts in history must not be separated from the faith which witnessed to them. The narrowness of the reaction to hellenism with its failure to recognize the great contribution that hellenism had to make to the world doubtless in the event condemned Israel to the ghetto, but there were those who did not lose heart because the end did not come as the author of this book expected it would. Alongside the developing Rabbinism with its lowered temperature, the belief survived that one day God would act, as act he did. The realized eschatology of Christianity leaves room for a final end which, near or far, will be the ultimate justification of the faith which produced the Book of Daniel.

I

CHAPTER ONE

1 ¹In the third year of the reign of Jehoiakim king of Judah, Nebuchadnezzar king of Babylon came to Jerusalem and besieged it. ²And the Lord gave Jehoiakim king of Judah into his hand, with some of the vessels of the house of God; and he brought them to the land of Shinar, to the house of his god, and placed the vessels in the treasury of his god. ³Then the king commanded Ashpenaz, his chief eunuch†, to bring some of the people of Israel, both of the royal family and of the nobility, ⁴youths without blemish, handsome and skilful in all wisdom, endowed with knowledge, understanding learning and competent to serve in the king's palace, and to teach them the letters and language of the Chaldeans. ⁵The king assigned them a daily portion of the rich food which the king ate, and of the wine which he drank. They were to be educated for three years, and at the end of that time they were to stand before the king. ⁶Among these were Daniel, Hananiah, Mishael, and Azariah of the tribe of Judah. ⁷And the chief of the eunuchs gave them names: Daniel he called Belteshazzar, Hananiah he called Shadrach, Mishael he called Meshach, and Azariah he called Abednego.

8 But Daniel resolved that he would not defile himself with the king's rich food, or with the wine which he drank; therefore he asked the chief of the eunuchs to allow him not to defile himself. ⁹And God gave Daniel favour and compassion in the sight of the chief of the eunuchs; ¹⁰and the chief of the eunuchs said to Daniel, 'I fear lest my lord the king, who appointed your food and your drink, should see that you were in poorer condition than the youths who are of your own age. So you would endanger my head with the king.' ¹¹Then Daniel said to the steward* whom the chief of the eunuchs had appointed over Daniel, Hananiah, Mishael, and Azariah; ¹²'Test your servants for ten days; let us be given vegetables to eat and water to drink. ¹³Then let our appearance and the appearance of the youths who eat the king's rich food be observed by you, and according to what you see deal with your servants.' ¹⁴So he hearkened to them in this matter, and tested them for ten days. ¹⁵At the end of ten days it was seen that they were better in appearance and fatter in flesh than all the youths who ate the king's

† Or 'court official'.   * Possibly 'guard'.

23

rich food. 16So the steward took away their rich food and the wine they were to drink and gave them vegetables.

17 As for these four youths, God gave them learning and skill in all letters and wisdom; and Daniel had understanding in all visions and dreams. 18At the end of the time, when the king had commanded that they should be brought in, the chief of the eunuchs brought them in before Nebuchadnezzar. 19And the king spoke with them, and among them all none was found like Daniel, Hananiah, Mishael, and Azariah; therefore they stood before the king. 20And in every matter of wisdom and understanding concerning which the king inquired of them, he found them ten times better than all the magicians and enchanters that were in all his kingdom. 21And Daniel continued until* the first year of King Cyrus.

THE FIRST CHAPTER of the book is introductory to the whole and, in particular, to the stories about Daniel and his companions contained in chapters 2–6. It tells who the hero of the book is and how he came to be in the position of responsibility and trust in which the God of Israel could use him for his high purposes. It makes it clear from the outset, however, that, though God's servants may indeed be right to give their service to the wider world in which they may find themselves, nevertheless there are limits to their participation in the life of that world which may make it necessary for them to show their loyalty to their faith by a refusal to compromise. The assurance given in this chapter is that God will honour such loyalty.

It may be inferred that the book thus introduced was meant to be relevant to a situation, in which men of Jewish faith were becoming increasingly conscious of the great world which needed their service and promised them scope for their gifts of character and ability, but the claims of which were often difficult to reconcile with those of that unseen environment which their ancestral faith would not allow them to forget. In the story of Daniel it is the fortune of war which brings him to one of the centres of world power, and in that he is typical of the multitude of his compatriots who had to share the experience of exile after their state collapsed before the Babylonian conqueror. But in the centuries that followed, those catastrophic centuries when Babylon was replaced by Persia and Persia by Macedonia and the Hellenic successor states, there were other causes than war that led to the dispersal of the Jews over the face of the earth. The love of

* 'Was still alive in.'

adventure, the lure of commercial gain, the desire to share in the life of the wider world were compelling motives which led many a Jew to pass beyond the narrow confines of his homeland. The Book of Daniel had its primary, urgent message for a time of supreme crisis, but it had also a relevance for many times and places which made the demand for loyalty in real but less spectacular ways.

Furthermore it may be said that the book does more than issue a challenge; it reflects the loyalty of men who found themselves acting in a certain way, because, being who they were, there seemed nothing else to do. The stories of the Book of Daniel paint an ideal of steadfastness and courage intended to be a challenge to action; they also indicate to us the presence of men of flesh and blood who in the day of ordeal, or in times of lesser tension, were found faithful and formed links in the great chain of witness.

[1-2] In a book of this kind, in which stories are told primarily for their inspirational value, what concerns us chiefly is the historical reality of the contemporary situation, which the author has in view and in which he and his first readers were involved, rather than the question as to what degree of historicity can be assigned to the *dramatis personae* who occupy the stage in the literary invention and to the events which are narrated of them. The actors may have their place in history or they may not; what first claims our attention is the relevance of the stories to the day for which they were recorded. Moreover, it is as we ponder that, that this ancient book of witness may come to have something of significance to say to our own day and generation.

It is of no great consequence, therefore, that the very first statement in chapter 1 can be shown to be inaccurate. Indeed it would for our purpose be a waste of time if we were to concern ourselves unduly with the attempts which have been made to prove the contrary. In making the assertion that, in the third year of the reign of Jehoiakim, Jerusalem was besieged by Nebuchadnezzar and that Jehoiakim was captured, the author was in all probability not drawing on independent evidence, but was simply combining in a way that seemed satisfactory to himself the statements he found in II Chron. 36.6–7 and in II Kings 24.1ff. Unfortunately Jer. 25.1 (cf. 46.2) makes it clear that Nebuchadnezzar did not become king of Babylon till the fourth year of Jehoiakim, while from Jer. 36.9 it appears that Jehoiakim was still independent a year later and that there was at that time no occupation of Judaean territory by enemy troops. Moreover II Kings 24.1–2 does not imply, as the author of Daniel seems to think, that Jehoiakim's period of submission to Nebuchadnezzar dated from the beginning of the former's reign or that the raiding activities referred to amounted to a regular siege. Indeed the story of Nebuchadnezzar's siege of Jerusalem during Jehoiakim's reign and his capture of that king seems to be apocryphal and may represent a confused memory of what actually happened to Jehoiakin. Neither in Jeremiah nor in II Kings, which must be regarded as our primary authorities (Jer. 22.18–19 is an instance of unfulfilled prophecy) is there any evidence that Jehoiakim suffered the fate implied in II Chronicles and in Daniel. The ante-dating of the first capture of Jerusalem to the reign of Jehoiakim may possibly have had as its motive the desire to harmonize as nearly as possible the prophecy of Jer. 29.10 (cf. II Chron. 36.21) about a seventy years' captivity with the date of Cyrus's capture of Babylon and the consequent release of the Jews. The number seventy was certainly important to the author, because later in his book he was to claim the authority of revelation for his interpretation of seventy years as seventy weeks of years, i.e. as seventy times seven. That all this was in his mind here, however, is mere supposition. All that really matters is that the hero of the book is given a setting in the Babylonian exile, that is to say in a situation of opportunity and testing. The writer is not even concerned with the hope of a return from the exile, because the problem he is actually concerned with is not that of men who were filled with nostalgia for their homeland. The reference to the depositing, presumably in the temple of Marduk, of the sacred vessels taken from the temple at Jerusalem (cf. II Chron. 36.7, 10, 18–19), besides being a possible side allusion to the spoiling of the temple by Antiochus Epiphanes, is intended to clear the way for the incident described in chapter 5.

Nebuchadnezzar (inaccurate spelling of Nebuchadrezzar, Nabū-kudurri-usur, which is found in Daniel and in certain other instances of the occurrence of the name in the Old Testament) is correctly represented here as the neo-Babylonian king who captured Jerusalem, though it was actually in the reigns of Jehoiakin and Zedekiah that the successive blows fell. Elsewhere in the Book of Daniel it is thought to be possible that he has attracted to himself traditions or legends which belonged more properly to Nabonidus (Nabunāid), the last king of the neo-Babylonian dynasty. The depositing of the sacred spoils of the temple at Jerusalem in the temple of Marduk was in accordance with custom, since vessels and other furniture looted from captured temples were regarded as retaining their sacred character which must not be violated.

It may not be without significance that Babylonia here is called the land of Shinar, a name associated in Hebrew memory with the kingdom of Nimrod the mighty hunter (Gen. 10.10), and still more with the impious builders of the so-called tower of Babel (Gen. 11.2), and the name of the land to which, in the bizarre vision of Zechariah (Zech. 5.11) Wickedness was to be banished. From the very outset, then, it is hinted that the environment of the Jewish exiles, whose adventures are to be told, contains an element hostile to faith. As the story goes on, it is not surprising to find this hostility concentrated, where one might expect to find it, at the Babylonian court.

[3–5] The land of exile was to be for some of the exiles the land of opportunity. We are told how the Babylonian king set about recruiting for his civil service. The RSV translation represents the more probable view that only two classes of recruits are referred to here, both belonging to the Israelite exiles. The Hebrew, it is true, could also be understood in the sense that there were three classes, *viz.* Israelites, members of the Babylonian royal family and members of the Babylonian nobility (the word used here is of Persian origin). It is much more likely, however, that the author's intention is to indicate that, in the selection of candidates from the mass of foreign captives, only young men of high rank were considered. It was only in Jewish court circles and among the Jewish aristocracy that the king would expect to obtain lads with the combination of physical and intellectual qualities that he sought. The three-year period of training to which they were to be subjected corresponds to what is known from Greek sources to have been customary among the Persians. As for the subject-matter of the prescribed education, what was presumably intended by the phrase 'letters and language of the Chaldaeans' was either the neo-Babylonian language of the court, or, still more probably, the sacred Sumerian language along with the highly complicated cuneiform script and the sacred myths and rituals and omen texts characteristic of Babylonian religion. It is strange that the author feels no incongruity in this introduction of the Jewish lads to the ambiguous world of heathen thought and practice. He wishes, however, to create the situation where presently Babylonian wisdom will be beaten on its own ground and, perhaps without realizing it, ignores the difficulty which his story involves.

The word 'Chaldaean' (taken from the Greek rendering of the
Hebrew *kaśdim* and corresponding more accurately to the original
kaldu) belongs properly to the people which proved such a thorn in
the flesh to the Assyrians in the latter part of the eighth century under
Merodach-Baladan (Marduk-appal-iddina) and which, in the following century under Nabopolassar (Nabium-apil-uṣur) the father of
Nebuchadrezzar, was to join with the Medes in bringing about the
fall of Nineveh, and subsequently was to win empire for itself under
the neo-Babylonian dynasty. Here and in most other occurrences of
the word in the Book of Daniel, as also in Herodotus and later Greek
writers, it acquired a secondary meaning, being applied to a particular class of Babylonian sages, practised in astrology and the magical
arts. This may have happened because, in later times, when the
original Chaldaean element had largely merged in the general
population, it was mainly certain priestly circles which continued to
claim Chaldaean descent. The use of the word 'Chaldaean' in this
restricted sense is an undoubted anachronism wherever it has reference to the period when the Chaldaean dynasty was in power. This is
one of the indications that the literary form at least of these stories is late.

During the course of training prescribed for them as court pages
the candidates were to be pensioners of the royal table and have their
rations assigned to them (cf. Jehoiakin—J. B. Pritchard, *ANET*,
p. 308).

[6–16] The stage now being set, the hero of the book and his three
companions are introduced, first by their Hebrew names, which,
whether the coincidence is accidental or not, all appear in Ezra-
Nehemiah, and then by the Babylonian names which they are said
to have received from the commander of the eunuchs in whose charge
they had been placed. It is true that all four Hebrew names are theo-
phoric, Daniel meaning 'God has judged', Hananiah 'Yahweh has
been gracious', Mishael 'Who is what God is?' and Azariah 'Yahweh
has helped', and that in the names which are substituted there are
hints of sinister associations—in the case of Belteshazzar, Balatṣu-
uṣur, 'May he protect his life', a false etymology (cf. 4.5) connecting
the name with Bel, though, of course, Bel may indeed be the sup-
pressed subject of the verb *uṣur*. There is, however, no explicit suggestion here that a Jew in such a case would see a challenge to his
faith on the part of the pagan authority, any more than in the
story of Joseph, where there is a similar change of name (see Gen.
41.45) and where the hero actually marries into a priestly family. If

the author intends a disapproving allusion to Jason and Menelaus, the contemporary hellenizing high-priests of the Maccabaean period and their like, he does his best to make it as little obvious as possible. If Saul of Tarsus could be proud enough of his Roman citizenship to assume a Roman name, we must accept it as possible that no sinister meaning was normally suspected behind such a change.

The first crisis in the fortunes of Daniel and his companions arose from the circumstance that, as we have seen, they were expected, like all the other candidates in training as court pages, to eat the food and drink the wine from the royal table, which had doubtless been associated in some way with idolatrous worship. The food certainly would not have been prepared in the correct Hebrew fashion and might even have consisted of animals regarded by Hebrew law as unclean.

It is true that scruples such as we are told the Jewish lads felt might have manifested themselves in the days of the Babylonian exile, as they have been felt by the orthodox among the Jews throughout Jewish history. Perhaps the closest parallel to the situation described in the Book of Daniel is to be found in the Book of Tobit which refers to the exile of the northern tribes (1.10, 11): 'When I was carried away captive to Nineveh, all my brethren and those that were of my kindred did eat the bread of the Gentiles: but I kept myself from eating, because I remembered God with all my soul.' Compare Judith 12.1–4, Jubilees 22.16 and the interesting account in Josephus, *Life* 3 (14), where we hear of certain Jewish priests in Rome who avoided defilement with Gentile food by living solely on figs and nuts.

At the same time, it is difficult not to believe that the author of the Book of Daniel put this story in the forefront of his book in view of the fact that loyalty to the food laws had become an issue of life and death for many pious Jews during the struggle with Antiochus Epiphanes. We read in I Macc. 1.62–63: 'Many in Israel were fully resolved and confirmed in themselves not to eat unclean things. And they chose to die, that they might not be defiled with the meats, and that they might not profane the holy covenant: and they died.' On the other hand, it may be admitted that, unlike Antiochus and his minions, the official in charge of Daniel and his friends is not unsympathetic to their scruples, but is afraid to make an exception in their favour because of possible consequences to himself. An under-official, however (if the translation of an obscure word given above is approximately correct), proves more accommodating and agrees to a trial period, at the end of which we are told that Daniel's faith was abundantly vindicated. The suggestion intended by the author is, not that a course of asceticism is good for the health of both body and mind, but that God honours the loyalty of his servants. So far the supreme test of loyalty has not been applied, but there is evidence of a stoutheartedness which will approve itself in grimmer situations.

Now, it is just here, where this chapter makes the test of loyalty for the Jew a matter of scrupulous observance of the rigid dietary laws, that perplexity arises with respect to our appropriation of the Old Testament witness. There is no doubt at all where the Jew stands, if he cleaves strictly to the orthodox faith. This is the law and unswerving obedience to it at whatever cost will be blessed by God. In II Macc. ch. 7 we read of the seven brothers and their heroic mother who were matryred one after the other at the bidding of Antiochus Epiphanes for their refusal to defile themselves by eating unclean food and who believed that God would vindicate them by their resurrection. The story is probably legendary, but the conception of such loyalty reflects historical fact and is the counterpart of what we find in the Book of Daniel.

The difficulty of appropriation which this story in chapter 1 presents to us is twofold.

First there is the more general consideration that in real life it is very frequently not true that loyal obedience is rewarded by worldly success. Only too often the man who is loyal to principle and defies the world's way meets with crushing defeat. That the author of the Book of Daniel knew this quite well is shown by the magnificent utterance in 3.18. We may be permitted to draw the conclusion that he held the faith, which we may indeed share, that, whether worldly success be granted or not, God does indeed honour the loyalty of his servants. Instead of saying this, however, in an abstract, theological way, with all the necessary safeguards, he proclaims the truth in story form. This is a favourite Hebrew way of proceeding. A. C. Welch in an illuminating comment on Ps. 91 (*The Psalter*, 1926, pp. 110–12) deals with this very difficulty presented by Hebrew thought and points out that, 'when it is taken literally, the psalm is patently at variance with all experience'. The misfortunes of life do not discriminate between the good and the bad. We are not to suppose, however, that the psalmist was unaware of this. 'In terms of his own time and in Eastern imagery the psalmist embodied his sense of the infinite worth of the inner life through its hold on God.'

But, secondly, Daniel and his friends show their loyalty by making an issue of a point in the ceremonial law. That is to say, the emphasis here is laid precisely upon that aspect of Judaism which seems to us the least important. For the orthodox Jew, on the other hand, the issue has always been and still remains a vital one. Strict adherence to the food laws has proved one of the most certain methods by which the Jew has preserved his distinctness from the rest of the world. When Daniel and his companions are represented as taking this line, one can recognize it as witness to God, whose will it was that Israel should preserve its uniqueness and the way of life which was guarded by regulations such as these. It may be matter for regret that Judaism and Hellenism could not have learned from each other without the fearful clash of wills made inevitable by the folly of Antiochus and the Hellenizers in Jerusalem. But, things being as they were, the Jewish stand for principle was fraught with tremendous consequences for the future of the world and, in that moment of history, the very narrowness of the Jew was meritorious.

We may also recognize that obedience to rules, which we may not recognize as having in themselves absolute significance, may nevertheless be of great spiritual value as an expression of brotherly tact and consideration for others. There may be occasions when such obedience is fitting in a certain place and at a certain time. This is especially true in situations where to claim a liberty for oneself may involve inflicting an injury on someone who is not able to share our point of view. This is an issue which had not arisen when the Book of Daniel was written. The freedom which was being claimed by the emancipated hellenizing Jews was not the freedom with which Christ was to make men free. It was the issue which St Paul hammered out with reference to the situation in Corinth (see I Cor. 10), where some Christians were flaunting their emancipation from the belief that to eat food which had been offered in idol-temples before being sold in the market was to expose oneself to demonic influence. St Paul speaks to them with gentle raillery. They are very proud of their 'knowledge'. Knowledge, however, is apt to inflate people. It is only love that is truly constructive. 'Hence, as to the eating of food offered to idols, we know that "an idol has no real existence", and that there is no God but one.' The trouble is that there are weaker brothers who are not emancipated in their thinking. If they are led by stronger brothers to set aside a regulation in which they still believe, then they suffer injury in conscience. The ultimate question to consider is, not what things are lawful—the answer to that question may in certain cases not be the same for everybody—but what things best serve the fellowship. ' "All things are lawful", but not all things are helpful. "All things are lawful", but not all things build up.' The governing principle is, then, the principle of love. In another epistle (Rom. 14.1ff.) St Paul writes: 'Let us then pursue what makes for peace and for mutual upbuilding. Do not for the sake of food, destroy the work of God. Everything is indeed clean, but it is wrong for anyone to make others fall by what he eats; it is right not to eat meat or drink wine or do anything that makes your brother stumble.'

The significance of the story in Dan. 1, then, is best understood, first, if we consider its own witness to the value of loyalty to principle, and, secondly, if we bring that witness into relation to the New Testament handling of a related, though by no means identical problem. It is true that we must listen carefully to what the author of the Book of Daniel actually says and not try to make him say anything else. But there is also a word which God may wish to speak to us through this story and it is perhaps wise to set it in the wider context provided by Christian experience.

When we read the history of the past, we may often have the feeling that the battles were fought on the wrong ground and for the wrong issues. At the same time it may well be better in the end that certain battles should have been fought than that men should have felt that there was no issue worth fighting for. The martyrs of the Maccabaean period, whose sacrifice is probably reflected in these stories of loyalty which occupy the first half of the Book of Daniel, did Israel's religion a great service and that service was not forgotten.

[17–21] According to the story, God does not only honour the loyalty of the young Jewish captives by enabling them to come through the test with flying colours; they also receive intellectual gifts which put them in a class by themselves at the Babylonian court and lead to their employment in the royal service. Emphasis is laid on the special endowment of Daniel in his ability to explain visions and dreams. Thus the way is prepared for what is to follow and, in particular, for the service which Daniel is to render at the royal court on more than one occasion. The writer is expressing his conviction that Israel's religion is superior to the pagan religions, for all the prestige which was associated with the latter. It is all very well for us to see that clearly now. It was not so easy when the Jews were faced with a dominant civilization which mocked at Jewish scruples and offered a broader and more cultivated existence and, indeed, seemed to have all the pomp and circumstance on its side. Babylon and Greece—they both in their day seemed to be on the winning side. The temptation to be impressed by, and to make terms with, the world is still with us, and a faith like that of this old Jewish writer can still speak to us of the loyalty and the courage which are needed to meet the world's challenge.

The concluding verse can be interpreted as meaning that Daniel was still alive in the first year of King Cyrus and need not be regarded as contradicting 10.1. It is unlikely that the reference to Cyrus is meant to remind readers of Cyrus's Edict enabling the Jews to return to their homeland. That is not a special concern of this writer who looks forward to a great climax to Israel's long travail.

II

CHAPTER TWO

2 ¹In the second year of the reign of Nebuchadnezzar, Nebuchadnezzar had dreams; and his spirit was troubled, and his sleep left him. ²Then the king commanded that the magicians, the enchanters,* the sorcerers, and the Chaldeans be summoned, to tell the king his dreams. So they came in and stood before the king. ³And the king said to them, 'I had a dream, and my spirit is troubled to know the dream.' ⁴Then the Chaldeans said to the king,† 'O king, live for ever! Tell your servants the dream, and we will show the interpretation.' ⁵The king answered the Chaldeans, 'The word from me is sure: if you do not make known to me the dream and its interpretation, you shall be torn limb from limb, and your houses shall be laid in ruins. ⁶But if you show the dream and its interpretation, you shall receive from me gifts and rewards and great honour. Therefore show me the dream and its interpretation.' ⁷They answered a second time, 'Let the king tell his servants the dream, and we will show its interpretation.' ⁸The king answered, 'I know with certainty that you are trying to gain time, because you see that the word from me is sure ⁹that if you do not make the dream known to me, there is but one sentence for you. You have agreed to speak lying and corrupt words before me till the times change. Therefore tell me the dream, and I shall know that you can show me its interpretation.' ¹⁰The Chaldeans answered the king, 'There is not a man on earth who can meet the king's demand; for no great and powerful king has asked such a thing of any magician or enchanter or Chaldean. ¹¹The thing that the king asks is difficult, and none can show it to the king except the gods, whose dwelling is not with flesh.'

12 Because of this the king was angry and very furious, and commanded that all the wise men of Babylon be destroyed. ¹³So the decree went forth that the wise men were to be slain, and they sought Daniel and his companions, to slay them. ¹⁴Then Daniel replied with prudence and discretion to Arioch, the captain of the king's guard, who had gone out to slay the wise men of Babylon; ¹⁵he said to Arioch the king's captain, 'Why is the decree of the king so severe‡?' Then Arioch made

* Possibly 'exorcisers'.   † Hebrew adds 'in Aramaic', indicating that the text from here to end of ch. 7 is in Aramaic.   ‡ Possibly 'peremptory'.

34

the matter known to Daniel. [16]*And Daniel went in and besought the king to appoint him a time, that he might show to the king the interpretation.

17 Then Daniel went to his house and made the matter known to Hananiah, Mishael, and Azariah, his companions, [18]and told them to seek mercy of the God of heaven concerning this mystery, so that Daniel and his companions might not perish with the rest of the wise men of Babylon. [19]Then the mystery was revealed to Daniel in a vision of the night. Then Daniel blessed the God of heaven. [20]Daniel said:

'Blessed be the name of God for ever and ever,
    to whom belong wisdom and might.
[21]He changes times and seasons;
    he removes kings and sets up kings;
he gives wisdom to the wise
    and knowledge to those who have understanding;
[22]he reveals deep and mysterious things;
    he knows what is in the darkness,
    and the light dwells with him.
[23]To thee, O God of my fathers,
    I give thanks and praise
for thou hast given me wisdom and strength,
    and hast now made known to me what we asked of thee,
    for thou hast made known to us the king's matter.'

24 Therefore Daniel went in to Arioch, whom the king had appointed to destroy the wise men of Babylon; he went and said thus to him, 'Do not destroy the wise men of Babylon; bring me in before the king, and I will show the king the interpretation.'

25 Then Arioch brought in Daniel before the king in haste, and said thus to him: 'I have found among the exiles from Judah a man who can make known to the king the interpretation.' [26]The king said to Daniel, whose name was Belteshazzar, 'Are you able to make known to me the dream that I have seen and its interpretation?' [27]Daniel answered the king, 'No wise men, enchanters, magicians, or astrologers can show to the king the mystery which the king had asked, [28]but there is a God in heaven who reveals mysteries, and he has made known to King Nebuchadnezzar what will be in the latter days. Your dream and the visions of your head as you lay in bed are these: [29]To you, O king, as you lay in bed came thoughts of what would be hereafter, and he who reveals mysteries made known to you what is to be. [30]But as for me, not because of any wisdom that I have more than all the living has this mystery been revealed to me, but in order that the interpretation may be made known to the king, and that you may know the thoughts of your mind.

31 'You saw, O king, and behold, a great image. This image, mighty and of exceeding brightness, stood before you, and its appearance was

* Read 'who asked the king for time' (based on Theodotion and the Syriac, which omit 'and went in').

frightening. ³²The head of this image was of fine gold, its breast and arms of silver, its belly and thighs of bronze, ³³its legs of iron, its feet partly of iron and partly of clay. ³⁴As you looked, a stone was cut out by no human hand, and it smote the image on its feet of iron and clay, and broke them in pieces; ³⁵then the iron, the clay, the bronze, the silver, and the gold, all together were broken in pieces, and became like the chaff of the summer threshing floors; and the wind carried them away, so that not a trace of them could be found. But the stone that struck the image became a great mountain and filled the whole earth.

36 'This was the dream; now we will tell the king its interpretation. ³⁷You, O king, the king of kings, to whom the God of heaven has given the kingdom, the power, and the might, and the glory, ³⁸and into whose hand he has given, wherever they dwell, the sons of men, the beasts of the field, and the birds of the air, making you rule over them all—you are the head of gold. ³⁹After you shall arise another kingdom inferior to you, and yet a third kingdom of bronze, which shall rule over all the earth. ⁴⁰And there shall be a fourth kingdom, strong as iron, because iron breaks to pieces and shatters all things; and like iron which crushes, it shall break and crush all these. ⁴¹And as you saw the feet and toes partly of potter's clay and partly of iron, it shall be a divided kingdom; but some of the firmness of iron shall be in it, just as you saw iron mixed with the miry clay. ⁴²And as the toes of the feet were partly iron and partly clay, so the kingdom shall be partly strong and partly brittle. ⁴³As you saw the iron mixed with miry clay, so they will mix with one another in marriage, but they will not hold together, just as iron does not mix with clay. ⁴⁴And in the days of those kings the God of heaven will set up a kingdom which shall never be destroyed, nor shall its sovereignty be left to another people. It shall break in pieces all these kingdoms and bring them to an end, and it shall stand for ever; ⁴⁵just as you saw that a stone was cut from a mountain by no human hand, and that it broke in pieces the iron, the bronze, the clay, the silver, and the gold. A great God has made known to the king what shall be hereafter. The dream is certain, and its interpretation sure.'

46 Then King Nebuchadnezzar fell upon his face, and did homage to Daniel, and commanded that an offering and incense be offered up to him. ⁴⁷The king said to Daniel, 'Truly, your God is God of gods and Lord of kings, and a revealer of mysteries, for you have been able to reveal this mystery.' ⁴⁸Then the king gave Daniel high honours and many great gifts, and made him ruler over the whole province of Babylon, and chief prefect over all the wise men of Babylon. ⁴⁹Daniel made request of the king, and he appointed Shadrach, Meshach, and Abednego over the affairs of the province of Babylon; but Daniel remained at the king's court.

THE SECOND CHAPTER fulfils the expectation aroused by the first chapter that Daniel's special endowment with wisdom and with the skill to interpret dreams will be given scope at the Babylonian court. Quite apart from the revelation regarding the course and climax of world history which the chapter is to record and which forms its kernel, it has the secondary but important aim of demonstrating the superiority of the God-given wisdom which is at Daniel's disposal to all the vaunted insight which the sages and diviners of Babylon claim to possess by the exercise of human reason or through their control of magical techniques, and, further, of showing that in the event the world is forced to recognize this superiority.

That there is an element of wishful thinking in the expectation that the world will make this acknowledgment cannot be denied. In actual fact the world is seldom ready to admit the bankruptcy of human wisdom. But, as we already saw in chapter I, when the Jew tells a success story, he is often merely resorting to a vivid and memorable way of saying what we would say otherwise with greater theological caution but less memorably. The representation of Nebuchadnezzar as admitting the superiority of Daniel's God and of the wisdom that he communicates through his servant should in the last resort be understood as the writer's way of emphasizing the truth of the revelation he has recorded. The Jew was convinced of the superiority of his own religion to the religions of the heathen nations and he enjoyed telling stories which described what he would have liked to happen in the way of recognition of that religion. That there were pagans who were attracted by the Jewish faith and discipline is undoubtedly true, but that the superiority of the Jewish religion was admitted in high places as handsomely as is here described is not to be insisted on as historical fact. Even Cyrus, for all his toleration of other religions, did not go as far as Nebuchadnezzar is represented as doing here. It is clear that the Second Isaiah expected great things from Cyrus: it is equally clear that, whatever the decree of Cyrus meant, it did not involve that acknowledgment of Yahweh's lordship that the prophet hoped for. It is incredible, then, that Nebuchadnezzar should have made the admission recorded in v. 47 of this chapter. Nevertheless, a story of the kind told here is an impressive witness to the belief of the Jewish people in the control of the events of history by Israel's God and to their confidence that by his favour they were possessors of the only true wisdom.

One is reminded of the somewhat similar narrative in Gen. 41 which tells how the Egyptian Pharaoh had a dream which troubled him, and how, as in the story under consideration, a Hebrew youth, endowed with the gift of interpretation by God, is able to interpret the dream and so confound all the magicians and wise men of Egypt who had shown their complete incapacity to solve the riddle. Their discomfiture is mentioned, but not underlined, in the Joseph story. The interest of the author there is in hurrying on to the next episode, in which Joseph, having by his skill won for himself a position of great authority and influence, is able to carry out famine-relief measures, which, in the event, through the overruling providence of God, ensure the survival of the ancestors of the chosen people. The story of Joseph has the characteristics of the historical novel, the narrative moving on from episode to episode in ordered fashion. In the Book of Daniel the chapter under consideration has a certain completeness in itself and Daniel's success over the wise men is not incidental to the narrative, but is, as it were, underlined as a leading motif in what the author has to tell. He wishes by a vivid story to make it as clear as he can that paganism is bankrupt in spite of its magnificent façade of reputed wisdom and learning.

At the same time it would be a mistake to suppose that this particular story, like the other stories in the Book of Daniel, is designed merely to illustrate a thesis or to reflect a general attitude of the Jews over against the pagan world. It is quite true that these stories belong to a type of which there are many examples. Yet they have been brought together in the Book of Daniel in days of great tension and crisis to encourage men to stand firm in their loyalty. Moreover in chapter 2, it is not merely Daniel's success in interpreting the king's dream which is important. The place given to the content of the dream, linking, as it does, this chapter with chapter 7 and indeed with the theme of the concluding chapters of the book, reflects the writer's conviction that in his own day, which is the real point of perspective for understanding the book's main purpose, history was swiftly moving towards its climax. It may be true, as Hölscher maintains, that the apocalyptic literature in general is the product of that class of the wise men in Judaism which was interested in legendary and visionary material and in every variety of esoteric knowledge. Yet there is an urgency in the Book of Daniel, as compared with books like Proverbs and Ecclesiasticus on the one hand and books like Enoch and Jubilees on the other, which suggests a link with the older prophecy.

Material which in part may have a wider relevance has been drawn together and made relevant to a particular situation.

[1-13] The discrepancy between 1.5 and 18 and 2.1 need not be taken seriously, since the dates in this book do not imply a genuine historical interest.

Among the many stories of warning dreams dreamt by royal personages the one which is most closely parallel to Nebuchadnezzar's dream recounted in this chapter is that of the dreams which terrified Nabonidus, the last neo-Babylonian king (see the Istanbul Stela: J. B. Pritchard, *ANET*, p. 308ff.). Indeed, the parallels between what we are told of Nebuchadnezzar in the Book of Daniel and what we learn of Nabonidus from other sources are such as to have suggested the theory that behind our canonical Book of Daniel lie Babylonian traditions about Nabonidus which have been transferred to the earlier and better-known monarch. It is known that Nabonidus had a quarrel with the Babylonian priests which made them ready to transfer their loyalty to Cyrus. This may possibly be reflected in the account here of Nebuchadnezzar's threat against the wise men. The setting up of the image in the Plain of Dura is compared with Nabonidus's erection of a statue of Sin in the temple of Eḫulḫul. The years which Nabonidus spent at the oasis of Teima, doubtless for political reasons, may be reflected in the account of Nebuchadnezzar's madness. The parallels, it must be admitted, are not on the whole very close, but some colour is lent to the theory by the interesting fact that fragments of a dream of Nabonidus have turned up at Qumran and it is known that the Book of Daniel was of particular interest to the Dead Sea Community, a community which was living in expectation of the last things.

However this may be, we read in the story before us that King Nebuchadnezzar summoned various categories of experts, who belonged to the establishment of royal courts, to help him in his predicament. It is unnecessary that we should concern ourselves further with the attempt to differentiate between these categories on philological grounds, as it is improbable that the author of the book could have done so himself. The translation represents an attempt to do justice to what evidence there is. The first word in the list is one which is used of the Egyptian magicians in the story of Joseph. The Chaldaeans mentioned here are obviously the class of practitioners in magic and esoteric wisdom referred to in 1.4. The author of our book here and elsewhere, like other authors of similar tales, enjoys embellishing his narrative with picturesque lists of names of people and things (cf. especially chapter 3).

In v. 4 the text, as we now have it, seems to say that the Chaldaeans (representative of the whole body of wise men) spoke to the king in Aramaic.[1] Actually, however, from this point until the end of chapter 7, the Aramaic language is used exclusively, not only for the speeches, but for the narrative as well. It is, therefore, almost certain that the adverb translated 'in Aramaic' was originally a marginal comment, drawing attention to the linguistic change, which has wrongly been incorporated in the text. Whatever the explanation of the linguistic change from Hebrew to Aramaic and from Aramaic back to Hebrew in chapter 8, it seems to have no obvious bearing on the problems of interpretation.

From the outset Nebuchadnezzar appears to be sceptical of the ability of the wise men to do what was asked of them. In fact he has a shrewd suspicion that all they are capable of doing is to apply the techniques laid down in their books of divination, given a dream to apply them to. The demand, therefore, that the wise men should supply both dream and interpretation provides the king with a convenient test of their competence, if not of their honesty. Daniel's success in passing the test triumphantly goes some way towards making it plausible that the king should accept so readily his interpretation of the dream. The view, however, that the king applies a test does not require the support of the translation of certain words in v. 5 as 'The thing is gone from me'. Philology seems rather to justify the RSV translation, 'The word from me is sure', i.e. 'I have made a final decision'.

Nebuchadnezzar is not deceived by the appeal of the Chaldaeans for more time. He knows evasion when he sees it and insists on the test he has proposed. If they fail to meet it, they will be dealt with with the utmost rigour. Indeed there is only one sentence they can expect (cf. Esth. 4.11). Aware of their own inability, the Chaldaeans play for time, but make it all too clear by what they say that they have no contact with the source of revelation (cf. Jer. 23.18) and that their magic arts are worthless human devices. The king promptly orders the destruction of all the wise men of Babylon and, although

[1] Aramaic had apparently succeeded Accadian as the *lingua franca* of the Near East by the end of the eighth century BC (see II Kings 18.26) and it was eventually superseded by Greek. It was still the principal vernacular in Palestine in the second century BC, though the Dead Sea Scrolls show that Hebrew was also familiar in certain circles.

Daniel and his companions have not been summoned along with the
others to give their advice, the story demands that they be included
in the doom pronounced on the class of wise men as a whole. It is not
necessary to press the difficulty that Daniel and his companions have
so far been ignored; for the sake of dramatic effect the intervention
of Daniel at a late stage in the proceedings is more effective than if
he had been involved earlier, serving better, as it does, to throw
into relief the superiority of the wisdom at Daniel's disposal.

[14–23] Daniel first demonstrates his tactfulness by doing the
right thing in the critical situation in which he and his companions
find themselves. He appeals to the man who has been charged with
execution of the judgment passed on the wise men, namely Arioch,
the captain of the king's bodyguard, and asks him for an explanation
of the king's peremptory (RSV prefers the translation 'severe')
decree. Arioch—if we may accept a slight emendation of the text of
v. 16 based on Theodotion and the Syriac—presumably acts as the
intermediary between Daniel and the king, who grants Daniel's
request for time (or, possibly, for an appointment).

At this point the story brings in Daniel's three companions.
Daniel himself takes the lead, but they are given the task of praying
to God for help to solve the mystery of the king's dream. It should be
noted that the divine title used here is 'God of heaven', of which
Montgomery, after pointing out that it was the Jewish equivalent of
the Phoenician Ba'al Šamēn, goes on to state that 'the term was dis-
owned in Israel's religion, but was revived after the Exile, when it
became the title by which the Persian government recognized the
Jewish God. It was generally used by the Jews only in external
correspondence, and finally fell into disfavour again as too similar to
Zeus Ouranios.'

The prayer of Daniel and his companions is answered by the
disclosure of the secret of Nebuchadnezzar's dream to Daniel in a
vision by night, though, for reasons of literary art, the reader is still
kept in the dark. The corresponding Hebrew expression is used by
Eliphaz (Job 4.12ff.) where he describes his uncanny experience and
tells how a word came to him 'amid thoughts from visions of the
night'. The vision (ḥazōn) was regarded as a higher medium of
revelation than the dream, which might be vague and deceptive,
whereas in the vision a voice spoke clearly. The same distinction is
probably intended in Num. 12.6–8, where a contrast is drawn between the prophets, to whom God makes himself known in a vision

(*mar'ā*, not *ḥazōn*, the emphasis being on *seeing*), and speaks in a dream (though it must be admitted that the word 'speak' is here used), and Moses, to whom God speaks mouth to mouth and not in riddles. As an afterthought, however, it is also said that Moses beholds the form of God. In Dan. 7 we read that Daniel has a dream, but the writer immediately adds 'visions of his head' or 'visions that came into his head'. He is not left to vague surmise.

Daniel's immediate reaction to the revelation is to express his gratitude in a psalm or hymn of thanksgiving which, as Bentzen points out, is reminiscent in its phraseology of passages in the Psalms (41.14), Job (12.12, 13), Nehemiah (9.5) and Esther (1.13). It is by no means, however, a mere cento of quotations but is an original poem which fits beautifully into its context. It starts with the thought of God's mysterious being (referred to in the word 'name') which calls for man's adoration. Wisdom and might belong to him (cf. Job 12.13), i.e. he has knowledge and the power to do what he wills. Then there is emphasis on God's control of history which anticipates the content of the king's dream. Moreover, before we are told in the record of Daniel's own dream (7.25) that the little horn, representing Antiochus Epiphanes, was one who would plan 'to change the times and the law', we read here of the God of Israel who 'changes times and seasons'. It is this God who is able and willing to reveal his wisdom to those who are properly called the wise, because they are dependent for their knowledge on the only true source of wisdom (cf. v. 30 below). There is nothing so hidden or mysterious that it is inaccessible to God's knowledge. Compare Ps. 139.12 ('Even the darkness is not dark to thee, the night is bright as the day; for darkness is as light with thee') and Ps. 36.10, where God's light is represented as the light by which men see ('in thy light do we see light'), and Wisd. 7.26, where we are told that Wisdom is 'a reflection from the everlasting light'. There is a passage in the New Testament (I John 1.5) where God is actually identified with light ('God is light and in him is no darkness at all'), and C. H. Dodd, who thinks it unlikely that the author of the Johannine Epistles is the same as the author of the Fourth Gospel, considers that here is a thought which stands in some relation to the thought of Platonism and of Zoroastrianism and of the Hermetic philosophy. In the Fourth Gospel it is not God but the Logos who is identified with light (cf. 1.9; 3.19; 8.12; 9.5 and 12.46). The poem in Daniel finishes with an acknowledgment of the source of the knowledge which Daniel, as the representative Israelite, now possesses.

E. W. Heaton, in his commentary, suggests that the section vv. 14–23 'develops the theme of wisdom beyond the immediate needs of the story', and goes on to say that 'it may be suspected that the writer reveals here something of his own characteristic point of view', which Heaton believes to have been that of the typical scribe. It may be granted that the author of Daniel, like every educated Hebrew, must have been steeped in the thought of the Wisdom books, since no doubt the wise men as a class had much to do with what education was given to the young. It has even been suggested (by Fichtner, *TLZ* 74, 1949, pp. 75–80) that Isaiah may have been a wisdom teacher in Jerusalem before he was a prophet. The suggestion, however, that vv. 14–23 interrupt the connection between v. 13 and v. 24 cannot be accepted. It is true that there may be some confusion in the text as we have it, since it seems to represent Daniel as forcing his way without ceremony into the king's presence (v. 16), which would be a very awkward anticipation of Daniel's correct procedure in v. 24. Hebrew narrative writers, however, are frequently guilty of inconsistencies and, in any case, a very slight emendation here would obviate the difficulty and has been suggested above. It is really essential to the purpose of the author that some account should be given of the way in which Daniel obtains the knowledge which was to prove so vital on this occasion. What has to be made clear is, not that Daniel is a wiser man than the Babylonian sages and practitioners of the magic arts, but that the credit for what he is able to do belongs entirely to God, as Daniel himself confesses. H. Kosmala (*Hebräer-Essener-Christen*, 1959, p. 222) draws attention to the way in which the theology of the Essenes, as illustrated in the *Hodāyot* from Dead Sea Cave I and in the Book of Discipline, follows in particular the teaching of Job and the Psalms in laying emphasis on the link between the power of God and the possession by certain men of divine wisdom, and points out that the same connection of thought is found in this passage in the Book of Daniel. We are here on one of the lines of development which leads from the Old Testament to the New Testament, the theology of the Essenes possibly forming a link between the two.

[24–25] Arioch snatches at the chance to escape from his disagreeable duty and loses no time in introducing Daniel into the king's presence. The inconsistency with 2.16, as it stands in the

Massoretic Text, and with chapter 1, in that Daniel is introduced to the king as if for the first time, is probably not to be taken too seriously, and can in part, as we saw, be removed by emendation.

[26-30] The king, addressing Daniel by his Babylonian name Belteshazzar, puts the same question to Daniel as he has already put to the professional wise men, and Daniel immediately dismisses the possibility that any of them could have supplied the desired information. He himself, he declares, has been granted a supernatural power of interpretation by the God who sent the dream to Nebuchadnezzar. Like Joseph, who said (Gen. 41.16), 'It is not in me; God will give Pharaoh a favourable answer', Daniel explicitly disclaims the possession of any superior wisdom or command of technique in his own right which would distinguish him from anybody else. It is all of God, if he is able to disclose the secret of the dream. There is a God, who, because he controls the future, can make it known, and it has been his wish to reveal something to the king, and this he has done through a dream. The dream, however, requires a fit interpreter. The difference between the wise men and Daniel is, not a difference of genius or skill, but simply the fact that God has chosen to use Daniel and not the wise men who have nothing but their worthless manuals of dream interpretation to guide them.

The first and most important thing that Daniel tells the king about his dream is that it is eschatological in character. It concerns what is to happen at the end of the present age. The phrase used here and again in 10.14, literally 'in the end of the days', recurs in various contexts but always seems to denote the end of a perspective of history, 'the *closing period* of the future so far as it falls within the range of view of the writer using it' (S. R. Driver, Camb. B., p. 26). Sometimes the phrase refers to the closing days of history before the Messianic culmination when God will bring in his kingdom (see especially Isa. 2.2 = Micah 4.1). That seems to be the meaning here. The king is being told by God how history is moving towards its consummation, and we are given to understand that the dream was sent to him because his mind was anxiously revolving thoughts about the destiny of the world.

[31-36] Daniel now describes the king's dream. In his dream he became aware of a colossal statue or image standing before him. Montgomery (ICC, p. 186) says that there were no literary models for our author to imitate in his creation of this piece of symbolism.

The huge statues of Babylonian art and the famous colossi of Egypt might well have acted as prototypes. Herodotus (I, 183) tells of a statue of Bel at Babylon twelve cubits high and Nabonidus is said to have set up an image of Sin in the temple of Eḫulḫul. There is no suggestion here, however, that the image of Nebuchadnezzar's dream was an idol. A more likely parallel might be found in the allegorical figures representing the world as a huge man which, as Reitzenstein tells us, appear in ancient literature (*Studien zum Antiken Synkretismus aus Iran und Griechenland*, 1926), and, though it is impossible to trace the connection, this may conceivably be the source of the symbolism.

The image is of a very remarkable kind, constructed, as it is, of different metals in a descending series with the peculiar feature that the feet are the weakest part, being partly of iron and partly of clay or (as Montgomery suggests) of tile-work or ceramic. It has been plausibly suggested that the meaning is that a core of clay was covered with metal (cf. Bel and the Dragon, v. 7, 'clay within and brass without'), but it must be admitted that the weakness of the structure would not then have been visible to the onlooker. The weakness of the image, resting indeed on an insecure foundation, is shown when a mysterious stone, quarried without human agency, is seen to strike against its feet with the result that the whole structure dissolves in a thousand fragments and is blown away like the cloud of chaff from a threshing-floor. Then suddenly, with the fantastic sequence of dream symbolism, the stone grows and grows until it dominates the whole scene.

Such is the dream. From the description of the image and its strange fate Daniel proceeds immediately to the interpretation.

[37–45] The four parts of the image made of four different metals are explained as representing four successive kingdoms. The head of gold, indeed, is identified with Nebuchadnezzar himself, but he obviously stands for the Babylonian kingdom as its most outstanding monarch.

In the writer's thought here there is an unmistakable reminiscence of the idea of the four ages, their degeneration being represented by the descending scale of values of the four metals after which they are named, gold, silver, copper or bronze and iron. There is just a hint in Gen. 4 of the belief that the course of history is a degeneration, but, as is well known, the clearest statement of the theory appears in two famous passages in classical literature, *viz.* Hesiod, *Works and*

Days 109–201 (where the number of ages is actually given as five owing to the interpolation of an age of demigods) and Ovid, *Metamorphoses* I, 89–150. Parallels occur in Hinduism, Buddhism and Zoroastrianism, though, in the case of the Zoroastrian or Parsee theory of the periods of history, there are chronological difficulties which make it doubtful whether it is relevant to the interpretation of the present passage.

Here in Daniel, however, the idea of degeneration is purely secondary. Indeed the circumstance that there are four metals does not seem to be of any great consequence either, the important point being that the successive kingdoms of this world, representing the attempted deification of human power, were destined to be brought to an end by something that was not of this world. What is of most importance, not only for the interpretation of this chapter, but for the interpretation of the whole book, is to determine what the fourth kingdom stands for. There is no doubt at all, as we have seen, about the identification of the first kingdom with the neo-Babylonian Empire. The great majority of modern scholars likewise agree that the fourth kingdom is that of the Greeks. That this view is correct might be difficult to demonstrate on the basis of chapter 2 taken by itself, but, when the parallel vision of chapter 7 and the visions of the concluding part of the book are taken into account, a case can be made out which should convince anyone who is not committed to another view in spite of the internal evidence of the book itself.

It is undoubtedly true that, when men looked back from the vantage point of early Christianity, they saw in the tremendous event of the founding of the Church the fulfilment of the promised triumph of God's kingdom as it had been foreseen by Daniel. It is further understandable that others down the ages should feel that the triumph depicted in Nebuchadnezzar's dream and in Daniel's vision had not yet been adequately fulfilled, and should, therefore, have attempted to find in the Book of Daniel the clue to an imminent climax in their own day. There is a sense in which all history stands in immediate relation to the *eschaton*. But all this should not prevent us from looking fairly and squarely at what the book itself says. As we shall see, the evidence points unmistakably to a date which may be very closely determined within the reign of Antiochus IV Epiphanes for the composition of the book as we have it now and makes it clear that the climax of history was regarded as being imminent at that particular time. That the expectation was not literally fulfilled is a fact which has to be honestly faced. Failure here has been responsible for the deplorable history of the interpretation of this book and has done much to obscure the message which the book has for its own, and indeed for every, age. Yet we should not fail to realize that, even when it has been misinterpreted, the very anxiety to make it relevant to each new age, is a sign that it has not been completely misunderstood. Much harm has been done, and is still being done, by the refusal to recognize a truth which an absurd interpretation of Scripture is in its own mistaken way seeking to conserve.

If the fourth kingdom is Greece, it is clear that the third kingdom must be Persia; and then there seems to be no choice but to regard the second kingdom as the apocryphal Median kingdom, for the existence of which, between the Babylonian and Persian Empires, there is absolutely no trace in contemporary records. The Median kingdom of actual history, which had played its part in destroying Nineveh in 612, was incorporated in the kingdom of Persia in 550 by Cyrus when he defeated Astyages. It is only in the Book of Daniel, and in writings dependent upon it, that we meet with the mysterious and baffling figure Darius the Mede who owes his supposed existence to a historical blunder. It is true that Josephus informs us that he was a kinsman of Cyrus and a son of Astyages and that he had another name among the Greeks, but Josephus is merely making the best of a bad job, and the same has to be said of all the other attempts to give Darius the Mede a foothold in history. We possess contemporary records and they show that there is no place at all between the fall of the neo-Babylonian dynasty and the assumption of power by Cyrus the Persian for a Median kingdom. One or both of two explanations may account for the mistake. There is evidence that in pre-Maccabaean times there was a belief, reflected in certain Greek writers and possibly of Persian origin, that the series of kingdoms begins, not with the Babylonian Empire as in Daniel, but with the Assyrian, the historical successor of which was the Median. What the author of Daniel has done, then, is simply to take the original series and substitute Babylonian for Assyrian, no doubt because the Babylonians had had a more decisive influence on the fate of Judah than the Assyrians ever had, failing to notice that he thereby made nonsense of the sequence. Another decisive influence in determining the sequence in the Book of Daniel may have been such a passage in prophecy as that preserved in Isa. 21.2–4:

A stern vision is told to me;
   the plunderer plunders,
   and the destroyer destroys.
Go up, O Elam,
   Lay siege, O Media. . . .
   The twilight I longed for
   has been turned for me into trembling.

A late writer, like the author of the Book of Daniel, might very easily
conclude that such a prophecy must in the course of events have been
fulfilled. Moreover a vague, popular, but accurate tradition may
have existed to the effect that a Darius once captured Babylon, and
so it would be concluded that that must have been the name of the
founder of the supposed Median Empire which was interpolated between the neo-Babylonian and the Persian. The Darius of this tradition, however, would be the great Darius Hystaspis, the successor of
Cambyses, who did recover Babylon from rebels who had seized it
after the death of Cambyses, but was a Persian and not a Mede.
However that may be, enough evidence is already in our possession
to make it virtually certain that no further evidence could establish
the historicity of a Median kingdom as occurring between the Babylonian and the Persian.

In the interpretation of his dream to the king Daniel, as we have
seen, specifically identifies the image's head of gold with Nebuchadnezzar himself, selected as the representative monarch of the first
kingdom. He addresses him with a Persian royal title, *viz*. king of
kings, which, however, is actually used of Nebuchadnezzar in Ezek.
26.7 and, therefore, may not be used anachronistically of the Babylonian monarch. It is more important to notice that an authority ex-
tending over both men and nature is here attributed to Nebuchadnezzar such as is almost exactly paralleled in Jer. 27.6–7; 28.14.
Heaton, following a suggestion of Bentzen's, sees in this a reflection
of the Babylonian New Year Festival at which one fixed element in
the ceremonies was the recitation of the Epic of Creation in honour
of the creator god Marduk, whose representative the king was supposed to be. Whether or not the author of the Book of Daniel was
aware of and intended this connection of thought is uncertain, though
that in some way, like other biblical writers, he has knowledge of
Babylonian and related mythologies seems likely in view of the symbolism of chapter 7. Whether there is a connection between this
thought of royal sovereignty over nature and the custom of having
menageries at Oriental courts in ancient times, not to speak of the

familiar bas-reliefs depicting kings enjoying the pleasures of the chase, it is impossible to say. It will be remembered that an interest in the flora and fauna of the natural world is attributed to Solomon (I Kings 4.33; cf. Jer. 27.5–6; Bar. 3.16).

In the interpretation the second and third kingdoms are dismissed in a single verse. The interest of the writer is clearly in the fourth kingdom, and that, of course, is because the fourth kingdom was contemporary to himself and he was filled with the confident hope that the Jews were about to be delivered from its hated sway by a divine intervention.

It is emphasized that the fourth kingdom, the kingdom of the Greeks, corresponds to the iron of the image, and this is taken seriously as symbolizing its ruthless character. Bevan in his commentary draws attention to the quaint suggestion of Jerome, for whom the iron represented Rome, that the Greek Empire was identified with brass, 'because brass is the most resounding of metals, and thus symbolizes the eloquence of the Greek language'! Actually, on the interpretation to which by the evidence we seem to be committed, it was a very different aspect of the Greek Empire that impressed the author of the Book of Daniel.

He also finds a double appropriateness in the curious feature of the description that the feet and the toes (the toes are mentioned only in the interpretation) are composed of a mixture of iron and potter's clay. It signifies, first, that the fourth kingdom is to be a divided or composite kingdom. After the death of Alexander the Greek Empire did break up and, eventually, the two successor kingdoms which were of most consequence to the Jews were the Seleucid power to the north and the Ptolemaic to the south. By the second century the former (i.e. the Seleucid) power had clearly by the victory of Antiochus III proved its superiority over its Ptolemaic rival at the battle of Paneas (198 BC), so much so that Palestine had passed from the Ptolemaic into the Seleucid sphere of influence. We must, therefore, conclude that the iron represents the Seleucid kingdom and the clay the Ptolemaic. Secondly, however, the mixture of iron and clay is explained as symbolizing certain intermarriages between the Seleucid and Ptolemaic royal families to which reference will have to be made later (see ch. 11). These intermarriages had not led to stable friendship between the houses thus linked together. Montgomery can scarcely be right in thinking that there is here a reference to the well-known policy of Alexander of encouraging the fusion of races and setting an example to his followers by himself contracting marriages with non-Hellenic women. The question of the conservation of the purity of the Greek race can have been of no concern to a Jew. It is difficult to understand what Montgomery means by describing Alexander's attempted fusion of races and cultures as 'the revival of the Tower of Babel'. One would have thought that it might have been regarded as a reversal of the process initiated by the dispersal of mankind associated in Jewish belief with the story of the Tower of Babel, a reversal, however, taking place in a way that would undoubtedly be 'abhorrent to Judaism'.

In his interpretation Daniel finally comes to the mysterious stone quarried without human agency which strikes the image on the feet, its most vulnerable part, and in a moment reduces it to a heap of fragments so small and light that they are all winnowed away by the wind. This is said to have happened 'in the days of those kings', by which is meant the kings of the fourth kingdom, not the kings of all four kingdoms. It is a result of the figure employed in the dream, *viz.* an image, that the four kingdoms are represented as if they were all present contemporaneously and vanished at one and the same time. This should not be pressed. Chronological sequence is clearly introduced in the interpretation.

The grotesque growth of the stone in the dream is explained as meaning the establishment of an eternal kingdom. Jeffery (*IB*) well says, 'Its standing *for ever* is the universality of the kingdom in time, just as the mountain filling the earth was its universality in space.' It is not clear whether, when we are told that the sovereignty of this kingdom is not to be left to another kingdom, there is any implication that the kingdom which is to be set up is that of Israel as the People of God. That may well have been in the the writer's mind, but the thought is not expressed unambiguously until we come to chapter 7. All that we can say at this point is that it was Daniel's God who was going to set up this everlasting kingdom and was therefore able to reveal what he was about to do. The closest parallel in Scripture to the fantastic growth of the stone into a mountain is to be found in the famous prophecy of Isa. 2.1ff. (= Micah 4.1ff.):

> It shall come to pass in the latter days
>> that the mountain of the house of the Lord
> Shall be established as the highest of the mountains,
>> and shall be raised above the hills.

Daniel's assertion of the reliability of the dream as a revelation of the future, though ostensibly intended for Nebuchadnezzar, was doubtless also intended for the readers of the book. For them the announced collapse of the world power before the onset of the divine kingdom was imminent, as it was not for Nebuchadnezzar. It was they upon whom the end of the ages was about to come, and so they could rest serene in the certainty that it was God's will that was about to be accomplished. There was apparently an expectation in the East, in connection with the theory of the four kingdoms, that a fifth or Oriental monarchy would sweep away the Greek Empire. There was also in certain quarters the expectation that the rising power of Rome was destined to be the fifth monarchy. Dionysius of Halicarnassus, the contemporary of Livy, gives the succession of empires as Assyria, Media, Persia, Macedonia and Rome, and it is familiar knowledge how Virgil hailed the foundation of the Roman Empire by Augustus as the climax of history planned by the gods far back in the past. The author of the Book of Daniel is expressing the belief that there is going to be a final end to man-made empires. This is to be no fifth monarchy to which a sixth or a seventh might succeed.

[46–49] The end of the story shows us Nebuchadnezzar capitulating completely. He accepts Daniel's interpretation without question and apparently offers Daniel divine honours. His payment of homage to Daniel might merely have meant the reversal of the homage a subject was expected to pay to the king. The use, however, of the terms sacrifice and incense shows that more is implied. It is odd that Daniel should be represented as accepting what is virtually worship, if we consider the attitude of the Jew to the worship of anything other than God alone. But we must not take this feature of the story too solemnly. We may suspect almost a touch of humour here. The Jew who was so often in the position of the inferior liked to indulge in the fantasy of having the tables turned on occasion. Montgomery, too, rightly recalls the story in Josephus of an apocryphal visit of Alexander to Jerusalem, representing him as doing obeisance before the high-priest of the Jews and, when asked by Parmenio for the reason of his surprising action, as replying, 'I did not adore him, but that God who hath honoured him with his high-priesthood.' Nebuchadnezzar, at all events, follows up his action by confessing Daniel's God to be the supreme God. It is possible that the author has in mind such passages as the one in Isa. 49.23 where it is promised that kings would bow with their faces to the ground to Israel and would lick the dust of their feet.

The chapter ends with the promotion of Daniel and his friends, the friends presumably to minor prefectures, while Daniel himself, being put in authority over the whole province of Babylon, remains at court or in the royal chancellery, whichever is the significance of the phrase which, translated literally, means 'in the gate of the king'. A similar expression is used in the version of the story of Aḥiḳar in the Elephantine Papyri where the meaning is that Aḥiḳar was keeper of the seal to Sennacherib (*viz.* 'at the gate of the palace'); but in Esth. 2.21, where we are told that Mordecai was sitting at the King's gate, the intention seems to be to represent him as haunting the palace gate. Appropriately enough Daniel was not only given the highest civil post under the king, but was placed as prefect over the whole corps of wise men and practitioners of the magic arts. How an Israelite, while remaining true to his ancestral faith, could accept such a position does not seem to have occurred to the author, any more than it did to the author of the story of Joseph. It is all part of the subordination of all human wisdom to the wisdom which is conferred by God.

III

CHAPTER THREE

3 ¹King Nebuchadnezzar made an image of gold, whose height was sixty cubits and its breadth six cubits. He set it up on the plain of Dura, in the province of Babylon. ²Then King Nebuchadnezzar sent to assemble the satraps, the prefects, and the governors, the counsellors, the treasurers, the justices, the magistrates, and all the officials of the provinces to come to the dedication of the image which King Nebuchadnezzar had set up. ³Then the satraps, the prefects, and the governors, the counsellors, the treasurers, the justices, the magistrates, and all the officials of the provinces, were assembled for the dedication of the image that King Nebuchadnezzar had set up; and they stood before the image that Nebuchadnezzar had set up. ⁴And the herald proclaimed aloud, 'You are commanded, O peoples, nations, and languages, ⁵that when you hear the sound of the horn, pipe, lyre, trigon, harp, bagpipe, and every kind of music, you are to fall down and worship the golden image that King Nebuchadnezzar has set up; ⁶and whoever does not fall down and worship shall immediately be cast into a burning fiery furnace.' ⁷Therefore, as soon as all the peoples heard the sound of the horn, pipe, lyre, trigon, harp, bagpipe, and every kind of music, all the peoples, nations, and languages fell down and worshipped the golden image which King Nebuchadnezzar had set up.

8 Therefore at that time certain Chaldeans came forward and maliciously accused the Jews. ⁹They said to King Nebuchadnezzar, 'O king, live for ever! ¹⁰You, O king, have made a decree, that every man who hears the sound of the horn, pipe, lyre, trigon, harp, bagpipe, and every kind of music, shall fall down and worship the golden image; ¹¹and whoever does not fall down and worship shall be cast into a burning fiery furnace. ¹²There are certain Jews whom you have appointed over the affairs of the province of Babylon: Shadrach, Meshach, and Abednego. These men, O king, pay no heed to you; they do not serve your gods or worship the golden image which you have set up.'

13 Then Nebuchadnezzar in furious rage commanded that Shadrach, Meshach, and Abednego be brought. Then they brought these men before the king. ¹⁴Nebuchadnezzar said to them, 'Is it true, O Shadrach, Meshach, and Abednego, that you do not serve my gods or

53

worship the golden image which I have set up? ¹⁵Now if you are ready when you hear the sound of the horn, pipe, lyre, trigon, harp, bagpipe, and every kind of music, to fall down and worship the image which I have made, well and good; but if you do not worship, you shall immediately be cast into a burning fiery furnace; and who is the god that will deliver you out of my hands?'

16 Shadrach, Meshach, and Abednego answered the king, 'O Nebuchadnezzar, we have no need to answer you in this matter. ¹⁷If it be so, our God whom we serve is able to deliver us from the burning fiery furnace; and he will deliver us out of your hand, O king.* ¹⁸But if not, be it known to you, O king, that we will not serve your gods or worship the golden image which you have set up.'

19 Then Nebuchadnezzar was full of fury, and the expression of his face was changed against Shadrach, Meshach, and Abednego. He ordered the furnace heated seven times more than it was wont to be heated. ²⁰And he ordered certain mighty men of his army to bind Shadrach, Meshach, and Abednego, and to cast them into the burning fiery furnace. ²¹Then these men were bound in their mantles, their tunics, their hats, and their other garments and they were cast into the burning fiery furnace. ²²Because the king's order was strict and the furnace very hot, the flame of the fire slew those men who took up Shadrach, Meshach, and Abednego. ²³And these three men, Shadrach, Meshach, and Abednego, fell bound into the burning fiery furnace.

24 Then King Nebuchadnezzar was astonished and rose up in haste. He said to his counsellors, 'Did we not cast three men bound into the fire?' They answered the king, 'True, O king.' ²⁵He answered, 'But I see four men loose, walking in the midst of the fire, and they are not hurt; and the appearance of the fourth is like a son of the gods.'

26 Then Nebuchadnezzar came near to the door of the burning fiery furnace and said, 'Shadrach, Meshach, and Abednego, servants of the Most High God, come forth, and come here!' Then Shadrach, Meshach, and Abednego came out from the fire. ²⁷And the satraps, the prefects, the governors, and the king's counsellors gathered together and saw that the fire had not had any power over the bodies of those men; the hair of their heads was not singed, their mantles were not harmed, and no smell of fire had come upon them. ²⁸Nebuchadnezzar said, 'Blessed be the God of Shadrach, Meshach, and Abednego, who has sent his angel and delivered his servants, who trusted in him, and set at naught the king's command, and yielded up their bodies rather than serve and worship any god except their own God. ²⁹Therefore I make a decree: Any people, nation, or language that speaks anything against the God of Shadrach, Meshach, and Abednego shall be torn limb from limb, and their houses laid in ruins; for there is no other god who is able to deliver in this way.' ³⁰Then the king promoted† Shadrach, Meshach, and Abednego in the province of Babylon.

* Probably 'If our God . . . furnace, he will. . .' or 'But if there is need . .' (Plöger).
† Or 'left in office'.

THE STORY IN this chapter is a simple one simply told. Daniel, who was the hero in chapter 2, is surprisingly not mentioned at all, and the stage is occupied by his three companions, referred to by their Babylonian names, who courageously defy an order of King Nebuchadnezzar rather than compromise their loyalty to their God. By a miracle they are delivered from a dreadful death. Astounded at this evidence of the power of God, the pagan king decrees that worship of the God of Shadrach, Meshach and Abednego shall henceforth be permissible.

There are two ways of regarding this story, both of them legitimate.

On the one hand, we can apply the form-critical method and treat it as an example of a familiar *genre*, the martyr story. The very fact that Daniel is not mentioned suggests that it was originally independent of the cycle of stories about Daniel, and has been somewhat artificially united with them, though, of course, to bring Daniel into this chapter as worthy of punishment for loyalty to a God whom Nebuchadnezzar, according to the previous chapter, had acknowledged so handsomely, would have seemed very strange. However this may be, we have here the familiar situation of the tyrant who acknowledges no authority but his own and is liable to fly into paroxysms of rage at the slightest opposition. Over against him, to all appearance completely at his mercy, are the three confessors who are faced with the choice between inevitable death, if they hold to their loyalty to God, and an act of compromise which would save their lives. They unhesitatingly choose death rather than compromise. The martyr story takes two forms. Either the martyr is faithful unto death and the reward is reserved for another world or a miracle takes place and the martyr's faith is visibly justified. To the former type belongs the story of the martyrdom of the seven heroic brothers and their mother who are all put to a most painful death and are supported in their agony by the hope of a blessed resurrection (II Macc. 7). To the latter type belongs the present story in which faith is justified by manifest miracle. It is quite likely that there is no essential difference in ultimate meaning between these two types of story. They may merely represent two different ways of saying that God will honour the loyalty of his servants. Indeed the link between the two types of story seems to be provided by the magnificent 'But if not' of v. 18. The martyr must stand firm whether a miracle takes place or not. Indeed where, as here, the justification takes the form of a miraculous deliverance, the story may actually be meant to encourage those who have no expectation of a literal miracle, but recognize in the symbolism of the miracle story one way of expressing the faith in which they are inflexibly prepared to die.

The other method of interpretation, which in a sense includes the former, is to see this story, for all that it belongs to a familiar type with its summons to loyalty in every age, as acquiring a particular meaning and made relevant to a particular situation through the setting in which we find it here. It is not impossible that the story may reflect the memory of some earlier testing of Jewish loyalty, for example under Nabonidus, the historical evidence about whom represents him as something of a religious fanatic, or under one of the later Persian kings. The polemic against idolatry in Second Isaiah and in the Epistle of Jeremy, however, meets the challenge of paganism with the weapons of ridicule and satire and suggests that the danger to faith came not so much from the threat of persecution as from the appeal of idolatrous worship to the senses. It may well be, as has frequently been suggested, that the author of our story had in mind in writing it the splendid words in Second Isaiah (Isa. 43.1–2): 'Fear not, for I have redeemed you; I have called you by name, you are mine. When you pass through the waters I will be with you; and through the rivers, they shall not overwhelm you; when you walk through fire you shall not be burned, and the flame shall not consume you.' When, however, we compare this with Ps. 66.10–12: 'For thou, O God, hast tested us; thou hast tried us as silver is tried. Thou didst bring us into the net; thou didst lay affliction on our loins; thou didst let men ride over our heads; we went through fire and through water; yet thou hast brought us forth to a spacious place'—we can see that we have to do with cultic language which has a general reference to the trials of the faithful rather than to a specific historical situation. In the Book of Daniel, on the other hand, all the different stories, including this one about the blazing furnace, whatever their original reference, seem to be brought into relation to the persecution of the Jews under Antiochus Epiphanes by whose deliberate policy the Jews were ordered to violate the regulations of their sacred law and apostatize from their ancestral faith on pain of death (I Macc. 1.44–50). It is true that Jer. 29.22 makes it clear that burning as a punishment was not unknown in the time of Nebuchadnezzar, but there is no suggestion there that the incident referred to had anything to do with religious persecution. The problem of loyalty, of course, does not belong to any one period of Israel's history, but it seems to have become particularly acute in the period of crisis under Antiochus Epiphanes, when it was seen in relation to the expected climax of history as the ultimate test that would determine whether or not a man belonged to the age to come or to the age that was about to pass away.

[1–7] The date given for the incident recounted in this chapter in the LXX, *viz.* the eighteenth year of Nebuchadnezzar's reign, is doubtless borrowed from Jer. 52.29, so as to give a plausible reason for this unusual ceremony. The dates in the Book of Daniel are of little historical interest.

The erection of an image or statue of gold is profusely illustrated in the commentaries. Perhaps the most relevant references given are that to Herodotus I, 183, where we read of two statues of gold, one of Zeus and another (dated to the time of Cyrus) of a man, twelve cubits high, and that to the image of Apollo at Daphnae which was set up by Antiochus Epiphanes and to which indeed a veiled reference might be seen here. The El Grecoesque proportions of the image have attracted attention. It is possible that the figure is to be thought of as not very realistic and more like a totem pole. Montgomery compares it with 'a stele only partly sculptured, where the stone is decorated at the top with the relief of the bust of a human body'.

It can have been of no importance to the readers of the story where the Plain of Dura was supposed to be. The word 'dura' suggests a circular enclosure of some kind and is common in place names. Possibly a locality in the neighbourhood of Hillah is intended. A piece of local colour like this may conceivably indicate a traditional element in the story.

The author goes on to tell of the ceremony of dedication of the image which can be illustrated from Babylonian and Assyrian inscriptions. The list of high officers of the realm, summoned by the king to attend, is obviously given with relish and repeated in the next verse for good measure. As the majority of the titles are Persian, the writer is clearly at no pains to avoid anachronism. Similar lists of officials, however, appear in Assyrian inscriptions. The details are of interest to the philologist, whereas the author uses the titles as a rhetorician for their effect.

These representatives of the many provinces of the empire are summoned to do obeisance to the image which presumably (vv. 12, 14, 18) represents a god and not the king. As the Babylonian king, however, was thought of as the representative of Marduk it is not inappropriate

in this connection to remember the worship of the Emperor, which
was used to consolidate the Roman power, and the earlier deification
of the hellenistic monarchs which set a model for the Romans. Judith
3.8 credits Nebuchadnezzar with a similar policy and furnishes a close
parallel to Dan. 3.

It is possible to make too much of the policy of hellenization to
which this story is supposed to be an allusion. Antiochus Epiphanes did
not embark on a policy of the hellenization of all Jews everywhere but
required conformity only from the Jews of Jerusalem and neighbourhood as a punishment for their rebellion. The policy of hellenization
seems to have been initiated by a powerful party among the Jews
themselves who sought the sanction and support of Antiochus. But
the issue for the loyal Jews was that between the world and their own
conscience and that is the issue in the story under consideration.
Nebuchadnezzar symbolizes the authority of the world which comes
into conflict with the authority of God (cf. Acts 5.29).

The list of musical instruments once more illustrates the author's
partiality for sonorous lists of names. We should certainly not suppose
that anything in the nature of a modern orchestra is intended. If
sūmpōnyāh is the bagpipes its sound would not blend very well with
that of the other instruments! What is of interest is that several of the
names of instruments mentioned here are Greek. In particular, the
first instance in Greek literature of the use of the word συμφωνία
(= *sūmpōnyāh*) as a musical instrument occurs in the second century
B C and actually in connection with Antiochus Epiphanes, who according to Polybius seems to have shocked public opinion by dancing to its
barbarous strains. The use of Greek terms makes it highly improbable
that the form in which this story lies before us is to be dated before the
third century B C at the earliest.

It has been suggested that the sounding of musical instruments as
a prelude to the act of worship may be intended as a blasphemous
parody of the blaring of trumpets on the Jewish New Year's Day. The
martyrs were thus expected on this view to take part in a kind of black
mass or witches' sabbath.

The punishment by burning in Israel was reserved for certain ex-
ceptional offences. It can be documented in Egypt, while, as we have
already seen, there is actually a reference in Jer. 29.22 to the burning
of two Jewish prophets, Zedekiah and Ahab, by Nebuchadnezzar for
some unspecified offence. The martyrdom of the seven brothers (II
Macc. 7) is a very relevant illustration. Montgomery is doubtless

correct in describing the furnace as 'similar to our common lime-kiln, with a perpendicular shaft from the top and an opening at the bottom for extracting the fused lime'. This would explain both the way in which the victims were put into the furnace and the circumstance that the king could see what was happening inside.

[8–12] This section tells of the accusation brought by certain Chaldaeans against Shadrach, Meshach and Abed-nego who had refused to conform like all the other officials summoned to the Plain of Dura. Unlike the informers of chapter 6 who engineered everything from start to finish, these men—whether the word 'Chaldaean' is used here racially or of a special class of wise men previously referred to it is impossible to determine—took advantage of a situation which they had not themselves brought about. We are not told what their motive was, whether jealousy or the hope of some personal advantage in recognition of their zeal for the honour of the king, but they represent an unpleasant concomitant of tyranny which is only too familiar. The accusation they made was not a false one, since the men had undoubtedly refused to conform to the king's order, but it was definitely malicious (better than 'slanderous', though the Aramaic phrase, derived from a similar Assyrian one, can mean 'to slander'). The Jews had been appointed to positions of influence and the informers clearly wished to represent them to the king as disloyal and unworthy of his trust.

[13–18] On hearing the accusation, the king falls into the typical rage of the Oriental tyrant whose will is thwarted, but, rather surprisingly, he gives the Jews a second chance. This, however, is merely a necessary device, so as to bring the tyrant and the accused face to face and to give the latter the opportunity to make their confession in public. It is not to be supposed that the author's intention is to represent the king in a favourable light. In fact he now makes the arrogant and blasphemous claim which the Rabshakeh made when threatening Hezekiah (Isa. 36.13ff.), the claim to the possession of a human power so great that there is no divine power to which the victims can turn for help. We see here the worldly power absolutely confident that there is no limit to its authority. The confessors reply boldly, but what they say has proved unusually difficult to translate. The meaning seems to be something like this: 'If our God whom we worship is able to save us, then he will do so', or possibly, 'there is a God who can and will deliver us'. At the same time, they know well that God for some good reason may not choose to deliver them, and so they make the splendid affirmation: 'But if not, be it known to your majesty that we will neither worship your god nor worship the image which you have erected.' In a very real sense the climax of the chapter is reached here. The tyrant is defeated on ground of his own choosing, whether God intervenes to work a miracle or not, just as the Satan was defeated when Job justified God's faith in him. The human spirit, unconquerable through reliance on God, has been able to defy the worst that the earthly power can do. That, of course, is where the similar story in II Macc. 7 leaves the matter. The author here, however, like the author of the Book of Job, prefers to conclude with a manifest vindication of the heroes of his story. But that he had reached a faith beyond the need of a manifest vindication is plain from v. 18 and it is this that makes it easier for us to appropriate the message of the chapter. Although nothing is said in this chapter of the hope which is said to have supported the martyrs of II Macc. 7 in their terrible ordeal, we should not forget Dan. 12.2–3 (see below), where the hope of resurrection for faithful martyrs does break through.

[19–23] The element of caricature in the story is maintained. Any fire at all would have served the tyrant's purpose, but it has to be represented as an unnecessarily hot one! Possibly to suggest that the king was not quite as sure of his power as he professed to be, we are told that the most muscular men in his army were sent for to act as executioners. The feature of the story that the men were not stripped of their clothing before execution may have it as its aim to heighten the miracle that was to follow. The garments detailed, however, may be their ceremonial dress worn over their ordinary clothes. It is scarcely adequate poetic justice that the executioners are killed by the heat instead of the informers, but this feature of the story is evidently intended to make the tyrant's power seem ridiculous. It is at this point that the long interpolation in the LXX known as the Song of the Three Children is introduced.

[24–30] The mention of Nebuchadnezzar's alarm and excitement as the first indication that something unusual has happened is extremely effective as a piece of story-telling. Apparently the king alone sees the mysterious companion of the dauntless three as they walk about quite unharmed in the furnace, their bonds fallen off or burned off. The king seeks from the courtiers who are with him confirmation that only three men had been thrown into the furnace, and declares that the fourth figure is like 'a god', which expression is interpreted in v. 28 by the king himself as meaning 'an angel'. There is no doubt at all that the idea that the fourth figure in the furnace is Christ is impossible and, indeed, contrary to the plain meaning of the author. The *bar 'ᵉlāhīn* here is one of a class of beings who are called in Hebrew the *benē 'ᵉlōhīm* and are to be thought of as attendants upon the deity, members of his court and messengers sent on his behests. Other names for them are *mal'ākīm* (messengers or angels) and *qᵉdōshīm* (holy ones), while collectively they are called *ṣᵉbā' hash-shamayim* (the host of heaven): see Gen. 6.2; Job 1.6; 38.7; I Kings 22.19; Ps. 148.2. There is further evidence in the inscriptions from Karatepe and Ugarit. It is necessary to distinguish from the *benē 'ᵉlōhīm* the *mal'āk Yahweh*, who was regarded as an appearance of Yahweh himself.

Nebuchadnezzar now approaches the door of the furnace and calls the confessors out by the title of servants of the Most High God (*'ᵉlahā 'illayā*), the *'el 'elyōn* or *'elyōn* (Θεὸς ὕψιστος) of Gen. 14.19, 20 and Num. 24.16; Deut. 32,8; Ps. 18.14, etc.; Isa. 14.14. Compare also the Phoenician deity Ἐλιοῦν καλούμενος ὕψιστος vouched for by Philo of Byblos (see Eusebius, *Praep. Evang.*, I 10, §12f.). 'This monotheistic term', Montgomery remarks, 'became current in circles more or less influenced by Judaism.' It is peculiarly appropriate here with its suggestion that the pagan king has had at least a glimpse of the truth about God. The astonishing nature of the miracle is emphasized by the statement that not a trace of burning was to be detected on the bodies, hair or even clothing of the men. In a brief doxology Nebuchadnezzar declares that the God of Shadrach, Meshach and Abed-nego has sent his angel to protect them. Thus, from the mouth of a pagan king, tribute is paid to a God whose protecting presence is with his people in every danger. Bentzen (Introd. to Comm., p. 10) very wisely points out that the danger which besets the Jewish faith in God's power to work miracles of deliverance was that men should indulge in a kind of escapism, but, as we have already seen, v. 18 of this chapter shows that the author avoids the temptation of wishful thinking. He is a realist, even though he chooses to say what he has to say in the form of a story with a happy outcome. Von Gall (quoted by Bentzen, p. 39) may be right in thinking that the author is even alluding here to the newly born hope of eternal life and God's ability to save his faithful ones in death. In this connection it is worth quoting Weiser's remark in his Commentary on the Psalms where he says with reference to Ps. 66 that God brings his people, not by a *via triumphalis*, but by a *via crucis*.

Nebuchadnezzar proclaims the religion of the confessors to be

legitimate within his realm. This may be intended as an encouragement to the Jews who were suffering under the ban on their religion
put into force by Antiochus Epiphanes. It is sometimes urged that
Nebuchadnezzar is not represented here as hostile to the Jews but
only to the three confessors who had disobeyed him and that he is,
therefore, not a very suitable type to represent Antiochus. It has to be
pointed out, however, that the policy of Antiochus was not anti-
Semitic but was rather a political move against a certain section of the
Jews who had defied him. Perhaps the story of the heroic confessors is
more relevant to the second-century situation than is sometimes recognized. We are told that, as the result of Nebuchadnezzar's change of
heart, the men were promoted in the province of Babylon, though
what that involved is left entirely vague. Whether the author really
hoped or expected that Antiochus would exhibit the openness to conviction of a Nebuchadnezzar it is impossible to say. Perhaps, however,
the author is saying what he has to say in despite of the hard facts of
history.

IV

CHAPTER FOUR

4 ¹King Nebuchadnezzar to all peoples, nations, and languages, that dwell in all the earth: Peace be multiplied to you! ²It has seemed good to me to show the signs and wonders that the Most High God has wrought toward me.

³How great are his signs,
   how mighty his wonders!
His kingdom is an everlasting kingdom,
   and his dominion is from generation to generation.

4 I, Nebuchadnezzar, was at ease in my house and prospering in my palace. ⁵I had a dream which made me afraid; as I lay in bed the fancies and the visions of my head alarmed me. ⁶Therefore I made a decree that all the wise men of Babylon should be brought before me, that they might make known to me the interpretation of the dream. ⁷Then the magicians, the enchanters, the Chaldeans, and the astrologers came in; and I told them the dream, but they could not make known to me its interpretation. ⁸At last Daniel came in before me—he who was named Belteshazzar after the name of my god, and in whom is the spirit of the holy gods—and I told him the dream, saying, ⁹'O Belteshazzar, chief of the magicians, because I know that the spirit of the holy gods is in you and that no mystery is difficult for you, here is the dream which I saw; tell me its interpretation. ¹⁰The visions of my head as I lay in bed were these: I saw, and behold, a tree in the midst of the earth; and its height was great. ¹¹The tree grew and became strong, and its top reached to heaven, and it was visible to the end of the whole earth. ¹²Its leaves were fair and its fruit abundant, and in it was food for all. The beasts of the field found shade under it, and the birds of the air dwelt in its branches, and all flesh was fed from it.

13 'I saw in the visions of my head as I lay in bed, and behold, a watcher, a holy one, came down from heaven. ¹⁴He cried aloud and said thus, "Hew down the tree and cut off its branches, strip off its leaves and scatter its fruit; let the beasts flee from under it and the birds from its branches. ¹⁵But leave the stump of its roots in the earth, bound with a band of iron and bronze, amid the tender grass of the field. Let

63

him be wet with the dew of heaven; let his lot be with the beasts in the grass of the earth; 16let his mind be changed from a man's, and let a beast's mind be given to him; and let seven times pass over him. 17The sentence is by the decree of the watchers, the decision by the word of the holy ones, to the end that the living may know that the Most High rules the kingdom of men, and gives it to whom he will, and sets over it the lowliest of men." 18This dream I, King Nebuchadnezzar, saw. And you, O Belteshazzar, declare the interpretation, because all the wise men of my kingdom are not able to make known to me the interpretation, but you are able, for the spirit of the holy gods is in you.'

19 Then Daniel, whose name was Belteshazzar, was dismayed for a long time, and his thoughts alarmed him. The king said, 'Belteshazzar, let not the dream or the interpretation alarm you.' Belteshazzar answered, 'My lord, may the dream be for those who hate you and its interpretation for your enemies! 20The tree you saw, which grew and became strong, so that its top reached to heaven, and it was visible to the end of the whole earth; 21whose leaves were fair and its fruit abundant, and in which was food for all; under which beasts of the field found shade, and in whose branches the birds of the air dwelt—22it is you, O king, who have grown and become strong. Your greatness has grown and reaches to heaven, and your dominion to the ends of the earth. 23And whereas the king saw a watcher, a holy one, coming down from heaven and saying, "Hew down the tree and destroy it, but leave the stump of its roots in the earth, bound with a band of iron and bronze, in the tender grass of the field; and let him be wet with the dew of heaven; and let his lot be with the beasts of the field, till seven times pass over him"; 24this is the interpretation, O king: It is a decree of the Most High, which has come upon my lord the king, 25that you shall be driven from among men, and your dwelling shall be with the beasts of the field; you shall be made to eat grass like an ox, and you shall be wet with the dew of heaven, and seven times shall pass over you, till you know that the Most High rules the kingdom of men, and gives it to whom he will. 26And as it was commanded to leave the stump of the roots of the tree, your kingdom shall be sure for you from the time that you know that Heaven rules. 27Therefore, O king, let my counsel be acceptable to you; break off your sins by practising righteousness, and your iniquities by showing mercy to the oppressed, that there may perhaps be a lengthening of your tranquillity.'

28 All this came upon King Nebuchadnezzar. 29At the end of twelve months he was walking on the roof of the royal palace of Babylon, 30and the king said, 'Is not this great Babylon, which I have built by my mighty power as a royal residence and for the glory of my majesty?' 31While the words were still in the king's mouth, there fell a voice from heaven, 'O King Nebuchadnezzar, to you it is spoken: The kingdom has departed from you, 32and you shall be driven from among men, and your dwelling shall be with the beasts of the field; and you shall be made to eat grass like an ox; and seven times shall pass over you, until you have learned that the Most High rules the kingdom of men

and gives it to whom he will.' ³³Immediately the word was fulfilled upon Nebuchadnezzar. He was driven from among men, and ate grass like an ox, and his body was wet with the dew of heaven till his hair grew as long as eagles' feathers, and his nails were like birds' claws.

34 At the end of the days I, Nebuchadnezzar, lifted my eyes to heaven, and my reason returned to me, and I blessed the Most High, and praised and honoured him who lives for ever;

> for his dominion is an everlasting dominion,
> and his kingdom endures from generation to generation;
> ³⁵all the inhabitants of the earth are accounted as nothing;
> and he does according to his will in the host of heaven
> and among the inhabitants of the earth;
> and none can stay his hand
> or say to him, 'What doest thou?'

³⁶At the same time my reason returned to me; and for the glory of my kingdom, my majesty and splendour returned to me. My counsellors and my lords sought me, and I was established in my kingdom, and still more greatness was added to me. ³⁷Now I, Nebuchadnezzar, praise and extol and honour the King of heaven; for all his works are right and his ways are just; and those who walk in pride he is able to abase.

THE THEME OF this chapter is summed up in v. 25 in what is to be Nebuchadnezzar's discovery after he has been disciplined by God, *viz.* that 'the Most High is sovereign over the kingdom of men, giving it to the man of his choice', a discovery that is relevant for every age. That this is the theme of the chapter should be borne in mind as we seek to understand the symbolic language that is used. The theme is one which is common in the Old Testament, the theme of *hybris*. In Isa. 10.5ff. we are told how the Assyrian king oversteps what is permissible to an earthly ruler and invites the judgment of God. In Isa. 14 we read of a king of Babylon (J. M. Wilkie, *JTS* New Series II/1, April 1951, pp. 36–44, suggests that the king referred to is Nabonidus) who says:

> I will ascend above the heights of the clouds,
> I will make myself like the Most High.

In Ezek 28.1ff. we learn that the prophet is told to denounce the king of Tyre because of his arrogant assumption that he is divine.

Now, it is quite true that the imagery of the passage in Ezek. 28 seems to have been inspired by what is said in chapters 17 and 31 in which kingdoms and their rulers are compared to trees. Chapter 17 concludes with the thought that the replanted Judah will become a noble cedar, 'and all the trees of the field shall know that I the Lord bring low the high tree, and make high the low tree, dry up the green tree, and make the dry tree flourish'. Even more relevant is the magnificent description of Pharaoh king of Egypt and his multitude in chapter 31 as a cedar in Lebanon, where the actual language employed is closely similar to what appears here in Daniel. It concludes:

> The plane trees were as nothing
>   compared with its branches;
> no tree in the garden of God
>   was like it in beauty.
> I made it beautiful
>   in the mass of its branches,
> and all the trees of Eden envied it,
>   that were in the garden of God (vv. 8–9).

It is this reference to Eden which leads Heaton (p. 149) to say, 'Underlying these complex passages (e.g. in Isaiah and Ezekiel, see above) it is not unreasonable to suspect that there lies a mythological theme connected with Eden, "the garden of God". Possibly they reflect a legend about "the first man", who acquired wisdom and set himself on an equality with God.' Heaton also declares (p. 146), 'The temptation of rulers is . . . the temptation of all mankind.' It is true, of course, that themes which originally concerned the king have not seldom been democratized in the Old Testament, but, as a matter of strict exegesis, there is no hint at all in the text that this is so in Dan. 4. It may be granted that the sin of *hybris* is by no means confined to kings. In Genesis 3.5, as Heaton points out, the original human pair are told by the tempter, 'Ye shall be as God'. But that is not what the author of Daniel is concerned to say. It is possible that primeval man is thought of as a king (cf. Gen. 1.28; Ps. 8.6, 7), though by no means certain; it is a very different thing to assume that, when a king is being discussed, we must assume that there is also an allusion to man in general. The Book of Daniel is directed against the challenge of an authority which does not recognize that it is subordinate to the authority of God. At the same time it is legitimate for the preacher to remind his hearers that Everyman, in so far as he forgets the divine authority, falls under the divine judgment.

[1–9] In v. 29 of chapter 3 at the end of the story of the three confessors mention was made of a decree of Nebuchadnezzar making their religion a legitimate one in the province of Babylon. The next episode, which tells of the great king's strange madness, is somewhat artificially set in the form of an epistle of Nebuchadnezzar which refers to a dream of the king dated by the LXX in the same eighteenth year of the reign in which the previous episode took place. The fiction of an epistle, however, is not maintained very consistently, because from vv. 19–33 there is a curious relapse into the third person, and then, in the last four verses of the chapter (34–37) there is a return to the first person. It is possible to detect reasons for the inconsistency and fortunately the general interpretation is unaffected by this stylistic peculiarity.

Nebuchadnezzar begins his communication to his realm with a little doxology which anticipates the words with which the narrative closes (cf. v. 34) and is reminiscent especially of Ps. 145.13. He then goes on to tell how a period of carefree prosperity had been broken in upon by a disturbing dream. Incidentally the same autobiographical note is struck as we may recall in Eccles 1 and 2. The dreams of kings cannot be other than portentous and so Nebuchadnezzar had called in his corps of diviners and wise men with the same result as on the previous occasion. This prepared the way for Daniel or Belteshazzar (whose name is erroneously stated to contain the name of the god Bel; cf. p. 28) to make his appearance at the psychological moment. The idea is once again to throw into relief the bankruptcy of Babylonian wisdom. Daniel is described as possessed by the spirit of the holy gods. We may appropriately compare Ezek. 28.3: 'You are indeed wiser than Daniel, no secret is hidden from you.' Though the word *'elāhin* is plural, it is not necessary to regard this as a polytheistic expression; even paganism was becoming familiar with the concept of a supreme deity and the word might possibly be translated as 'deity' here. Daniel was received courteously and invited to solve the problem of the dream which the king proceeded to describe.

[10–18] The most obvious source of Nebuchadnezzar's dream is, as has already been said, Ezek. 31.2–18, a passage which Montgomery (followed by Jeffery) curiously enough applies to Assyria rather than to Egypt on the basis of an impossible reading in v. 3. The Egyptian Pharaoh is compared to a cedar of Lebanon. If we seek to go back behind the imagery employed here, it may be that it is correct to recognize the mythology of the world-tree, which, in ancient Oriental belief, grew in the midst of the earth and overshadowed the whole world. To what extent such a myth would be consciously present to the mind of Ezekiel or to the author of Daniel is uncertain; mythological language has a strange power of surviving the actual myth which originally created it. There would certainly be something appropriate in the description of a ruler who claimed world power under the figure of a tree spreading over the whole world. Montgomery (p. 228) refers to the similar dreams of Astyages the Mede (Herodotus, I. 108) and of Xerxes (7.19), which symbolize extensive rule by a spreading tree. In particular, Cyrus is foretold under the figure of a vine spreading over the whole of Asia. Bentzen refers to a building-inscription of Nebuchadrezzar in which Babylon is compared to a spreading tree.

The king tells how in his dream he saw coming down from heaven a watcher, a holy one, who gave the command to hew down the tree and lop off its branches. A mystery is sometimes made as to who are addressed in this and certain other similar occurrences of plural imperatives (cf. Isa. 40.1; Jer. 5.1). The explanation may simply be that here we have an imperative corresponding to the third person plural used impersonally. The word 'watcher' ('*îr*) is explained as meaning 'a wakeful one' and is translated variously, by the LXX as ἄγγελος, by Aquila and Symmachus as ἐγρήγορος and by Jerome as *vigil*, while Theodotion is content to transliterate as εἴρ. The addition to 'watcher' in the text 'and a holy one' seems merely to indicate the supernatural character of this mysterious being. The qualification has nothing to do with the later distinction between loyal and fallen angels. In his detailed note on the subject (pp. 231–3), Montgomery refers to the considerable role played by the Watchers in the inter-testamental literature and to a possible occurrence in the Zadokite fragment. He quotes Meinhold as drawing attention in this connection to 'the eyes of the cherubs' in Ezek. 1 and 'the seven, which are the eyes of the Lord, which run to and fro through the whole earth', Zech. 4.10, and goes on to trace a still closer parallel with the Watchers (*haššomerîm*) and the Remembrancers of the Lord (*hammazkîrîm 'eth-Yahweh*) of Isa. 62.6. Bousset (*Die Rel. des Jud.*³, 1926, note on pp. 322–3) suggests some connection with the Ζωφασημίν (= Ζωφασαμίν), Heaven-watchers of Philo Byblius. Bousset thinks that originally the watchers were conceived of as members of a college of (star-?) gods.

The announcement of doom made by the watcher was of a drastic character. The tree was to be felled to the ground and stripped until it became a mere log. Nothing but the stump was to be left and that was to be bound with a band of iron.[1] As there is no evidence that it was a custom in antiquity to protect a stump in this way, it is probable that here, as happens elsewhere in parables, the meaning of the symbolic

[1] The word usually translated 'bronze' may conceal a verb—'and let it luxuriate in the meadow grass' (suggestion of G. R. Driver).

language is permitted to emerge. Certainly in the words that follow
the meaning of the dream is almost explicitly stated by the king himself, who sees the pathetic figure of one who is living the life of the
beasts, after his mind has lost its human character, without realizing
that he is seeing himself as he is about to become. The period described vaguely as seven times may be a period of seven years (cf. 7.25,
where it is usual to explain the period indicated as three and a half
years) or possibly it is merely implied that a certain period of time is to
pass.

The declaration that 'the sentence is by the decree of the watchers,
the decision by the words of the holy ones' may reflect the influence of
the Babylonian belief in the rule of the world by fate (*'Fata regunt
orbem, certa stant omnia lege'*, Manilius IV, 14), but fate is neutralized
by the words which immediately follow and proclaim that 'the Most
High rules the kingdom of men', an utterance which Montgomery well
describes as 'one of the immortal sentences of the Hebrew Scriptures'.
Moreover, when Daniel gives the interpretation, he substitutes in
v. 24 'a decree of the Most High' for 'the decree of the watchers'. The
watchers really constitute the divine council.

Nebuchadnezzar, it should be noticed, has been given the main
truth he has to learn without any interpretation, but a general truth
has little influence until it is appropriated by the individual. Nebuchadnezzar must first learn humility before he can make the general truth
of God's sovereignty truly his own. We may infer that a similar act of
appropriation would have to be made by those for whose encouragement in a time of crisis this story was told.

That God can set up in a position of power the lowliest of men is a
commonplace of Scripture (see Job 5.11; the song of Hannah, I Sam.
2.7–8; Ps. 113.7–8; the Magnificat, Luke 1.52). There must have been
many examples in the ancient East of men of low degree who rose to
positions of dazzling eminence. In Hebrew tradition Joseph was a
shining example of this.

Nebuchadnezzar, having recounted his dream, invites Daniel to
interpret it, expressing his confidence that Daniel, unlike the dis-
credited wise men, is endowed with a spirit which will make this
possible.

[19–27] Daniel, knowing as he does to whom the dream is applicable and shrinking in dismay (or, possibly, embarrassment) from en-
lightening the king, is courteously encouraged to speak. Vying with
the king in courtesy, Daniel prefaces his interpretation with words of

good omen. Perhaps this is more than mere politeness. As we see from
v. 27, a possibility of escape is still open. The Hebrew view was a denial
of fate. We may recall that the prophetic denunciation of judgment
was conditional.

   Daniel's interpretation of the dream follows. The dream is recapitulated and its relevance to Nebuchadnezzar is shown. There has
been a great deal of discussion about the strange malady which is
foretold as about to befall the king. That there is such a mania as
zoanthropy (by which is meant a mental derangement and not, of
course, a metamorphosis) does not prove the historicity of the story.
Indeed there is no record of Nebuchadnezzar's having had leave of
absence from his royal duties on account of insanity. The possibility
has to be considered that the account of the dream and madness of
Nebuchadnezzar is actually a reminiscence of what was told of
Nabonidus, the last Babylonian king, especially of his strange retire-
ment to the oasis of Teima at a critical time in his empire's fortunes.
D. N. Freedman (*BASOR* 145, pp. 31ff.) writes: 'It would appear
certain that the original story which underlies the present text of
Dan. 4 concerned Nabonidus rather than Nebuchadnezzar. . . . Behind Dan. 4 there is a story of the third (or an earlier) century, originat-
ing in Babylon. The substitution of "Nebuchadnezzar" for "Nabonidus" most likely took place after the story was brought to Palestine,
since the more accurate tradition presumably persisted in Babylonian
circles, where information about Nabonidus was available. There is
no reason to suppose that the Palestinian author of the present Book
of Daniel was responsible for this shift. By his time apparently all
memory of Nabonidus had been lost in Palestine, and he simply
transmitted the tradition as it had come down to him.' For further
information on this, see J. T. Milik, *Ten Years of Discovery in the*
Wilderness of Judaea, Engl. transl., SBT 26, 1959, pp. 36–7, and
F. M. Cross, *The Ancient Library of Qumran*, 1958, pp. 123–4.

   Of some interest as showing how shadowy popular traditions about
the great tend to be is the odd story to which Bevan, Montgomery,
Bentzen and Jeffrey all refer. It appears, we are told, in Eusebius,
Praep. Evang., IX, 41.6 and is there attributed to Abydenus who
quotes Megasthenes as his authority. The story relates how Nebuchad-
ezzar, while on the roof of his palace, was seized by a prophetic
cstasy and announced that a Persian male (Cyrus) would be aided
by the son of a Median woman (Nabonidus) to bring about the en-
slavement of the men of Babylon. Nebuchadnezzar curses the traitor

in words which are reminiscent of the judgment which is pronounced upon himself by the watcher in the Book of Daniel. Having uttered the curses Nebuchadnezzar vanishes! All this goes to make it clear that both the story in Daniel and the story of Abydenus are legendary in character. How the stories are related to each other it is impossible to say. The author of Daniel may be indebted to tradition for part of his material, but he has almost certainly used it freely and artistically to convey the great lesson he has to teach, a lesson which, as Heaton vividly phrases it, was 'rarely . . . more sorely needed than when Israel, like King David of old, faced a new and more terrifying Goliath in the middle of the second century B C'.

Daniel's interpretation, as has been said, concludes by leaving the door open for Nebuchadnezzar to avert the threatened disaster. But, even if the disaster must first come, there is always the stump of the tree and that means, Daniel declares to the king, 'that your kingdom shall be sure for you from the time that you know that Heaven rules'. It should be noted that here for the first time, and for the only time in the Old Testament, the word 'heaven' is substituted for God, a usage which is found frequently in later literature, inter-testamental and Rabbinic, and in the New Testament. It is a sign, not merely of a reverent avoidance of the title 'God', but of a tendency of religions to assimilate and use language which united instead of dividing. The Book of Daniel stands for an attitude to the pagan world of the second century B C which was not completely antagonistic. The author clearly shared the violent opposition to Antiochus Epiphanes which was characteristic of the Maccabees and of their followers, but none of the Oriental potentates who figure in the stories he tells, neither Nebuchadnezzar nor Belshazzar nor Darius the Mede, is made into a portrait of Antiochus, even though some of the things that are said about them and their actions could not fail to make men think of Antiochus and were doubtless intended to do so. There is still something in this book of the larger outlook of Deutero-Isaiah and of Jonah.

It is interesting to find Daniel advising the king to seek to avert the coming disaster by the practice of meritorious works. The word translated 'righteousness' is ṣidqā (Heb. ṣᵉdāqā), which in later Hebrew almost came to mean 'alms-giving' and we can see that the doctrine here is identical with what is said in Eccles 3.30: 'alms maketh an atonement for sins'. The word translated 'break off' is the same word which later in the Targums and in Syriac came to have the meaning 'redeem' and that meaning is just possible here. The commentators at this point make the obvious contrast between the Jewish and the Christian view of good works which is suggested by the passage before us. It is unfortunate when the Christian doctrine of justification by faith is presented in such a way that the challenge of the moral law is obscured. The problem is to find the right place for morality. In the present context we have to think of a minimum demand being made of Nebuchadnezzar. That 'righteousness' was coming to mean the showing of charity and kindness to the needy is a sign that the Jews, along with their growing insistence upon conformity to the ceremonial law, were not forgetting the simple benevolence which meant that religion was being brought down into the ordinary relationships of daily life. It is not altogether fair when Charles (Comm., p. 97) says that, 'as the chief Hebrew virtue righteousness degenerated in course of time into the mere act of almsgiving, so the chief Christian grace ἀγάπη, caritas, "charity", incurred the same fate.' What we miss in this view of the religious life represented in the exhortation addressed to Nebuchadnezzar should not make us blind to what is there. Good works are not to be despised. What Christianity supplies is a new motive for performing them.

[28–33] Nebuchadnezzar did not take advantage of the respite of a year granted to him. At the end of that time he was, we are told, walking on his palace roof from which he could look out over the city which he had embellished with so many wonderful buildings. His pride in his achievement (a pride which is reflected in known inscriptions of the king) is doubtless intended to imply the arrogance which calls for judgment. Just as he reached the pinnacle of worldly success the blow fell. A mysterious voice from heaven, the bat qōl of later Jewish thought, repeated the doom pronounced by the watcher in the dream and the king was immediately seized by the malady which had been foretold. Montgomery draws attention to the parallel between the description of Aḥiḳar in the story about that sage and what we are told here about the mad king's uncared-for appearance.

Still more remarkable is the parallel in the Prayer of Nabonidus found at Qumran (Burrows, More Light on the Dead Sea Scrolls, p. 400) which tells how the king was laid low at Teima by an inflammation of some kind and during his seven years' illness had to be segregated from human society. We are told that upon his repentance, a Jewish seer urged him to give glory to the name of the Most High God, whereas at the beginning of his illness he had prayed to idols. This parallel seems to make it almost certain that the Nabonidus legend has had something to do with the moulding of the stories in the Book of Daniel.

[34–37] Nebuchadnezzar's recovery of sanity is interestingly described as the result of an upward look to God by which the king recognized God's sovereignty. Bevan and Montgomery followed by Jeffery draw attention to the similarity between this feature of the story and what we are told of the Bacchant queen in Euripides, *Bacchae* 1265ff. Bevan adds, 'The resemblance is the more remarkable because the Bacchants, like Nebuchadnezzar, are in some sort assimilated to animals—they not only wear the skins of beasts but also suckle young fawns and wolves.'

The doxology which follows contains various scriptural allusions (e.g. Ps. 145.13; Isa. 40.17; Isa. 24.21). Nebuchadnezzar acknowledges that God is sovereign and does not abide man's question. As soon as he does this, the relative right of his own sovereignty is recognized. Life went on for him as it had done before and his power was even greater than it had been. His acknowledgment of Daniel's God is more generous than what he had to say of the God of the three confessors. This time he had not only witnessed the power of God, he had felt it in his own person.

V

CHAPTER FIVE

5 ¹King Belshazzar made a great feast for a thousand of his lords, and drank wine in front of the thousand.

2 Belshazzar, when he tasted the wine, commanded that the vessels of gold and of silver which Nebuchadnezzar his father had taken out of the temple in Jerusalem be brought, that the king and his lords, his wives, and his concubines might drink from them. ³Then they brought in the golden and silver vessels which had been take out of the temple, the house of God in Jerusalem; and the king and his lords, his wives, and his concubines drank from them. ⁴They drank wine, and praised the gods of gold and silver, bronze, iron, wood, and stone.

5 Immediately the fingers of a man's hand appeared and wrote on the plaster of the wall of the king's palace, opposite the lampstand; and the king saw the hand as it wrote. ⁶Then the king's colour changed, and his thoughts alarmed him; his limbs gave way and his knees knocked together. ⁷The king cried aloud to bring in the enchanters, the Chaldeans, and the astrologers. The king said to the wise men of Babylon, 'Whoever reads this writing, and shows me its interpretation, shall be clothed with purple, and have a chain of gold about his neck, and shall be the third ruler in the kingdom.' ⁸Then all the king's wise men came in, but they could not read the writing or make known to the king the interpretation. ⁹Then King Belshazzar was greatly alarmed, and his colour changed; and his lords were perplexed.

10 The queen, because of the words of the king and his lords, came into the banqueting hall; and the queen said, 'O king, live for ever! Let not your thoughts alarm you or your colour change. ¹¹There is in your kingdom a man in whom is the spirit of the holy gods. In the days of your father light and understanding and wisdom, like the wisdom of the gods, were found in him, and King Nebuchadnezzar, your father, made him chief of the magicians, enchanters, Chaldeans, and astrologers, ¹²because an excellent spirit, knowledge, and understanding to interpret dreams, explain riddles, and solve problems were found in this Daniel, whom the king named Belteshazzar. Now let Daniel be called, and he will show the interpretation.'

13 Then Daniel was brought in before the king. The king said to

Daniel, 'You are that Daniel, one of the exiles of Judah, whom the king my father brought from Judah. [14]I have heard of you that the spirit of the holy gods is in you, and that light and understanding and excellent wisdom are found in you. [15]Now the wise men, the enchanters, have been brought in before me to read this writing and make known to me its interpretation; but they could not show the interpretation of the matter. [16]But I have heard that you can give interpretations and solve problems. Now if you can read the writing and make known to me its interpretation, you shall be clothed with purple, and have a chain of gold about your neck, and shall be the third ruler in the kingdom.'

17 Then Daniel answered before the king, 'Let your gifts be for yourself, and give your rewards to another; nevertheless I will read the writing to the king and make known to him the interpretation. [18]O king, the Most High God gave Nebuchadnezzar your father kingship and greatness and glory and majesty; [19]and because of the greatness that he gave him, all peoples, nations, and languages trembled and feared before him; whom he would he slew, and whom he would he kept alive; whom he would he raised up, and whom he would he put down. [20]But when his heart was lifted up and his spirit was hardened so that he dealt proudly, he was deposed from his kingly throne, and his glory was taken from him; [21]he was driven from among men, and his mind was made like that of a beast, and his dwelling was with the wild asses; he was fed grass like an ox; and his body was wet with the dew of heaven, until he knew that the Most High God rules the kingdom of men, and sets over it whom he will. [22]And you his son, Belshazzar, have not humbled your heart, though you knew all this, [23]but you have lifted up yourself against the Lord of heaven; and the vessels of his house have been brought in before you, and you and your lords, your wives, and your concubines have drunk wine from them; and you have praised the gods of silver and gold, of bronze, iron, wood, and stone, which do not see or hear or know, but the God in whose hand is your breath, and whose are all your ways, you have not honoured.

24 'Then from his presence the hand was sent, and this writing was inscribed. [25]And this is the writing that was inscribed: MENE, MENE, TEKEL, and PARSIN. [26]This is the interpretation of the matter: MENE, God has numbered the days of your kingdom and brought it to an end; [27]TEKEL, you have been weighed in the balances and found wanting; [28]PERES, your kingdom is divided and given to the Medes and Persians.'

29 Then Belshazzar commanded, and Daniel was clothed with purple, a chain of gold was put about his neck, and proclamation was made concerning him, that he should be the third ruler in the kingdom.

30 That very night Belshazzar the Chaldean king was slain. [31]And Darius the Mede received the kingdom, being about sixty-two years old.

THIS CHAPTER IS a simpler one than the foregoing. Chapter 4 told how Nebuchadnezzar was punished for his arrogance and pride and, through the punishment this brought upon him, was brought to an acknowledgment of the sovereignty of God over even the greatest earthly sovereign. But then the Nebuchadnezzar of the Book of Daniel, like the Nebuchadrezzar of history as we know him from his own inscriptions, was a pious monarch and was able to learn from the disaster which overtook him. Belshazzar, on the other hand, is represented as a frivolous character who thoughtlessly committed the act of sacrilege. Certainly he is not accused of persecuting the Jews as such any more than Nebuchadnezzar or Darius the Mede. None of the potentates in these stories is represented as a persecutor. Yet, when we read in chapter 1 how Nebuchadnezzar took away the vessels of the temple and how later Belshazzar put them to sacrilegious use, it is difficult not to believe that there is intended a veiled reference to the plundering of the temple treasures by Antiochus Epiphanes (I Macc. 1.20–28), not to speak of the earlier attempted sacrilege of Heliodorus (II Macc. 3). The story is designed to make it plain that sacrilege is liable to bring swift and condign punishment on the transgressor.

The question of the historicity of this story has been much discussed. Although there is a certain amount of literary support for the biblical story, that cannot be allowed to outweigh the unambiguous inscriptional evidence. A contemporary inscription of Cyrus himself makes certain things abundantly clear. 'Without any battle, he (i.e. Marduk) made him (i.e. Cyrus) enter his town Babylon, sparing Babylon any calamity. He delivered into his (i.e. Cyrus's) hands Nabonidus, the king, who did not worship him (i.e. Marduk)' (Pritchard, *ANET*, pp. 315–16). And then we are told how Cyrus was welcomed by the entire population. Even if we make all allowances for the exaggeration of a victor wishing to make the most of his popularity with a vanquished people, it is evident that the story in Herodotus and Xenophon, repeated by Josephus, about the capture of Babylon by the diversion of the Euphrates into another channel is pure romance. On the other hand it is known that Belshazzar (*Bēl-shar-uṣur*) was a historical person, the son of the last Babylonian king Nabonidus, who acted as regent of Babylon for several years before its fall, while his father was absent at the oasis of Teima in Arabia. But he was never actually king, though a certain royal dignity was accorded him, the crucial evidence being that on several occasions the New Year Festival could not be held in

the temple of E-sagila, because apparently Belshazzar was not quali-
fied to take the place of Nabonidus. In the story before us in the Book
of Daniel, however, Belshazzar is represented as acting in every way
as a king with full authority. He is moreover described as the son of
Nebuchadnezzar, whereas, since Nabonidus was a *novus homo*, and
there is no proof or even likelihood that he married into the royal line,
it is no more than a desperate resource to argue that Belshazzar may
have been somehow or other the grandson or descendant of Nebuchadnezzar. The probabilities are all the other way. It is true that Herodotus (I. 188) tells us that the last king of Babylon was Labynetus the son
of Labynetus and Queen Nitocris. Dougherty (in his book *Nabonidus
and Belshazzar*) argues that the first Labynetus is not Nebuchadnezzar
as is generally supposed nor the second Labynetus Nabonidus, but that
Herodotus is really referring to Nabonidus and his son Belshazzar.
But this, if true, would not help greatly, since the Cyrus inscription
makes it clear that Nabonidus was still king when Babylon was surrendered and since there is no contemporary evidence that Belshazzar
was killed at the time of the fall of the city. It seems reasonable to suppose that the author of Daniel was in much the same position as
Herodotus and Xenophon of having to depend on vague traditions
and has built up his story out of elements of those traditions, without
feeling under any obligation to test their historicity as a modern
historian instinctively would or, indeed, without having the means to do
so that are now available. Like Xenophon he is writing what we may call
a romance, but he is doing so, not to entertain, but with a view to convey
to his readers a conviction which had been borne in upon him and
which, through his witness, might serve to strengthen his readers'
faith and their power of resistance in critical days. This is not history
but story-telling for the communication of religious truth. At the same
time it is not necessary to deny that the book may contain genuine
reminiscences of historical fact, while it is clear that the author has had
access to a good deal of authentic information about the customs
observed at Oriental courts. The accompanying local colour,
however, is no proof of the historical accuracy of the events
narrated.

[1-4] The story begins in much the same way as the Book of Esther
with the account of a fabulous banquet. The tradition that this banquet took place on the very eve of the fall of the city is also found in
Herodotus and Xenophon, and in Josephus who follows the Bible
narrative. That judgment is made to follow so swiftly on this scene of

careless festivity adds to the effectiveness of the tale as an encouragement to the readers for whom it was intended. The picture given here of the feasting customs of the Babylonian court need not be questioned. The evidence we have refers mainly to Persian times, but it is not unlikely that Babylonian practices were similar. Athenaeus, who tells (in the *Deipnosophistae* IV, 145) that the Persian king usually dined alone or with a very few companions, also admits an important exception. 'Sometimes,' he says, 'on the occasion of a public holiday, all dine in a single room with the king, in the great hall.' There is evidence that the king sat by himself at a table with his back to the wall and so would have all his guests before him as he drank and doubtless pledged them. The phrase translated in RSV 'when he tasted the wine' may possibly mean 'under the influence of the wine'. In the Book of Esther, it was 'when the heart of the king was merry with wine' that Ahasuerus forgot himself so far as to summon to the banquet his favourite Queen Vashti whom it was almost an insult to bring into that scene of revelry. If Herodotus is right, Babylonian custom permitted wives and concubines to attend, though there is some doubt about this. Montgomery (p. 250) wisely comments: 'Royal banquets in *fin de siècle* ages have been much the same the world over, and it is unnecessary to press antiquarian details for or against the historicity of our story.' The author wishes to increase the enormity of what Belshazzar now proceeded to do. He ordered the vessels of gold and silver which Nebuchadnezzar had taken from the temple in Jerusalem and had laid up in the temple of Marduk to be brought to grace the feast. Bentzen may or may not be correct in thinking that the feast is represented as being of an orgiastic and cultic character. Whether the occasion was secular or sacred, there was the invoking of the idol gods, and so the sacrilege of drinking from sacred vessels was increased by associating them with heathen worship.

[5–9] The most dramatic moment in the story is the supernatural appearance of the fingers of a human hand writing on the white plaster of the wall opposite the lampstand and, presumably above the king's head. It is just possible that the translation 'palm of the hand' in v. 5 is correct. This is precisely what the king would have seen if he was sitting with his back to the wall and happened to look up. We are not told immediately what was written on the wall. Instead of that the effect of the phenomenon upon the king is described. He exhibited the bodily signs of extreme fear and summoned the corps of wise men who were ordered to solve the mystery. Belshazzar showed the same pathetic

reliance on the professional magician as Nebuchadnezzar. Whoever is
successful in satisfying the king's curiosity and allaying his anxiety is,
in the manner customary in Oriental tales, promised extravagant
honours. Like Mordecai (Esth. 8.15) he is to assume the purple robe of
royalty and, like Joseph in Egypt (Gen. 41.42) to have the right to
wear a golden chain of honour round his neck—a typical Persian
decoration, it is said, but one which appears elsewhere. Last but not
least, he is to be elevated to one of the highest offices in the state,
though what exactly is meant by the word *taltī* or *taltā* is uncertain.
Various suggestions have been made, perhaps the most probable being
that the mysterious word is equivalent to the name of a Babylonian
official called *šalšu* (cf. Hebrew title *šālīš*) who seems to have been the
adjutant of the king or a high officer of some kind. Montgomery suggests that we might translate by 'Thirdling'. Another possibility is
that, as, at the beginning of the next chapter, Daniel appears as one of
three presidents set over the satraps, the office to which he was appointed by Belshazzar may have been continued to him by Darius the
Mede, and so this office of president may have been the office to which
the successful wise man might hope to attain. Still another suggestion
is that he was to hold the highest rank after the king and one other
(the queen-mother?). With our present knowledge the problem remains insoluble. At all events, the wise men, whatever the prize was
which was dangled before them, proved completely at a loss, and
this naturally added to the king's alarm.

[10–12] At this dramatic moment the 'queen' entered the banqueting hall, the clamour there having reached her ears (cf. Jer.
26.10) and warned her that something was amiss. That Belshazzar
sent for her, as the LXX states, seems less probable. It is generally
agreed that by 'queen' we are to understand 'queen-mother' and not
'consort'. Montgomery comments: 'The lady's masterful appearance
on the scene betokens rather the queen-mother than the consort',
while Jeffery says that 'She speaks to him of his father in a way that
suggests a mother speaking to a son rather than a wife to a husband.'
Josephus thinks she was Belshazzar's grandmother! As we are in the
region of tradition rather than of history, it is not unlikely that there is
some link between the lady who figures in this story and the Nitocris
of Herodotus (I. 94–96). B. Meissner (*Babylonien und Assyrien*, vol. I,
1920, pp. 74–75) recalls the notable careers of two queen-mothers
'Sammuramat (Semiramis)' and 'Naqia, the wife of Sennacherib',
who outlived Esarhaddon and was able to play a decisive part in

securing the accession of Assurbanipal. A Jewish writer would doubtless remember the important role of the queen-mother in the history
of the Judaean monarchy.

The queen-mother told Belshazzar of the existence of Daniel who
had played a notable part in the days of his 'father' Nebuchadnezzar.
In the very words which she had presumably heard Nebuchadnezzar
use of Daniel (Dan. 4.8, 9, 18) she described him as divinely inspired
(cf. II Sam. 14.20; cf. 16.23) and credited him with intelligence and
wisdom such as only God can bestow. She then recalled the position of
influence to which he was appointed by Nebuchadnezzar (2.48), a link
with chapter 1 being the mention of his Babylonian name Belteshazzar.
His pre-eminent qualities were then recapitulated as justifying his
being called in to deal with the emergency. His intelligence was defined
more precisely as enabling him to practise three skills, *viz.* the interpretation of dreams, the explanation of riddles and the loosing of
spells or (as in RSV) the solving of problems.

The riddles referred to are perhaps not so much the kind of conun-
drums that Samson put to the Philistines (Judg. 14.12ff.) or the Queen
of Sheba to Solomon (I Kings 10.1) as the dark parabolic sentences
which the prophets uttered (see Hab. 1.6a—against the Chaldaeans!).
Heaton rightly refers to Ecclus 39.1ff., especially 2 and 3, and Prov.
1.4–5 might also be instanced. Ps. 49 speaks (v. 4) of the solution of the
riddle of life and of the fate of those who are foolishly confident, declaring in a refrain:

> Man cannot abide in his pomp
> He is like the beasts that perish (vv. 12, 20).

Daniel's third skill is either the solving of problems such as the one
which perplexes Belshazzar (preferred by Montgomery in agreement
with Marti), or the loosing of spells, lit. loosing of knots (so perhaps
correctly Jeffery, following Bevan and Charles, who draws attention to
I Enoch 8.3: ἐπαοιδῶν λυτήριον).

[13–16] Daniel then entered and once more we get the confrontation of a heathen king and a Hebrew sage. Belshazzar treated Daniel
with the greatest courtesy, quoting the queen-mother's recommenda-
tion of him. He then expressed his confidence that Daniel would
succeed where the wise men had so signally failed and announced the
reward for success.

[17–23] Daniel brusquely waved aside the royal promise of reward.
Although he accepted reward later on, the refusal is perhaps a sign

of his incorruptibility, meant to indicate what the attitude of a
Jewish sage to a heathen potentate ought to be. Then Daniel, adopting
a sermonic style of speech, sternly rebuked Belshazzar. He first
pointed out the greatness of the power and opportunity which had
been granted to Nebuchadnezzar. The only effect on him was that he
became haughty and stubbornly presumptuous. Underlying the translation is the thought of the hardening of the heart which is here expressed passively. Various verbs are used in the Old Testament to
express this idea, sometimes the responsibility being laid on God,
sometimes on the individual himself, while sometimes the agent is not
indicated. The theological issue is not raised here. For his pride
Nebuchadnezzar invited the judgment which is described in the same
words as in chapter 4. In consequence of the judgment, however,
Nebuchadnezzar learned the truth of God's sovereignty. Belshazzar,
his 'son', however, had learned nothing from all this. To the sin of
pride he had added that of sacrilege. To sacrilege he had added the
sin of idolatry—commentators point out that the language here echoes
that of Deut. 4.28; Pss. 115.4–8; 135.16–17; it may be added that there
is a remarkably close parallel to the language of the Prayer of Nabonidus found in the Qumran Cave IV: 'You prayed to the gods made of
silver and gold, of bronze and iron, of wood, stone and clay'—and had
failed to give the glory to God as Nebuchadnezzar eventually did,
though he should have recognized that his very life was in God's
hands.

[24–28] The mysterious hand had written not so much in warning
as in judgment.

Daniel at last read the writing on the wall and gave the interpretation. In the Massoretic Text the inscription is given as *mene mene tekel
upharsin* (*u* = and + *parsin*). In LXX, Theodotion, Vulgate, Josephus
and Jerome, however, there are only three words, rendered with slight
variations. These are also given in the interpretation in the Massoretic
Text, vocalized as *menē*, *tekēl*, *perēs* and translated as meaning 'numbered', 'weighed' and 'divided'. The third is also understood as referring punningly to the Aramaic word for 'Persian', and so hinting at
the victory of Persia over Babylon. Commentators have felt the difficulty that the interpretation seems to imply a different and shorter
text for the inscription. The versions seem to support this. The difficulty is to explain why the discrepancy should have occurred. In 1886
Clermont-Ganneau (*Journal Asiatique*) made the suggestion that the
inscription actually contained a string of weight names, *viz. mēne*,

D.–F

tekel and *perēs* with the meaning mina, shekel and half-mina, the last named word being documented in the Mishna and other Jewish writings. It also appears from the Talmud, Ta'anith 21b that a man who was twice as good as his father could be jokingly described as 'a mina son of a half-mina', the half-mina being represented by *perās*! It seemed possible, then, that the inscription might be understood as a grimly humorous summing up of the kings of the neo-Babylonian Empire, five if the inscription as given in the Massoretic Text is taken as original (i.e. mene twice and upharsin = and two half-minas) or three if the shorter form is accepted. E. G. Kraeling (*JBL* 63, pp. 11–18) suggests that the five kings following Nebuchadnezzar were intended, *viz.* Evil-Merodach, Neriglissar, Labashi-Marduk, Nabonidus and Belshazzar. H. L. Ginsberg (*Studies in Daniel*, pp. 24–26) thinks that only three kings are referred to, those namely who are mentioned in the Old Testament, i.e. Nebuchadnezzar, Evil-Merodach and Belshazzar. More recently D. N. Freedman (*BASOR* 145, Feb. 1957) votes for Nebuchadnezzar, Nabonidus and Belshazzar in view of the new evidence about Nabonidus. C. C. Torrey ('Notes on the Aramaic Part of Daniel', in *Transactions of the Connecticut Academy of Arts and Sciences* 15, 1909, p. 241) follows Josephus who assumed that the inscription consisted of three words only which he translated as ἀριθμός, σταθμός, κλάσμα. The question as to why the Massoretic Text gives a longer version of the inscription has possibly been answered by Eissfeldt (*ZAW* 63, 1951, pp. 105–14) who points out on the basis of the Habakkuk Scroll from Qumran that an interpretation (*pešer*) need not correspond exactly to the actual language of what is interpreted. He therefore holds out for the original inscription as being *mene mene tekel upharsin*, and understands the first *mene* as a participle. The surface meaning would then be:

> Reckoned a mina, a shekel and two half-minas (or possibly, half-shekels).

He does not go into the question of what kings were thus designated.

This would mean that a string of words possibly expressing a popular summing up of the respective merits of a succession of Babylonian kings is represented as suggesting to Daniel three significant participial forms which he interpreted as in the Massoretic Text.

We are thus brought back finally to the solemn judgment which the words pronounced on the king. The theological significance of the passage, then, lies on the surface, however interesting the solution of the philological puzzle may be. In much the same way the interpretation of the divine name in Ex. 3.14 is more important theologically than the solution of the philological problem as to the original meaning of the name 'Yahweh'.

Daniel made the mysterious words immediately relevant to the situation of the king. The author of the book doubtless means to hint that the pride and sacrilegious conduct of Antiochus Epiphanes have invited immediate judgment. And so we press back to the writer's conviction that, in the crisis which faced the loyal and sorely tried Jews of his day, the Judge of all the earth could be counted on to do the right. The traditional materials are freely and imaginatively handled to convey this truth in the most impressive way possible. The *mašal* or parable which he has produced is unforgettable.

[29-31] The story closes with the king bestowing the promised reward upon Daniel—the wisdom granted by God to the Hebrew sage once again being vindicated—and meeting his fate that very night. We are back at something like the account of the fall of Babylon given in Herodotus and Xenophon, though in neither author is there any mention of Belshazzar's death. There may have been a tradition current of which this is the only relic. What is important for us is not the historical fact but the Belshazzar of legend, whose fate makes visible, as it did for those who suffered under Antiochus, the divine judgment upon arrogance and godless frivolity. The prophecies (Isa. 13.17ff.; 21.1-10, especially v. 5; Jer. 51.39, 57) that Babylon would fall to the Medes on a night of revelry were fulfilled in legend if not in fact. A prophet had foreseen it and cried, 'The twilight I longed for has been turned for me into trembling.' Even the faithful are awed when God's judgments are abroad in the earth. There is more than artistic truth here: we are in the presence of the ultimate judgment on history.

A single sentence describes the succession to the Babylonian throne of Darius the Mede. This Darius is almost certainly a figment of the writer's imagination. As we have seen, the prophets had foretold that Babylon would fall to the Medes and so there had to be a Median kingdom between the Babylonian and the Persian and there had to be a Median king to succeed Belshazzar. Every attempt to prove that there actually was such a monarch has failed. Astyages, the last king of the Median Empire will not fit. He had been conquered by Cyrus in 549 BC. Nor will Cyaxares II, the supposed uncle of Cyrus, suit any better. He is no more than an invention of Xenophon's. Gobryas, the renegade Babylonian who became a general of Cyrus, may have acted as governor of Babylon but was certainly never king. The successor of the historical Nabonidus was the historical Cyrus and there never was a Darius between them. But there was a Darius, Darius Hystaspis, who captured Babylon after the death of Cambyses in 520 BC and the tradition of this capture and the name of the conqueror, with which may have been associated some memory of his achievements, may have been attached to the apocryphal figure. There are thus actual historical reminiscences as possible ingredients in the story, but we are for all that once more in the realm of legend.

VI

CHAPTER SIX

6 ¹It pleased Darius to set over the kingdom a hundred and twenty satraps, to be throughout the whole kingdom; ²and over them three presidents, of whom Daniel was one, to whom these satraps should give account, so that the king might suffer no loss. ³Then this Daniel became distinguished above all the other presidents and satraps, because an excellent spirit was in him; and the king planned to set him over the whole kingdom. ⁴Then the presidents and the satraps sought to find a ground for complaint against Daniel with regard to the kingdom; but they could find no ground for complaint or any fault, because he was faithful, and no error or fault was found in him. ⁵Then these men said, 'We shall not find any ground for complaint against this Daniel unless we find it in connection with the law of his God.'

6 Then these presidents and satraps came by agreement to the king and said to him, 'O King Darius, live for ever! ⁷All the presidents of the kingdom, the prefects and the satraps, the counsellors and the governors are agreed that the king should establish an ordinance and enforce an interdict, that whoever makes petition to any god or man for thirty days, except to you, O king, shall be cast into the den of lions. ⁸Now, O king, establish the interdict and sign the document, so that it cannot be changed, according to the law of the Medes and the Persians, which cannot be revoked.' ⁹Therefore King Darius signed the document and interdict.

10 When Daniel knew that the document had been signed, he went to his house where he had windows in his upper chamber open toward Jerusalem; and he got down upon his knees three times a day and prayed and gave thanks before his God, as he had done previously. ¹¹Then these men came by agreement and found Daniel making petition and supplication before his God. ¹²Then they came near and said before the king, concerning the interdict, 'O king! Did you not sign an interdict, that any man who makes petition to any god or man within thirty days except to you, O king, shall be cast into the den of lions?' The king answered, 'The thing stands fast, according to the law of the Medes and Persians, which cannot be revoked.' ¹³Then they answered before the king, 'That Daniel, who is one of the exiles from Judah, pays

no heed to you, O king, or the interdict you have signed, but makes his petition three times a day.'

14 Then the king, when he heard these words, was much distressed, and set his mind to deliver Daniel; and he laboured till the sun went down to rescue him. 15Then these men came by agreement to the king, and said to the king, 'Know, O king, that it is a law of the Medes and Persians that no interdict or ordinance which the king establishes can be changed.'

16 Then the king commanded, and Daniel was brought and cast into the den of lions. The king said to Daniel, 'May your God, whom you serve continually, deliver you!' 17And a stone was brought and laid upon the mouth of the den, and the king sealed it with his own signet and with the signet of his lords, that nothing might be changed concerning Daniel. 18Then the king went to his palace, and spent the night fasting; no diversions* were brought to him, and sleep fled from him.

19 Then, at break of day, the king arose and went in haste† to the den of lions. 20When he came near to the den where Daniel was, he cried out in a tone of anguish and said to Daniel, 'O Daniel, servant of the living God, has your God, whom you serve continually, been able to deliver you from the lions?' 21Then Daniel said to the king, 'O king, live for ever! 22My God sent his angel and shut the lions' mouths, and they have not hurt me, because I was found blameless before him; and also before you, O king, I have done no wrong.' 23Then the king was exceedingly glad, and commanded that Daniel be taken up out of the den. So Daniel was taken up out of the den, and no kind of hurt was found upon him, because he had trusted in his God. 24And the king commanded, and those men who had accused Daniel were brought and cast into the den of lions—they, their children, and their wives; and before they reached the bottom of the den the lions overpowered them and broke all their bones in pieces.

25 Then King Darius wrote to all the peoples, nations, and languages that dwell in all the earth: 'Peace be multiplied to you. 26I make a decree, that in all my royal dominion men tremble and fear before the God of Daniel,

> for he is the living God,
>   enduring for ever;
> his kingdom shall never be destroyed,
>   and his dominion shall be to the end.
> 27He delivers and rescues,
>   he works signs and wonders
>   in heaven and on earth,
> he who has saved Daniel
>   from the power of the lions.'

28 So this Daniel prospered during the reign of Darius and the reign of Cyrus the Persian.

* Possibly 'musicians' or 'dancing girls'.
† Or 'in fear and trembling'.

OF ALL THE STORIES in the first half of the Book of Daniel the story of Daniel in the lions' den is the one which is the most difficult to date. As Heaton well remarks, 'the familiarity of the story of Daniel in the lions' den suggests that it belongs exclusively to no one age.' He goes on to argue that 'to a greater or less degree every man who believes in God shares Daniel's temptation to abandon his devotional practices'. The suggestion would seem to be that this chapter discloses its meaning apart from its setting in this particular book. It may be granted that up to a point this is so. A story like this one of Daniel's heroic witness for his faith at the court of Darius the Mede speaks directly to us and challenges all men everywhere to a like loyalty. Heaton rightly refers to A. C. Welch's comment (see *Visions of the End*, pp. 83f.) on Jeremiah's letter to the exiles (ch. 29) in which he counsels them to turn to God in prayer: 'Exiled Israel put God to the proof and, finding Him, practised the presence of God in their prayers.' It would be foolish to deny that Scripture does speak to us in this way. There is truth also in Bentzen's suggestion that stories like this one in chapter 6, and the similar one in chapter 3 are in a sense an 'embodying of sentences' (cf. Pss. 57.4–6; 91.13). Both in the Wisdom literature and in the Psalter are many pithy sentences which lend themselves to expansion into the story or the parable (*mašal*). The words of Ps. 57.5 and 7 ('I lie in the midst of lions that greedily devour the sons of men; . . . they dug a pit in my way, but they have fallen into it themselves') might almost have suggested the story of chapter 6 to an inventive story-teller!

It should not be forgotten, however, that these stories have been deliberately grouped together, whether or not they previously existed in separate form, and linked with the eschatological visions which follow, and we are not entitled to leave this fact out of account in our final assessment of the intention of the book. We can say this without ignoring in the least the common element which links the stories in Daniel to stories like those of Judith, Tobit, Susanna, Bel and the Dragon, and Aḥiḳar. The author of Daniel, however, chose these particular stories when he wished to issue a book to encourage those who were living and suffering in what he believed to be the ultimate crisis of history. There is a certain analogy with the parables of Jesus. We can, if we wish, treat them as belonging to the same *Gattung* as the stories told by the Rabbis, of which there are numerous examples in the Haggadic literature. In this way we may learn much about their form and their peculiar idiom. We must not forget, however, that they will not disclose their most urgent meaning unless we treat them as witnessing to the *eschaton*. They are stories of the coming Kingdom of God and not mere moral tales however edifying.

It is quite true that none of the heathen kings in these stories in the Book of Daniel is intended to be a portrait of Antiochus Epiphanes. It would have been dangerous to draw cartoons. Yet each story has something to say that is relevant to the day of crisis, and that is true of the story in chapter 6, even though Darius is more sympathetically portrayed than either of the other kings. No doubt there had been situations earlier during the exile and in the intervening centuries before the Maccabaean struggle when a story like that of Dan. 6 would have been relevant, but it came alive in a very special way when Jewish faith encountered what seemed to be the ultimate challenge.

Another suggestion made very tentatively by Bentzen (*Comm.*, pp. 55–56; *Bertholet-Festschrift*, 1950, pp. 58–64; *Eissfeldt-Festschrift*, 1947, pp. 57–60) is that behind the story of Daniel in the lions' den we ought to see the story of the descent of the hero into the Underworld, possibly the descent of the king, the lions being the demons to whose attacks he is exposed. It may be true that the language in which the story is told has mythological overtones, as perhaps some of the language we ourselves ordinarily use today has. But to say that the myth of a descent to Hades and return from Hades is the meaning of our story is a very different thing. A cultic death and resurrection is one thing. Dan. 6 speaks of the martyr death, which is something else. The story speaks of a God who can deliver from death and we know that it was at the time of the Maccabaean crisis that it was realized that God's deliverance might be by way of resurrection—a miracle of power and not just an acted mystery.

[1–9] The story begins by describing the position of pre-eminence that Daniel had attained under the new regime. As the reign of Darius the Mede is quite unhistorical, all that needs to be said about the number of satrapies which he is supposed to have instituted is that there may well be here some reminiscence of the fact that Darius Hystaspis was the great organizer of the Persian Empire. Herodotus (III.89) credits him with dividing it into twenty satrapies, a number which, according to Darius's own inscriptions, seems to have been later slightly increased. Unless we are to suppose that the word satrapy is here used of a smaller administrative division (as also in Esth. 1.1 and I Esd. 3.2: 127 satrapies; and Josephus X.11.4: 360), we must just recognize the fact that the author of our book is not concerned about historical accuracy. If so, our author is not peculiar in this. Montgomery points out that Greek authors are guilty of a similar inaccuracy. What the story tells us about the three presidents of whom Daniel is one may reflect some Persian administrative practice, but, once again, that is a matter of minor concern. The RSV translation of v. 2 (last clause) may be compared with Ezra 4.13. The meaning, however, may be 'that the king should not be overburdened' but should be set free from vexatious administrative detail. It is with a view to providing his colleagues with a ground for jealousy that Daniel is represented as likely to receive further promotion. His efficiency and reliability, however, were such that no charge could be brought against him in respect of the performance of his official duties. It then occurred to his rivals that he might prove to be vulnerable along the line of his known loyalty to his religion. The Persian word *dat* used here represents the Hebrew word *tōra* (see Ezra 7.10, 12, 14) or *mišpaṭ* (see Isa. 42.4; 51.4, where it appears as parallel to *tōra*). These words virtually mean religion thought of as the observance of a rule of life imposed by God. If Daniel's religion had been a vague religiosity, it would not have provided the opportunity his enemies sought.

No sooner had the thought occurred to them than the imperial officials decided to take action. That they were all involved in the plot is quite fantastic and is just one more indication that we are dealing with legend and not with sober history. The LXX, by confining the plot to Daniel's two co-presidents makes the story more plausible and, for that very reason, is not to be regarded as presenting the original text. The decree which the plotters persuaded the king to issue, even if it be regarded as referring only to cultic prayer, does not make the impression of belonging to the real world and is to be regarded as no more historical than Darius the Mede himself. That the decree should be issued is necessary to the plot of the story. It has the advantage, moreover, of suggesting to the reader the *hybris* and intolerance of the hellenistic kings. This is perhaps the kind of mad decree that Antiochus Epiphanes in one of his less responsible moments might have issued. That Medo-Persian law laid it down that a royal edict could not be revoked is stated also in the Book of Esther (1.19; 8.8) and in Diodorus Siculus (XVII.30) and may or may not be a matter of historical fact.

Two points of interpretation should be referred to. Preferable to 'came by agreement to' in v. 6 (cf. v. 11) would be 'watched for', but

scarcely 'came tumultuously', which in the circumstances would have
been quite ridiculous, or even 'thronging', an RSV alternative.
Further, the words translated 'sign', 'signed' in vv. 8, 9, 10 should perhaps be translated 'drafted'. Probably we are to understand that the
king had the document drawn up and then attached his seal. The
punishment for disobeying the edict was that the guilty person was to be
thrown into a lion pit which is rather absurdly thought of as of the
nature of a bottle dungeon. It was a common practice of the Assyrian
kings especially to indulge in lion hunts and we may suppose that the
animals would be kept in captivity and released when required for
sport.

[10–17] Daniel heard of the edict and realized at once that it was
directed against himself. Without any hesitation he decided to continue to do what he had been in the habit of doing. It was not a
question of flaunting his religion and so gratuitously courting trouble.
Rather was it that a man like Daniel was not prepared to lower his
flag when trouble threatened. He went up as usual to his roof
chamber (Judg. 3.20; I Kings 17.19; II Kings 1.2; 4.10; Jer.
22.14) which had lattice windows open towards the direction of
Jerusalem and said the stated prayers three times daily.

It is known from Solomon's prayer at the dedication of the temple
(I Kings 8) that it was customary when praying to face towards the
temple and this is confirmed by other Biblical evidence and by
Rabbinic injunctions. The custom of the qiblah became obligatory
upon Moslems, though they eventually faced towards Mecca rather
than towards Jerusalem. G. A. Smith (*Jerusalem . . . From the Earliest
Times to A.D. 70*, vol. II, 1908, pp. 396–7) writes of the devotion of
the Jews of the Dispersion towards Jerusalem: 'Exile only enhanced
the fervour with which Jerusalem was regarded; the pressure of the
heathen world but confirmed the discipline of which she was the
mistress. Just as . . . the Babylonian Captivity led to the exaltation
of the city above the sordid realities of her history to an idealism
richer than any prophet had dared for her before; so, through the
Greek dispersion, Jerusalem was raised to an even rarer sacredness
and endowed with a far wider empire of the spirit. Things now came
true which were then only seen in vision. . . . There was nothing
else like this in the ancient world, and all modern instances of so
wide a spiritual empire are only its imitations.' Jerusalem had
become a symbol of the intervention of the transcendent in history
and of men's response to it.

When the practice of praying three times daily became the rule is not known. Ps. 55.17 refers to prayer morning, evening and at noonday, but the Old Testament evidence is conflicting. Probably we should infer that by the time the Book of Daniel was written the later Jewish practice had already established itself.

Daniel was caught in the act by his enemies, who went immediately to the king, but, before accusing Daniel of a breach of the edict, reminded the king that he had indeed issued an irrevocable decree. They then triumphantly produced the name of the culprit. The king was furious when he found how he had been tricked. But, though he tried for the rest of the day to find some way round the legal difficulty, he finally had to yield to the importunity of the accusers and abandon Daniel to his fate. He did so, however, with an expression of the pious hope that the God to whom Daniel had been so faithful would even now deliver him. Daniel was flung into the lions' den, which was then sealed so that no interference could take place.

[18-24] The king spent a miserable night fasting and sleepless. Dawn found him at the lions' den anxious to find out what had been Daniel's fate. He called out to Daniel, addressing him significantly as servant of the *living* God and was overjoyed at receiving an answer from Daniel telling him that God had indeed intervened by sending an angel to shut the lions' mouths and proudly proclaiming his innocence in God's sight and in the king's sight. The parallel with chapter 3 in this as in a number of other points is striking. It is interesting that both these stories are referred to in Heb. 11.33 and 34 and are associated there with obvious references to the military exploits of the Maccabees and their followers. Heaton draws attention to this unconscious anticipation of the critical view accepted by modern scholarship. Like the three confessors of chapter 3, Daniel was found completely unharmed in spite of his ordeal. The *jus talionis* was then put into effect as in the case of Haman in the Book of Esther. Daniel's accusers along with their wives and families were thrown to the lions. Readers would doubtless see this barbarous punishment as in agreement with the injunction about the treatment of a false witness in the Torah (Deut. 19.16–19): 'you shall do to him as he had meant to do to his brother'. The author of our book had not learnt everything that God had to teach about the nature of justice.

[25-28] Chapter 6 finishes in much the same way as chapter 3. Darius issued a decree which went beyond that issued by Nebuchadnezzar. Men were not only not to speak against the God of the Jews,

they must actually reverence him. In hymnic language Darius celebrated him as the living and enduring God whose sovereignty is endless and who has proved himself to be a saving God by his deliverance of Daniel. The epithet 'enduring' as applied to God is, Montgomery points out, to be found in the Targum and occurs frequently in both the Rabbinic and the Samaritan literature. In an age when so much was changing it meant much to be sure that God at least would not change. It is an assurance that should mean much to us today.

An acknowledgment of God like this one attributed to Darius is what the Jews dreamed of, and the faith that, whether it was acknowledged by the pagan world or not, God was indeed sovereign supported them through the darkest days.

The chapter closes with the statement that Daniel's prosperity continued during the remainder of Darius's reign and on into that of Cyrus.

VII

CHAPTER SEVEN

7 ¹In the first year of Belshazzar king of Babylon, Daniel had a dream and visions of his head as he lay in his bed. Then he wrote down the dream, and told the sum of the matter. ²Daniel said, 'I saw in my vision by night, and behold, the four winds of heaven were stirring up the great sea. ³And four great beasts came up out of the sea, different from one another. ⁴The first was like a lion and had eagle's wings. Then as I looked its wings were plucked off, and it was lifted up from the ground and made to stand upon two feet like a man; and the mind of a man was given to it. ⁵And behold, another beast, a second one, like a bear. It was raised up on one side; it had three ribs in its mouth between its teeth; and it was told, "Arise, devour much flesh." ⁶After this I looked, and lo, another, like a leopard, with four wings of a bird on its back; and the beast had four heads; and dominion was given to it. ⁷After this I saw in the night visions, and behold a fourth beast, terrible and dreadful and exceedingly strong; and it had great iron teeth;* it devoured and broke in pieces, and stamped the residue with its feet. It was different from all the beasts that were before it; and it had ten horns. ⁸I considered the horns, and behold, there came up among them another horn, a little one, before which three of the first horns were plucked up by the roots; and behold, in this horn were eyes like the eyes of a man, and a mouth speaking great things. ⁹As I looked,

thrones were placed
  and one that was ancient of days† took his seat;
his raiment was white as snow,
  and the hair of his head like pure wool;
his throne was fiery flames,
  its wheels were burning fire.
¹⁰A stream of fire issued
  and came forth from before him;
a thousand thousands served him,
  and ten thousand times ten thousand stood before him;
the court sat in judgment,
  and the books were opened.

* Insert 'and bronze claws' with Hippolytus.
† Or 'one that was old in years'.

¹¹ I looked then because of the sound of the great words which the horn was speaking.* And as I looked, the beast was slain, and its body destroyed and given over to be burned with fire. ¹²As for the rest of the beasts, their dominion was† taken away, but their lives were prolonged for a season and a time. ¹³I saw in the night visions,

> and behold, with the clouds of heaven
>> there came one like a son of man,
> and he came to the Ancient of Days
>> and was presented before him.
> ¹⁴And to him was given dominion
>> and glory and kingdom,
> that all peoples, nations and languages
>> should serve him;
> his dominion is an everlasting dominion,
>> which shall not pass away,
> and his kingdom one
>> that shall not be destroyed.

15 'As for me, Daniel, my spirit within me§ was anxious and the visions of my head alarmed me. ¹⁶I approached one of those who stood there and asked him the truth concerning all this. So he told me, and made known to me the interpretation of the things. ¹⁷"These four great beasts are four kings who shall arise out of the earth. ¹⁸But the saints of of the Most High shall receive the kingdom, and possess the kingdom for ever, for ever and ever."

19 'Then I desired to know the truth concerning the fourth beast, which was different from all the rest, exceedingly terrible, with its teeth of iron and claws of bronze; and which devoured and broke in pieces, and stamped the residue with its feet; ²⁰and concerning the ten horns that were on its head, and the other horn which came up and before which three of them fell, the horn which had eyes and a mouth that spoke great things‡, and which seemed greater than its fellows. ²¹As I looked, this horn made war with the saints, and prevailed over them, ²²until the Ancient of Days came, and judgment was given for the saints of the Most High, and the time came when the saints received the kingdom.

23 'Thus he said: "As for the fourth beast,
> there shall be a fourth kingdom on earth,
>> which shall be different from all the kingdoms,
> and it shall devour the whole earth,
>> and trample it down, and break it to pieces.
> ²⁴As for the ten horns,
>> out of this kingdom
>> ten kings shall arise,
>> and another shall arise after them;

* Better 'because the horn was speaking arrogant words'.
† Or 'had been' (Plöger).
§ Read 'therefore' by a slight emendation.   ‡ 'Arrogantly'.

he shall be different from the former ones,
    and shall put down three kings.
25He shall speak words against the Most High,
    and shall wear out the saints of the Most High,
    and shall think to change the times and the law;
and they shall be given into his hand
    for a time, two times, and half a time.
26But the court shall sit in judgment,
    and his dominion shall be taken away,
    to be consumed and destroyed to the end.
27And the kingdom and the dominion
    and the greatness of the kingdoms under the whole heaven
    shall be given to the people of the saints of the Most High;
their kingdom shall be an everlasting kingdom,
    and all dominions shall serve and obey them."

28 'Here is the end of the matter. As for me, Daniel, my thoughts greatly alarmed me, and my colour changed; but I kept the matter in my mind.'

W ITH THIS CHAPTER we reach the heart of the Book of Daniel. It is related so closely to what precedes and also to what follows that, when one makes the obvious division of the book into the stories and the visions, it is very difficult to determine whether chapter 7 ought to be linked more closely with the former or with the latter. On the one hand, apart from the fact that, like most of the stories, it is written in Aramaic, there is not only a clear connection between the vision it describes and Nebuchadnezzar's dream in chapter 2: it also claims to say the last word about the brutal empires to which we have already been introduced in the stories about Daniel and his friends. On the other hand this chapter contains in semi-poetical form a more explicit version of the expectation hinted at in chapter 2, of which the elucidation and prosaic details are given in the concluding chapters. As we shall see later, another very important aspect of the situation is given in chapter 9 which will prove to have a vital bearing on our ultimate theological assessment of the Book of Daniel. Our present task, however, is to try and make what we can of the remarkable vision in chapter 7, composed, as it is, of elements with a history and complicated associations which have offered a challenge to interpreters and been the occasion of much ingenious scholarly research. The author of chapter 7 has been able to command a range of thought and imagery in which to clothe it, which invites one to look into the depths of religious thought and experience which preceded it and also forwards into later Jewish and Christian thought which drew so heavily upon it.

The first difficulty that has to be faced in interpreting this chapter is that of making up one's mind on the question of its unity. Part of the chapter is in plain prose, but the description of the tribunal (vv. 9-10), the section about the one like a son of man (vv. 13-14) and the interpretation of the whole vision (vv. 23-27) are rhythmical in style. That might point to disunity and lead to a theory of interpolation into an originally simple narrative. This radical solution, however, which suggests that the vision of the divine Judge holding tribunal and of the one like a son of man, who comes to the Ancient of Days and receives the dominion, had originally nothing to do with the vision of the four beasts, but has been artificially combined with it, does not commend itself. We can account for the abrupt changes of style by changes in the subject-matter or suppose that the author has drawn upon varied material in creating his total picture. Though a man of imagination and artistic sensibility, as is shown by the tremendous impact his book made on subsequent thought, he betrays, not only here but elsewhere in his book, a certain awkwardness in composition which may be regarded as a feature of his style as a writer. However clumsy certain of the transitions in chapter 7 are, then, to tear apart the chapter, as is proposed by some, would destroy the contrast which is surely intended between the symbolism of the beasts and the symbolism of the man-like figure, and would in the last resort leave 'the saints of the Most High' of the interpretation (v. 27) without a corresponding symbol in the vision.

It seems reasonable to regard vv. 21-22 as the ill-conceived attempt of an interpolator to add something to the vision to correspond to something in the later interpretation, through his failure to recognize that a tendency to such elaboration in the interpretation of a prophecy or a vision is not without parallel elsewhere in this kind of writing. Indeed if vv. 21-22 are omitted nothing essential is lost. Further, vv. 13-14 require vv. 11-12 before them, describing, as they do, what was made possible after the carrying out of the sentence upon the beasts, and in particular upon the fourth beast, a sentence which was presumably pronounced by the Ancient of Days alone and carried out by his agents, though this is not explicitly stated. It is only after the age of the bestial empires has been brought to an end that authority is delegated to the one like a son of man.

One should also be very hesitant about accepting the theory that there was an original version of this chapter which told of the succession of the four beasts without the further elaboration of the little horn which so clearly points to the tyranny of Antiochus IV Epiphanes. That is not, of course, to say that the author did not borrow the four kingdoms theory and use it for his own purpose. What the theory referred to (M. Noth, *ThSK* 98/99, 1926, pp. 143–63), which dates the original version in the time of Alexander the Great, fails to produce is a situation of sufficient urgency to account for the conviction that the supernatural destruction of the fourth kingdom was imminent. Alexander the Great did nothing to bring about such a sense of urgency in the mind of a Jew. Such a situation as seemed to demand swift divine intervention is symbolized by the little horn with its mouth uttering arrogant words. That is to say, without the symbolic reference to Antiochus Epiphanes who was challenging the authority of God as none of his predecessors had done, the chapter loses its point. That the author of the book, and of chapter 7 in particular, is writing at all is due to a conviction, which takes the form of a prophecy, that a climax in world affairs requiring the direct and final intervention of God is swiftly approaching. This consideration, *viz.* that a vision without the urgent symbol of the little horn would lack its necessary background, and would indeed be trivial, seems to outweigh the arguments brought forward by Noth.

Another issue now comes up for discussion, and this will involve us more deeply in the question of the meaning of the chapter. Put in prosaic terms, the meaning of the chapter is taken to be that the age of the oppressive empires is about to be terminated by the sovereign act of God and that, when his kingdom is brought in, delegated sovereignty will be given to the faithful among the Jews as the people of his choice. This information is conveyed to Daniel, according to the fiction of the book, first in the form of a remarkable vision with its successive scenes, and then in plainer language by the supernatural interpreter, who does for Daniel what Daniel, in the story of Nebuchadnezzar's dream in chapter 2, did for the Babylonian king. The question which now requires careful consideration is the extent to which we must pay heed to the possible overtones of the imagery which goes to make up the vision. In fact, if we recognize the ultimate source of the imagery which the writer employs, are we entitled to read more into the vision than the author himself does? It is quite true that the language in which the vision described in this chapter is clothed has a history and calls up in the mind of the scholar

D.–G

who has steeped himself in ancient religious thought and practice all kinds of suggestive associations. We may not, however, assume that the sum of these associations must have been present to the minds of those who read the composition in question or even to the man who used such imagery in his descriptions.

In his admirable commentary, which, whatever reservations we may have, makes an important contribution to the literature on chapter 7, Eric Heaton, following up certain suggestions of Bentzen which go back to Gunkel, has worked up an elaborate argument for the view that in chapter 7 the author draws heavily upon the imagery of the creation myth, as it appears in its Babylonian form, and in brief allusions here and there in the Old Testament itself, and also upon the biblical view of man's place in the universe which God has created. He accepts the view that there is a link between the varied elements of the chapter and the ceremonies of the Babylonian New Year Festival—whether these were known directly or indirectly to the Jewish author—one element in which was the recitation of the Creation Epic and another the annual re-enthronement of the king after being presented to Marduk. We are, therefore, asked to believe that the theme of chapter 7 is the new creation when God's kingdom is set up and the kingdoms symbolized by the beasts are either destroyed or deprived of their sovereignty, a delegated authority, in what must surely be a reflection of an enthronement scene, being given to one like a son of man, just as in Gen. 1.28 and Ps. 8.6ff. man is given an almost royal authority over the lower creation. We are further asked to consider the references to the creation myth in Ps. 74.13ff. and Ps. 89.9ff., in which Leviathan and Rahab represent the primaeval monster Tiamat of the Babylonian myth, and in the light of these to recognize here another example of God's salvation of his people being represented as a continuation of his victory over the dragon at the time of the creation.

There can be little doubt that the myths and rituals to which Bentzen and Heaton refer and which may have been mediated to Israel by way of Ugarit and the ancient religious practice of the Jebusite city which David converted into his capital, are the source of the imagery which appears in chapter 7 and indeed are the ultimate explanation of features in the vision to which Heaton does not refer. It will be necessary, however, to distinguish between all these associations and the actual use which the author makes of the imagery and what his readers would understand by it. At the same time there is a danger in reading too little as well as in reading too much, into the language, and perhaps we should in the last resort admit that we cannot be certain where the line ought to be drawn. It is also extremely hard to be objective with regard to a passage the ideas of which have had such a remarkable history of acceptance and adaptation in succeeding writers.

When one looks again at chapter 7 and what the writer actually says, it must be recognized that whatever reference to the creation is intended is not made explicit. It is true that the expression 'the great sea' would probably suggest to a reflective reader that $t^e h\bar{o}m$ or abyss upon which order had to be imposed when God created the universe. The creatures which are represented in the vision as issuing successively from it, however, do not bear any notable resemblance to the monsters of the creation myth, either in appearance or function, but are intended rather to symbolize the brutal nature of the empires with which the Jewish people had had to do in the course of the last few centuries of their history. The nearest we get to the creation myth is in the description of the fourth beast (see below). Yet, even so, there is no reference to an actual conflict between the deity and the dragon. This, of course, may be due to the fact that, in the original Ugaritic mythology, the slaying of Leviathan was not credited to El, between whom and the Ancient of Days of the vision in Dan. 7 there seems to have been some connection.[1] In much the same way God ($^e l\bar{o}h\bar{\imath}m$) in Gen. 1 does not take over the role of the slayer of the dragon but is elevated above the struggle, which is passed over in silence, though we know from various familiar allusions in the Old Testament that Yahweh could be represented as the actor in the mythological combat. What we find in Dan. 7 is the account of a judicial sentence, after which we learn that the fourth beast was killed—we are not explicitly informed by whom—and its carcase burned up.

Moreover, the contrast between the beasts and the one like a son of man to whom sovereignty is given over the nations has really no more than a remote connection with that sovereignty of man over the lower creation spoken of in Gen. 1; the beasts in Daniel are quite distinct from 'the fish of the sea, the birds of the air and every living thing that moves upon the earth', which all belong to God's creation as over against the powers of Chaos which *ex hypothesi* are signified here by the beasts out of the great sea. At the creation man

[1] Cf., p. 107.

is given sovereignty over the other creatures but not over the powers
of Chaos which are kept in check by God's creative will alone. The
most that can be said on the other side is that the first three beasts
live on tamed and harmless, the peoples they represent taking their
humble place with all the other Gentile nations under the sovereignty
of the saints of the Most High. But they belong to history and not to
nature.

It may be said, then, that while the imagery of this chapter seems
to bear some recognizable relation to the creation mythology, and
while it is true that in biblical thought creation and history are both
parts of one continuing divine activity, the main concern of Dan. 7
is with what God is about to do on the stage of history. Faced by what
he believes to be the culminating wickedness of the powers of this
world, which he sees as satanic in their brutality and depravity, the
author gives expression to his triumphant conviction that God is
about to intervene and replace the rule of tyranny by that of the
saints of the Most High which will be the embodiment of the purpose
and sovereignty of God. The problematic symbol, 'the one like a son
of man', may conceivably imply some thought in the author's mind
that the authority originally given to man over the lower creation is
now to be surpassed by the authority given to Israel over the nations.
His main point, however, would be that the tyrant nation symbolized
by the fourth beast was of a beastliness which demanded not control
but total destruction.

It should be recognized, however, that Heaton makes an excellent
point when he draws special attention to Ps. 74, a psalm which seems
to mirror a situation very similar to that in which the Jews found
themselves under the persecution of Antiochus Epiphanes. J. A.
Emerton ('The Origin of the Son of Man Imagery', *JTS* New Series
IX/2, 1958, p. 234) has pointed out that behind this Psalm and
certain others—46, 48, 76—we can detect a cultic situation like that
of the New Year Festival and some connection with apocalyptic
passages in the prophets (Zech. 12–14; Joel 3; Ezek. 38–39; Isa.
17.12–14 and 29.1–8). Ps. 74 describes a time when the temple has
been desecrated and when all the meeting places (synagogues?) of
God in the land have been burned. That last disaster points to a later
century than that of the Babylonian Exile. And the cry goes up:
'How long, O God?' One can agree that the Book of Daniel is very
like a prophetic answer to this appeal. Chapter 9, like this psalm,
may give us a clue to the spiritual condition to which the Book of

Daniel spoke and to those by whom the hope it kindled could be appropriated as a veritable word of God.

In Ps. 74, we must frankly recognize, the psalmist goes on to describe God's triumph over Leviathan in creation (vv. 12–17). Having reminded God of his creative triumph, the worshippers who use this lament plead with him not to 'deliver the soul of thy dove to the wild beasts', and the word which is used for wild beasts is the Hebrew word corresponding to the Aramaic term applied in Dan. 7 to the beasts which issue from the great sea. The wild beasts of the psalm, however, are not identified with Leviathan, though, of course, the more brutal side of nature may have been thought of as akin to that chaos which is forever raging behind its bars. Certainly the author of Daniel does not make explicit reference to the creation myth as the author of Ps. 74 unquestionably does. Indeed, if he is using the varied imagery of the New Year Festival, he may well be unaware of its origin, as he adopts it to indicate the nature of the dramatic transition which he believes is about to take place from a world ruled and dominated by a brutal tyranny to a world ruled by God in accordance with his settled purpose for human kind.

Before we pass on, however, to the detailed exposition of the chapter, we must look briefly at the contention of the stimulating article by J. A. Emerton to which reference has been made above (*art. cit.*, pp. 225–42). Accepting Bentzen's view that behind Dan. 7 lie the mythology and ritual practice of the New Year Festival and in particular the mythology of Ugarit, Emerton argues that the description of one like a son of man coming with the clouds of heaven suggests a divine rather than a human figure, clouds being in numerous instances in the Old Testament associated with a theophany. (He refers here to an article by A. Feuillet in *RB* 60, 1953, pp. 170ff. and 321ff., discussed by Coppens in *Wisdom in Israel and the Ancient Near East*, edited by Noth and Winton Thomas, 1955, pp. 33ff.) To state this point very briefly, Emerton suggests that in the Ancient of Days and in the one like a son of man we have the adaptation of a myth which originally told of two gods, probably El and Baal, Baal being originally the conqueror of the dragon. This would explain the cloud accompaniment of the one like a son of man. In the Ugaritic myth Baal was promoted by El after his victory. Emerton thinks that possibly in the manipulation of the mythology associated with Jebusite Jerusalem after its capture by David, Yahweh, the Hebrew God, in the first instance displaced, not El

Elyon but Baal, and only later, upon the final triumph of mono-
theism, was identified also with El Elyon. He suggests that through
some channel, which it is no longer possible accurately to identify,
the old mythology survived and remained available as the source of
imagery to be used in late apocalyptic writings. Emerton's contribution is a significant one and is worthy of the closest consideration.
He would, however, be the first to admit that, as used by the author
of Daniel, the polytheistic implications of the language are ignored
and the one like a son of man becomes at the most an angelic figure
who in some way symbolizes the faithful among the Jews through
whom the rule of God will become actualized in the world.

[1] We are told that the vision of this chapter came to Daniel in the
first year of Belshazzar king of Babylon. (After this verse throughout
the rest of the book, except in 10.1, Daniel is always represented as the
speaker. Actually, however, the anxiety and concern which are
attributed to Daniel are the anxiety and concern of the author himself, whom we can almost hear at times speaking *in propria persona*; cf.
especially ch. 9.) The vision of chapter 8 is dated in his third year. It
is in the first year of Darius the Mede that Daniel receives the explanation of the seventy years of Jeremiah's prophecy. A further experience
comes to Daniel in the third year of Cyrus, while, at the beginning of
chapter 11, there is a reference back to a supernatural event as having
taken place in the first year of Darius. As far as we can judge, these
dates have no significance other than that of giving a certain veri-
similitude to the referring of these *vaticinia post eventum* to the period of
the Babylonian Captivity. The real point of perspective, which
explains the stress under which the author is writing and which he
transfers to Daniel, is the time of the persecution of Antiochus, from
which he looks back, schematizing the history which is significant
for him, and from which he looks forward to the now imminent
climax.

[2–8] In the vision which Daniel now proceeds to describe he
sees the great sea churned up by the four winds of heaven and four
beasts emerging from it. It is probably true, as has been said above,
that by the great sea the author intends his readers to understand the
tehōm or abyss of Gen. 1 which corresponds philologically to the
Tiamat of Babylonian mythology (*Nammu* in Sumerian), but he does
not lay any emphasis upon this, because in v. 17, in the interpretation, the kingdoms which the beasts represent, arise out of the earth.
Jeffery (*IB*, p. 452, cf. Bevan, p. 120) is perhaps right in referring to

Isa. 17.12–13 and Jer. 6.23, where the turmoil of the nations is compared to the roaring of the sea. That is to say, the author of Daniel may be thinking more of the movements of history than of the creation of the universe. It is true that the mention of the four winds of heaven recalls the Epic of Creation. Here, however, the winds churn up the sea, whereas in the Babylonian Epic of Creation the four winds are instruments in the hand of Marduk to prevent Tiamat from escaping. The nearest we get in the Creation Epic to the four beasts of Daniel (for the possible connection between the fourth beast and Leviathan, see below) is in the description, repeated several times, of the monster companions of Tiamat who are described as:

the Viper, the Dragon, and the Sphinx,
the Great-Lion, the Mad-Dog, and the Scorpion-Man,
mighty Lion-demons, the Dragon-Fly, the Centaur.

(J. B. Pritchard's transl.)

This gives us the lion alone of the four beasts of Daniel. The difference has led to the suggestion that the author of Daniel may be drawing upon some myth otherwise unknown to us (so Eduard Meyer, *Urspr. u. Anf. des Christentums*, vol. II, 1921, p. 197), but perhaps we may allow a measure of originality to the author of Daniel, who may simply have chosen the bestial figures best suited to his purpose. We can still, even with our limited knowledge, detect a certain appropriateness in his symbolism.

In the vision, the four beasts which rise from the sea are clearly differentiated. There is an overwhelming measure of agreement among commentators that they represent symbolically the same four kingdoms as are represented in chapter 2, by the sequence of metals in the image, *viz.* the Babylonian, the Median, the Persian and the Greek. The author of the Ezra Apocalypse (II Esd. 12.11–12), who, understandably, when one remembers that he lived in the first century AD, preferred to interpret the fourth kingdom as Rome, appropriately symbolizing it by an eagle, makes it, however, abundantly clear that the Book of Daniel had given a very different interpretation.

The circumstance that the symbolism of chapter 2 is, as it were, static until the episode of the stone, which brings sudden and catastrophic movement into the picture, makes it less appropriate than the dynamic symbolism of chapter 7. It is quite obvious, of course, from the interpretation of chapter 2 that the kingdoms are

meant to be successive, and the same may be confidently asserted of
chapter 7, where the beasts do not arise from the sea simultaneously
(*pace* Gressmann, *Der Messias*, 1929, p. 366), but, with the exception
of the third beast, are specifically numbered, it being surely implied
that they come up on the land in succession. We may confidently
reject Gressmann's view that the four beasts represent the four main
successor kingdoms which followed upon the break-up of Alexander's
empire. Why should Daniel, who is represented as living in Babylon
during the Exile, begin his historical survey only after the death of
Alexander?

Coming now to the descriptions of the four beasts, we must first
take note of the ingenious, but by no means convincing, handling of
the text by H. L. Ginsberg (*Studies in the Book of Daniel*, ch. II,
pp. 5ff.), who transfers part of the description of the bear to the lion
and part of the description of the lion to the bear. The bear is thus
made to stand on two feet in human fashion (as bears frequently do!)
and to receive a man's mind, while the phrase which RSV translates
'was lifted up from the ground' is translated by Ginsberg as 'vanished
from the earth', a meaning which it manifestly does not have in the
present text. He seeks to justify the transposition partly on zoological
grounds, the hind feet of the bear being better adapted to the erect
posture than those of the lion. It is likewise argued by him that the
description of a gluttonous nature, which the text attributes to the
bear, should be transferred to the lion. All this somewhat arbitrary
handling of the text is to enable Ginsberg to claim that the Babylonian kingdom is represented in chapter 7 (i.e. in the emended text)
as having been destroyed when the empire passed from it. He thus
establishes a difference, so he claims, between the contemporary
historical situation implied by chapter 2 and that implied by chapter
7 and goes on from there to claim a pre-Epiphanian date for chapter
2 and an Epiphanian date for chapter 7. H. H. Rowley (*The Unity of
the Book of Daniel*: *HUCA* XXIII, Part One, pp. 250ff.; also in *The
Servant of the Lord and other Essays on the Old Testament*, pp. 250ff.)
acutely disposes of this supposed distinction between the dream and
the vision by pointing to 7.12, where it is clearly stated (on any
reasonable understanding of the words) that the first three beasts
were allowed to continue in life for a while after being deprived of
their sovereignty, no distinction between the lion on the one hand and
the bear and the panther on the other, such as Ginsberg claims, being
implied. It seems, then, that we are justified in taking the descriptions

of the first two beasts as we have them in the Massoretic Text.

The description of the first beast as a winged lion may be regarded as peculiarly appropriate for its identification with Babylon, not only because such creatures figured in Babylonian art (though also elsewhere), but because the lion is used as a symbol for Nebuchadnezzar in Jer. 50.44 (the references given by Jeffery are not conclusive), while the symbol of the eagle is used for Babylon in Ezek. 17.3 and in Heb. 1.8, where, however, the comparison with leopards and wolves is also used. It is difficult to be dogmatic about the rest of the description of the first beast. Heaton follows Montgomery and Bentzen in regarding it as probable that the allusion is to the fate which overtook Nebuchadnezzar, reducing him to the level of the beasts, followed by his restoration to human dignity (as described in ch. 4), when he humbled himself under the hand of God. Jeffery, on the other hand, thinks that the rampant posture given to the lion implies awkwardness, while 'a man's timid heart' is opposed to 'the fearless heart of a beast'. On balance the former solution of the problem commends itself.

The bear as a symbol for the Median kingdom has most probably been chosen because of its known ferocity (see Isa. 13.17–18) and the dread it aroused (Isa. 21.2ff.). The statement that 'it was raised up on one side and had three ribs in its mouth between its teeth' is obscure. There is probably here a cryptic allusion to Median greed for booty, while the bear's curious posture may imply aggressiveness rather than some kind of limitation of the effectiveness of the Medes as a power.

The third beast, a panther or leopard with four wings and four heads has, like the first, a heraldic character and is clearly intended to represent Persia. What precisely is the significance of the symbolism cannot now be determined. Either the four wings and the four heads mean the same thing and refer to the extension of the Persian Empire in all directions, or they signify different things, the wings symbolizing the swiftness in movement of the Persian armies (see Isa. 41.3) and the heads either implying extension as before, or representing the succession of the four Persian kings whose names appear in the Old Testament (so many commentators, following Dan. 11.2) or some other selection of Persian kings. Probably the circumstances that elsewhere in the book the horn is the symbol for a king (or a kingdom) should incline us to the view that the wings and heads signify swiftness and extension.

The fourth beast, which undoubtedly represents the Greek (Macedonian) kingdom of Alexander and his successors, is described as belonging to no identifiable class of animal and as being of horrible and alarming appearance. Bentzen (p. 61) thinks that the writer may have been inspired by the description of Leviathan which figures in the Ras Shamra mythology and may have survived in the Typhon of Apollodorus. However that may be, it should be obvious from the elaboration of detail which is now offered that we have come to what is of particular interest and, indeed, of urgent concern to the author, indicating, as it does, the situation which impelled him to write his book. To a lesser extent, but quite definitely, we observed a similar increase in detail in Daniel's interpretation of the image in chapter 2, when he came to the description of the fourth kingdom. The iron in the dream of chapter 2 has corresponding to it in chapter 7 the great iron teeth, while the brutality and ruthlessness of the fourth kingdom, as it seemed to a member of a subject race, is vividly portrayed.

It is generally agreed that the ten horns upon the creature's head represent ten kings, not contemporaries, but successive rulers. Interpreters have differed as to whether the succession should begin with Alexander the Great or not, and as to whether a mixture of Seleucids and Ptolemies is intended or an exclusive line of Seleucids (as is implied in the *Sibylline Oracles III*, 381–400). It is probable that the ten kings should be thought of as commencing with Seleucus Nicator, the founder of the Seleucid dynasty, and continuing in the same line down to the point at which Antiochus IV Epiphanes came to the throne. There is no doubt at all that he is the small horn springing up among the other horns, to make room for which three horns are rooted out. There has been endless discussion as to the identity of these horns and perhaps it does not greatly matter whom they represent. H. H. Rowley, who gives a masterly and exhaustive discussion of the whole historical problem of the fourth beast and its horns (*Darius the Mede and the Four World Empires in the Book of Daniel*, pp. 98–120), himself votes for Demetrius the son of Seleucus IV Philopator (who subsequently came to the throne as Demetrius I Soter, though our author could not know that), his brother Antiochus, who was killed in infancy, and Ptolemy VII Philometor, who, through his mother Cleopatra was nephew to Seleucus Philopator, and could, therefore, be reckoned as a Seleucid. This is probably the most satisfactory solution of the problem, but certainty is unattainable. Among recent commentators, Jeffery (*IB*, p. 456) prefers the selection Seleucus Philopator, Demetrius and Heliodorus, even though the last-named was no Seleucid. And so on! *Quot homines tot sententiae*!

The human character of the little horn is made clear by the eyes which appeared in it and the mouth speaking arrogantly. The reference to the eyes is elaborated in 8.23, where we read of the king of bold countenance. To illustrate the mouth speaking arrogantly reference is properly made to I Macc. 1.24; II Macc. 5.17 and, of course, to the monstrous challenge which, according to Dan. 11.36 Antiochus Epiphanes issued to God himself.

[9-14] From the contemplation of the horrid succession of monsters, which symbolizes for the author the course of human history from Nebuchadnezzar to Antiochus Epiphanes and which, as he himself experienced it in its closing phases, seemed to him to involve a blasphemous challenge to God's authority such as he could not ignore, the author now looks up and 'above the dim spot which men call earth' has a vision of the divine tribunal and of the Judge calmly passing sentence. One is strongly tempted to hold that here we have the description of an actual ecstatic experience, whatever may be said about some of the later visions.[1] That it is possible to suggest various sources for the imagery employed in the description does not disprove this. Such fusing of images to make a composite picture, conceivably achieved at the subliminal level, is precisely what one would expect. In Scripture itself, Job 1.6 and I Kings 22.19 might suggest the *mise en scène*, while Psalms like 9, 50, 82, 93, 96, 98 might make their contribution to the picture. It is conceivable that we should also reckon on the influence of Persian imagery. A highly probable link with Ugarit has been detected in the description of the divine Judge as 'Ancient of Days' (literally 'advanced in days'); for in the Aqhat poem (III. vi. 48) El is described as *mlk 'ab šnm*, i.e. 'the king, father of years'. The Ethiopic phrase *r'ĕsa mawâĕl*, 'the Head or Sum of days', of Enoch 46.1, 2, etc., is doubtless modelled on the title in Daniel, which may be regarded as meaning 'the Eternal' or 'the Everlasting'. If Emerton is right (see above) this venerable figure of the vision has probably its origin in the supreme god El of the Syrian pantheon.

---

[1] But S. B. Frost (*Old Testament Apocalyptic*, pp. 191-2) thinks that in the description of a genuine vision there would have been no detailed description of God, who would have been left as a mysterious, dimly glimpsed figure.

Much speculation has been devoted to the mention of thrones in the description of the judgment scene. If there were assessors there is no specific mention of them, though, of course, God is provided elsewhere in Scripture with his entourage (see references above, Job 1.6; I Kings 22.19; Ps. 82). Nor is there any definite suggestion in the text that the thrones were intended to be occupied later on by the one like a son of man or by representatives of the saints of the Most High, though the reader may have been expected to draw that inference for himself. It is true that in later thought about the judgment it was believed that the saints would have a part in it, but that is not conclusive for the intention of the author of Daniel. Jesus tells his disciples that they will 'sit on thrones judging the twelve tribes of Israel' (Matt. 19.28; Luke 22.30), but that is a different situation from the one described here. A more relevant passage is I Cor. 6.2: 'Do you not know that the saints will judge the world?' In Rev. 20.4, the seer of Patmos has a vision of thrones and seated upon them 'those to whom judgment was committed'. In Daniel's vision the interest is concentrated first upon the Judge alone and he is clearly God himself, the only God, whatever divine features in the long history of the imagery may have attached themselves to the figure of one like a son of man. There can be no doubt at all of our author's monotheistic faith. We are told in the vision that the dress and hair of the Ancient of Days are radiantly white. It may be due to a strange revival of an old belief at a new level that this descriptive feature is in Rev. 1.13–14 transferred to one like a son of man, while in Matt. 19.28 and 25.31, the glorious throne of judgment is occupied by the Son of Man himself.

The description of the throne here recalls the *merkābā*, the divine chariot of Ezekiel's vision (chs. 1 and 10) with its flames and wheels. Enoch 14.18–19 elaborates this: 'I looked and saw a lofty throne: its appearance was as crystal, and the wheels thereof as the shining sun . . . and from underneath the throne came streams of flaming fire.' The fire is a symbol of judgment and is associated in the Old Testament with theophanies. In Ps. 50, for example, devouring fire is said to precede God when he comes to judge his people. Even more relevantly in Ps. 97—one of the so-called Coronation Psalms— we are told of the divine King that

> righteousness and justice are the foundation of his throne.
> Fire goes before him,
>   and burns up his adversaries round about.

Cf. Mal. 3.2 and Isa. 30.27–28. Commentators rightly cite Deut. 33.2 and Ps. 68.18, both of which describe theophanies and refer to the multitude of the angelic attendants upon the deity. It is unlikely that the myriad myriads standing in the Judge's presence are meant to be those awaiting judgment (so Jeffery, p. 458); it is the bestial kingdoms, especially the fourth kingdom, that are about to be condemned. This is not the later conception of the Last Judgment.

The trial begins and we are told that the books are opened. Heaton suggests the possibility that the books have their analogy in the Tablets of Fate which Marduk appropriated after his battle with Tiamat and connects this with the fixing of the fates for the coming year in the New Year Festival. Even though he may be correct in deriving much of the imagery of the vision from the ceremonies of the New Year Festival, it is much more likely that the primary reference here is not to the Tablets of Fate but to the book of which we read that in it were recorded the evil deeds of men (Isa. 65.6) to which corresponded the 'book of remembrance' which 'was written before him (i.e. God) of those who feared the Lord and thought on his name' (Mal. 3.16). Cf. Ex. 32.33, Ps. 69.28 and Rev. 13.8 (where the book of life appears in a context similar to the present one). The Tablets of Fate had quite another purpose.

In v. 11 there is a reminder that this radiant vision had followed immediately upon the utterance of the arrogant words of the little horn. And then we are told of the fourth beast's being killed, how or by whom is not explicitly stated, and of its carcase's being burned up in the fire. That is the first thing that the author wishes to say urgently to his readers. The great tyrant is under the judgment of God and will pass suddenly like a phantasm of the night. The whole oppressive system of government which was imposed on subject peoples by the Seleucid power would utterly disappear at the *fiat* of God. And then the curious addition is made that the other beasts, that representing Babylon (*pace* Ginsberg) and those representing Media and Persia, get a further lease of life. Heaton quotes with approval Rowley's suggestion (*Darius the Mede*, p. 123) that the author of Daniel expects that these eastern peoples who had been swallowed up in Alexander's empire and had later been subject to the Seleucids will now regain their independence, but will not be allowed to tyrannize over other states. His own probably correct interpretation of their reprieve is that they are to become part of the nations who will become vassal to the saints of the Most High (vv. 14 and 27). That this hope was not fulfilled does not in the least prove that it was not entertained.

With v. 13 we reach a fresh scene in the drama. It might be felt that it follows more naturally upon vv. 9 and 10, as it is set in the same key as the description of the tribunal, whereas vv. 11 and 12 are set in a different key. The interposition, however, of vv. 11 and 12 is necessary to express the author's meaning. The celestial figure of one like a son of man does not appear until the sentence upon the fourth beast has been executed. The Ancient of Days who is the Judge acts in both scenes; the one like a son of man does not assume but is granted sovereignty.

The vision as we have it, whatever may have been the original associations of the imagery which is used, is of a man-like being escorted by the clouds of heaven and introduced into the presence of the Ancient of Days, a majestic and venerable King. It seems clear that what the author intends is a contrast between the one like a son of man and the beasts which issued from the abyss. As the kingdoms that are to pass away are symbolized by supernatural beasts, it seems appropriate that the symbol of what is to replace the bestial kingdoms should be both human and supernatural.

This new figure is introduced without explanation and we are left to conjecture whether or not it belonged to a tradition which could be taken for granted by the author of the Book of Daniel as familiar to his readers. Heaton (p. 183), correctly noting that the one like a son of man is represented in the vision as going to God, not descending from God, declares that 'the background of this scene is to be sought, not in the later apocalyptic ideas of the coming of the Messiah from heaven, but in the ideas associated in Israelite belief with the reigning king'. He goes on to expound his view that what we have in this vision is a reflection of an enthronement festival. That may be so (cf. Ps. 2)—though, as we have seen, Emerton thinks rather of the enthronement of a god like Baal—but the emphasis here is, not so much on the fact that the figure is in human likeness, as on the fact that those thus symbolized are the representatives of the kingdom of God; the man-like character of the kingdom, translated from the language of symbolism, means its divine character.

C. H. Dodd (whom Heaton quotes) puts forward the interesting view (*According to the Scriptures*, 1952, p. 117) that this passage and two of the Psalms (*viz.* 8 and 80) were used as testimonies for building up a theology by New Testament writers. Inasmuch as both Ps. 80

and Dan. 7 speak of the salvation coming to an Israel which has been suffering oppression and humiliation, while Ps. 8 starts with man 'in his weakness and insignificance', before telling how he has received royal dignity, we may agree with Dodd when he declares, 'To say, as it is often said, that the Old Testament knows nothing of a suffering Son of Man is inaccurate.' In Dan. 7, however, there is no suggestion that the author has even glimpsed the thought of vicarious suffering. Nor is there any suggestion in Jewish thought that, though there was indeed some *rapprochement* between the ideas of Messiah, Servant and Son of Man, the Servant was conceived of as a Suffering Servant. The Targum on Isa. 53 makes that clear. In spite of all that has been said to the contrary, it was probably Jesus himself who, when he appropriated the title 'Son of Man' as that best fitted to indicate who he was, fused it with the thought of a *Suffering* Servant and claimed no other Messiahship. (See William Manson, *Jesus the Messiah*, 1943, ch. VI.)

The interpretation of the vision implies a striking reversal of fortune which is to be brought about by the power of God. Jeffery wishes to see in the symbol of one like a son of man a secondary reference to the Messiah. 'In this book', he says, 'we find that king and kingdom interchange, and there is no *a priori* reason why this figure may not represent both the saints as a body and the saint of saints as an individual' (p. 461). We are on safer ground in doubting with Heaton (p. 184) whether the author of Dan. 7 is thinking of a Messianic leader at this point, but he invokes the principle of corporate personality to show how readily the thought of an individual Messiah might emerge from the corporate figure which appears here.

[15–18] Like Nebuchadnezzar in chapter 2, Daniel is represented as being in great confusion and anxiety of mind as a result of the vision. Just as the Babylonian king required Daniel as an interpreter, so Daniel in his turn has to depend on someone else whom, oddly enough, he finds among the angelic participants in a scene which has not yet taken place but which Daniel foresees in vision. We may perhaps see in this curious inconsistency a reflection of the absolute certainty in the author's mind that the celestial event he has described is virtually accomplished. Conversation with people seen in vision appears in Ezekiel's vision of the new temple (chs. 40ff.) and in the visions of Zechariah (chs. 1ff.). This becomes one of the conventions of later apocalyptic, and, indeed, angel interpreters play a big part in the remaining chapters of the Book of Daniel. No doubt there is justification for the view that this angelology is a literary device to explain how the gulf between God and man was bridged, in other words, to provide a theory of how revelation comes. We should not, however, conclude from the artificial character of the device that the conviction of the reality of revelation was not tremendously sincere. Indeed we shall not be far wrong in detecting in the perturbation of Daniel's mind a reflection of the author's stress of mind. He may use literary devices, but he is using them to describe a genuine religious experience.

In v. 15 a slight emendation gives 'therefore' instead of a reference to the body as the sheath of the soul. The American RSV prefers to retain the text and translates 'my spirit within me was anxious'. Bentzen and Montgomery and other modern commentators prefer the simple emendation which is also supported by the LXX.

The angel interpreter explains the four beasts as representing four kings, or possibly, with certain ancient versions, four kingdoms, which are to arise out of the earth. This suggests that the great sea of v. 2 is to be understood symbolically. The impressive scene described in vv. 9–10 is passed over in the interpretation and the scene which describes the coming of one like a son of man is translated into the assurance that the sovereignty is to be given to the saints of the Most High and never taken from them. The fact that the interpretation is given in such bald terms suggest that the interest of the writer is concentrated upon the certainty of the coming transformation rather than upon the mysterious details of the ecstatic experience which contributed to his conviction. Indeed, if the figure of one like a son of man had, in the intention of the writer, referred to an individual, it is difficult to believe that there would have been no reflection of this in the interpretation. Instead, it is clearly implied that the symbol which interests us so much because of its subsequent history was understood by the writer as signifying the saints of the Most High, who are the faithful among the Jews, with emphasis upon the power of God which was to operate through them when they would represent his triumphant rule.

[19–27] The urgent concern of Daniel, which conceals the concern of the writer, appears in his eagerness to know what was meant by the fourth beast. Its description is given in terms almost identical to those employed in v. 7. The insertion of the 'bronze claws' which was accepted in v. 7 on the evidence of Hippolytus may, of course, have been inserted by him on the basis of v. 19. It should be noted that the little horn of v. 8 has now outgrown the others.

It is very difficult to believe that vv. 21 and 22 are not an addition to the original text by someone who felt that there were features of the interpretation given by the angel in vv. 25–27 which did not seem to be sufficiently symbolized in the figure of one like a son of man in vv. 13–14. Certainly one might have expected that in the vision some action on the part of the little horn to follow up its arrogant words would have been included. The trouble is that the elaboration of the vision includes part of the interpretation, *viz.* the reference to the saints. It might be thought that vv. 21–22 are an earlier version of vv. 13–14 which has been misplaced and added in at this point. It is much more likely, however, that the verses have been written in by someone who knew the interpretation and had vv. 13–14 before him, so that he could allude to the Ancient of Days without further description. Who the saints are may be reserved till we come to v. 27.

The reply of the angel to Daniel's question about the fourth beast makes it clear that its difference from the other beasts corresponds to a difference between the kingdom it represents and the other kingdoms. We have already seen that it is undoubtedly the Macedonian-Greek empire of Alexander the Great and his successors that is thus characterized, and it is a sobering reflection that it was this empire, for all that it mediated to the ancient peoples of the East the achievements of Greek culture, that could appear, in the eyes of a member of a subject people, to be the worst of all tyrannies.

It is not necessary to discuss again the identification of the ten horns and the three. We are, however, told something more about the eleventh horn, which is now explained as a king who shall stand out in comparison with all his predecessors. We were told in the vision (v. 8) of the arrogant words of the little horn. We now learn that the king whom the little horn represents will speak blasphemously against God himself and will also direct his attack against the saints of the Most High. The word used is usually taken as meaning 'wear out', but it may come from a different Arabic root meaning 'afflict' or 'put to the test'. This seems to be a clear reference to the persecution of the Jews of Jerusalem and Judaea by Antiochus Epiphanes. That this is so is confirmed by the statement which immediately follows that this persecuting king 'shall plan to change times and the law'. It is generally agreed that this is a reference to the measures

D.–H

taken by Antiochus as described in I Macc. 1.41ff., the times referring
to the seasonal religious festivals of the Jews and the law to the
Mosaic Law (even though a Persian word is used here), in particular
the injuctions regarding circumcision and certain dietary rules which
became matters of issue between pious Jews and the Syrian authorities.
The power of the tyrant, however, was to be strictly limited to a
period of time defined mysteriously as a time, times and half a time.
Just as, in 4.25, the period of Nebuchadnezzar's madness is given as
seven times, which is usually understood as seven years, so here we
are doubtless meant to understand half that period, *viz.* three and a
half years. (Cf. Rev./12.14, forty-two months, an evident reference to
this passage.) Opinion is divided between the view that all that is
meant is that the persecution is to last for a very short time, and the
view that in this prophecy of a duration fixed for the persecution of
three and a half years we have a remarkably accurate forecast either
of the period from the desecration of the temple (15 Chislev 167 BC,
the setting up of the Abomination which appals; 25 Chislev 167 BC,
the first sacrifice upon the profaned altar) to the rededication of the
temple by Judas Maccabaeus (25 Chislev 164 BC), or of the period
from the punitive visit of Apollonius to Jerusalem in the summer of
168 BC (I Macc. 1.54, 59, 29) to the above-mentioned rededication of
the temple.

Unless we are to suppose that the later chapters of the book are
from a different author from the author of chapter 7, it would seem
that the mysterious indication of the time of endurance of persecution,
by whatever process of thought it was borne in upon the mind of the
author, provoked him to repeated attempts to predict to a day the
time of the end (see 8.14; 12.11, 12 and the repetition of the cryptic
period 12.7). Heaton's suggestion (pp. 50–51) that the author of
chapter 7, who in his view was also the author of chapters 1–6,
published his book after the plundering of the temple by Antiochus
in 169 BC and before the desecration of the temple in 167 BC, and
that the concluding chapters are from the pen of a disciple belonging
like him to the circles of the *Ḥasidim*, would certainly absolve the
author of chapters 1–7 (if that is all that he wrote) from being the
initiator of the tragic story of the human endeavour to determine the
time of the end which has continued all down the centuries. It would
seem, however, that it was not the plundering of the temple by Antiochus which led our author to produce his summons to faith and
endurance—the temple had been plundered more than once before

—but precisely its desecration, which was felt to be the proof that iniquity could go no farther, but must, by this supreme challenge to God's authority, bring down upon itself God's final judgment. It may be that after issuing his prediction that the persecution would last only a brief time (a time, times and half a time), the increasingly desperate plight of the Jews tempted him to a more precise determination of the period of endurance. It seems possible that the original book was chapters 1–7 and that it was supplemented, as the persecution went on, by additional visions issued in the form of broadsheets. The difference in literary elegance between the Aramaic portion and the Hebrew portion may be accounted for by the fact that the author was more at home in Aramaic than in Hebrew, but, for some reason unknown to us, chose to supplement the book in Hebrew, the language of revelation. We know from the discoveries made in the Dead Sea Caves that Hebrew was used freely alongside Aramaic. Conceivably the use of Hebrew gave a certain authority to a writing, which may explain why chapter 1 is also in Hebrew, though, in that case, it is difficult to understand why Hebrew was not used for chapter 7.

In v. 26 the interpretation makes brief reference to the bare fact of the judgment upon the tyrant and the destruction of his sovereignty. The author has not forgotten that in the vision it is the fourth beast that is destroyed, not just the little horn. In his thought, however, the evil of the fourth kingdom has become concentrated in Antiochus. There is no real inconsistency. We further learn that the sovereignty which is to be given to the people of the saints of the Most High will be greater than that which it replaces. The rule which God bestows will be universal.

Finally we are faced with the problem of determining what is meant by 'the people of the saints of the Most High'. It is usually assumed that the phrase must mean the Jews, or, more precisely, the faithful core of the Jewish people. Jeffery (p. 467) declares, 'The saints of course are the righteous Jews.' Noth, however, has revived an idea of Procksch and argued for his view with great cogency ('Die Heiligen des Höchsten', published 1955 in the *Mowinckel-Festschrift*, pp. 146ff.; English translation in *The Laws in the Pentateuch*, 1966, pp. 215ff.). He admits that in Ps. 34.10 the saints are faithful Israelites, but refuses to consider Ps. 16.3 and Dan. 8.24 as good evidence, since in both places the text is very uncertain. Coming to the actual interpretation of the vision in chapter 7 he rejects vv. 21–22

as being suspicious on literary grounds. In v. 25a he points out the
parallelism between the Most High and the saints of the Most High
and finds a meaning for the verb which governs the last named
expression which would suit the interpretation of the saints of the
Most High as heavenly beings. In v. 25b he thinks we have an addition by someone who supposed that the reference was to the faithful
Jews. In v. 27 he interprets the expression 'the people of the saints
of the Most High' as referring to heavenly beings, and supports this
interpretation by two passages in the *Hodayot*, the book of psalms,
from Qumran, arguing that the word in these two texts which other
translators have rendered by 'with' (*'im*) should be read as 'people'
(*'am*), thus obtaining phrases very like the present one, in which
'people' would be used of heavenly beings. This, he believes, weakens
the argument of those who insist that the word 'people' in v. 27
makes it necessary to take the reference as being to the Jewish
people, or, rather, to the faithful among the Jewish people. It may
be argued in reply that in both places (the references given by
Noth are to editions by Sukenik and the passages will be found
translated into English by T. H. Gaster in *The Scriptures of the Dead
Sea Sect*, pp. 142 and 147, where it will be noticed that he reads
the disputed word as *'im*, 'with' or 'in', not as *'am*, 'people') a
preposition is really required. Moreover, he can only get the desired
interpretation of v. 25a by violent textual surgery. The solution of the
problem may be that the writer thinks of the faithful among the Jews
as controlled by the heavenly powers, so that they can almost be
identified with them. God acts through his people who may thus be
called 'saints' (literally 'holy ones'), the name used elsewhere in the
book of celestial beings. It is perhaps significant in this connection
that in *The War of the Sons of Light and the Sons of Darkness*, the faithful
Jews will have celestial warriors mingled with them in their ranks
(see, e.g. Gaster, *op. cit.*, p. 275). One should perhaps not make too
much of the fact that in the vision the people of the saints of the Most
High is represented by one like a *man*, as 'man' here seems to be a
symbol for the celestial. The emphasis is on heavenly power which
acts through the faithful Jews as contrasted with the power of chaos
which acts through the kingdoms of this world.

[28] The concluding verse of the chapter suggests different things
to different people. Jeffery declares (p. 468), 'It is difficult to resist
the impression that this last verse has the coming chapters in mind.'
Heaton, on the other hand, thinks that the words 'Here the account

ends' may indicate that the book originally ended at this point. At all events, Daniel, in the verse as we have it, represents himself as perturbed by what he has just heard and he continues to ponder the matter. One may incline to the view that these words are intended to prepare us for the visions which follow.

VIII

CHAPTER EIGHT

8 ¹In the third year of the reign of King Belshazzar a vision appeared to me, Daniel, after that which appeared to me at the first. ²And I saw in the vision; and when I saw, I was in Susa the capital, which is in the province of Elam; and I saw in the vision, and I was at the river Ulai. ³I raised my eyes and saw, and behold, a ram standing on the bank of the river. It had two horns; and both horns were high, but one was higher than the other, and the higher one came up last. ⁴I saw the ram charging westward and northward and southward; no beast could stand before him, and there was no one who could rescue from his power; he did as he pleased and magnified himself.

5 As I was considering, behold, a he-goat came from the west across the face of the whole earth, without touching the ground; and the goat had a conspicuous horn between his eyes. ⁶He came to the ram with the two horns, which I had seen standing on the bank of the river, and he ran at him in his mighty wrath. ⁷I saw him come close to the ram, and he was enraged against him and struck the ram and broke his two horns; and the ram had no power to stand before him, but he cast him down to the ground and trampled upon him; and there was no one who could rescue the ram from his power. ⁸Then the he-goat magnified himself exceedingly; but when he was strong, the great horn was broken, and instead of it there came up four conspicuous horns toward the four winds of heaven.

9 Out of one of them came forth a little horn, which grew exceedingly great toward the south, toward the east, and toward the glorious land.* ¹⁰It grew great, even to the host of heaven;† and some of the host of the stars it cast down to the ground, and trampled upon them. ¹¹It magnified itself, even up to the Prince of the host; and the continual burnt offering was taken away from him, and the place of his sanctuary was overthrown. ¹²And the host was given over to it together with the continual burnt offering through transgression; and truth was cast down to the ground, and the horn acted and prospered. ¹³Then I heard a holy one speaking; and another holy one said to the one that

* Better 'the fairest of lands'.
† Better 'it pitted its strength against the host of heaven'.

spoke, 'For how long is the vision concerning the continual burnt offering, the transgression that makes desolate, and the giving over of the
sanctuary and host* to be trampled under foot?' 14And he said to him,
'For two thousand and three hundred evenings and mornings; then the
sanctuary shall be restored to its rightful state.'

15 When I, Daniel, had seen the vision, I sought to understand it;
and behold, there stood before me one having the appearance of a
man. 16And I heard a man's voice between the banks of the Ulai, and it
called, 'Gabriel, make this man understand the vision.' 17So he came
near where I stood; and when he came, I was frightened and fell upon
my face. But he said to me, 'Understand, O son of man, that the vision
is for the time of the end.'

18 As he was speaking to me, I fell into a deep sleep with my face to
the ground; but he touched me and set me on my feet. 19He said,
'Behold, I will make known to you what shall be at the latter end of the
indignation; for it pertains to the appointed time of the end. 20As for
the ram which you saw with the two horns, these are the kings of Media
and Persia. 21And the he-goat is the king of Greece; and the great horn
between his eyes is the first king. 22As for the horn that was broken, in
place of which four others arose, four kingdoms shall arise from his
nation, but not with his power. 23And at the latter end of their rule,
when the transgressors have reached their full measure, a king of bold
countenance, one who understands riddles, shall arise. 24His power
shall be great, and he shall cause fearful destruction, and shall succeed
in what he does, and destroy mighty men and the people of the saints.
25By his cunning he shall make deceit prosper under his hand, and in
his own mind he shall magnify himself. Without warning he shall
destroy many; and he shall even rise up against the Prince of princes;
but, by no human hand, he shall be broken. 26The vision of the evenings and the mornings which has been told is true; but seal up the
vision, for it pertains to many days hence.'

27 And I, Daniel, was overcome and lay sick for some days; then I
arose and went about the king's business; but I was appalled by the
vision and did not understand it.

WITH THIS CHAPTER the language changes back to Hebrew
and Hebrew is used exclusively till the end of the book. The
literary style of chapters 8 to 12 is noticeably inferior to that
of the Aramaic chapters. There is too a diminution in the imaginative
quality of the writing. In these concluding chapters, with the
exception of a long section of chapter 9, the author is mainly concerned with the actual history, especially the contemporary history
which would be familiar to his readers, and there would have been
little difficulty in penetrating the almost transparent disguise of the

* 'Fairest of lands' by a possible emendation. See Commentary on 8.9.

animal symbolism of chapter 8, even if the interpretation had not been supplied. The interpretation referred to is amplified in great detail in chapter 11, most of which is a straight piece of historical writing cast in the form of prophecy and, therefore, not unnaturally somewhat cryptic in its phrasing.

All this has suggested to many commentators that chapters 8 to 12 are from the pen of a different writer from the author of the Aramaic chapters, one who presumably came across the Aramaic book and, realizing its possibilities, edited and supplemented it to make it relevant to the situation in which the Jews found themselves during the persecution of Antiochus Epiphanes. We have seen, however, that it is by no means certain that chapter 7 ever existed in a pre-Epiphanian form, however true it may be that the author has borrowed much of his imagery from earlier writings. Moreover the difference in quality of writing between the Hebrew and the Aramaic chapters may be due to the writer's being more at home in Aramaic than in Hebrew. Though less skilful in the use of Hebrew, he may have felt that his detailed pronouncements on contemporary history would gain in authority by being written in the sacred language. The somewhat artificial symbolism of chapter 8 as compared with that of chapter 7 may merely indicate that behind the former there is an absence of ecstatic experience such as we may perhaps be justified in detecting behind the latter. A certain failure in inspiration, however, does not necessarily imply a difference of authorship, especially as it seems possible to find behind the whole book a single critical situation which provides the occasion for its composition. To offset the differences between the two main parts of the book, apart from the fact that chapter 7 belongs arguably to both, there are certain curious historical assumptions (for example about Belshazzar and Darius the Mede, as H. H. Rowley has pointed out[1]) and an identical attitude to Antiochus Epiphanes which bind the book together.

This argument, of course, can be met by an elaborate theory of interpolations, but the burden of proof seems to rest on those who deny unity of authorship, which provides the most natural hypothesis to account for the phenomena. The very awkwardnesses and inconsistencies to which attention is drawn may merely point to a certain quality of mind characteristic of the single author. It seems a weighty argument in favour of the unity of the book that it can, on the assump-

---

[1] *The Unity of the Book of Daniel*, pp. 264ff.

tion of its unity, be brought into relation to a situation sufficiently urgent to explain why someone felt that the time had come for a tremendous affirmation of faith. The earlier so-called pre-Epiphanian Book of Daniel which some critics postulate would lack such a motive for its composition, whereas all the material in it can easily be shown to have its relevance to the second-century situation, so long as we do not unreasonably insist that every tiny detail must have its point of correspondence in the contemporary circumstances and series of events. The stories of chapters 1 to 6 are relevant without being· allegorical.

[1–2] The ambiguity of the original language of these verses has led to a difference of opinion among scholars. It is difficult, on the ground of syntax alone, to be quite sure whether Daniel's presence in Susa was meant to be visionary or actual. The probability, however, is that, as the RSV translation implies, we are intended to think of him as transported in vision to what was the capital and one of the main residences of the Persian kings, situated midway between Ecbatana and Persepolis, and, therefore, chosen as a place suitable to be the scene of what is to follow. Commentators are doubtless right in suggesting that the author, here as in other places, is imitating Ezekiel, who more than once claims to have been the subject of miraculous—presumably visionary—transportation (see especially Ezek. 8.3 and 40.1ff.), and who locates his inaugural vision by the River Chebar (Ezek. 1.1), just as here Daniel represents himself as having been in the neighbourhood of the Ulai. It seems most improbable that the author both dated this vision in the third year of Belshazzar and intended the reader to understand that Daniel was actually in Susa. A visionary presence in Susa would be quite appropriate.

The Hebrew expression used in connection with Susa does not seem to indicate a part of the city (*viz.* the citadel) but apparently refers to its status as a capital city, presumably of the whole Medo-Persian Empire, though its narrower location is given as Elam. The Ulai may be the classical Eulaeus or perhaps a canal in the neighbourhood of Susa. In v. 2 the RSV translation might be improved upon. There seem to be almost equally good philological arguments for the alternative translations 'by the stream (or channel) of the Ulai' and 'by the Ulai gate', according as we understand *'ubal* as the equivalent of *yūbal* or as a mistake for *abullu*, an Accadian word for a city gate. Jeffery (p. 469) makes out a plausible case for the second view, which certainly makes it easier to understand why Daniel's location is first given as being Susa.

[3–8] We now come to Daniel's vision of the battle between the Ram and the Goat, representing respectively the Medo-Persian Empire and the Greek power which overthrew it. Both the ram and the goat are mentioned in the Old Testament as symbols of power, but perhaps there is an astrological reason for the choice of symbols here (see Bentzen, p. 69, following Burkitt), whereby Persia was thought of as under the zodiacal sign of Aries and Greece as sharing with Syria, the principal territory of the Seleucid monarchy, the zodiacal sign of Capricorn.

The ram is seen in vision as standing right in the centre of Persian territory, its two horns representing the successive kings of Media and Persia. The aggressive behaviour of the ram obviously symbolizes the irresistible campaigns of the Medes and the Persians. No account is taken of the Persian conquests to the east as far as India, but these may have been unknown to the author of the Book of Daniel or, at least, may have been beyond his range of interest.

The vision continues and Daniel becomes aware of the swift approach of another creature, a powerful he-goat, careering along from the west. As we are explicitly told later, this clearly represents the kingdom of Greece and its remarkable single horn the first king, Alexander the Great, the Macedonian dynasty that preceded him being ignored. Commentators rightly refer to I Macc. 1.1–4 for the extent of Alexander's conquest and to Isa. 41.3, where it is said of Cyrus, as it is said here of Alexander, that he advanced with such speed that his feet seemed not to touch the ground. The victory of the goat over the ram, symbolizing the victory of Alexander over Darius Codomannus, is represented as swift and decisive. Persia's previous display of strength is now matched by that of Alexander, the sudden end of whose reign is represented dramatically by the snapping off of the horn. It is evident that Alexander's swift removal from the stage of history when he was at the height of his power and the ensuing disintegration of his empire must have made a deep impression on men's minds and must have been assessed very differently according to the viewpoint from which it was regarded.

We should perhaps pause at this point to reflect soberly on the fact that, viewed from the perspective of this deeply religious member of a subject race who has given us the Book of Daniel, the great civilizing power of Greece, which spread Hellenism far and wide over the vast territories comprising the ancient East, is described under the figure of a beast and is compared with its Persian predecessor in world conquest merely in terms of power. Edwyn Bevan, one of the best interpreters of this whole period of human history, says of the Hellenism which entered these ancient lands along with the Macedonian army of Alexander: 'It was something of a sort incalculably, almost terribly, potent. It was a body of ideas.' He goes on to say how it had originated among the Greeks living in their little city-states. 'In these a kind of mental activity, hitherto unique among men, had been going on for the last few centuries before Alexander, and the result was a body of ideas, a way of thinking and feeling about the world which could not be paralleled anywhere else' (*Jerusalem under the High Priests*, p. 18). Another great historian, writing of Alexander himself, declares, 'He was one of the supreme fertilizing forces of history. He lifted the civilized world out of one groove and set it in another; he started a new epoch; nothing could again be as it had been. . . . Particularism was replaced by the idea of the "inhabited world", the common possession of civilized men. . . . Greek culture, heretofore practically confined to Greeks, spread throughout the world; and for the use of its inhabitants, in place of the many dialects of Greece, there grew up the form of Greek known as the *koine*, the common speech' (W. W. Tarn, *Alexander the Great*, vol. I, 1948, pp. 145–6).

Not a glimmer of all this appears in the Book of Daniel and, even though it must be admitted that it was a debased form of hellenistic culture which reached the Jewish people, we have here a glaring illustration of the way in which the benefits of a conquering civilization may be much more obvious to the conqueror than they are to the conquered. This is one of the tragic facts of human history which has been overlooked again and again by those who feel that they have great benefits to confer upon mankind and feel justified in forcing them upon those who see other values threatened and so are not willing to receive. It is easy enough for us to see that Alexander by his conquests and by his union of many states under a single rule gave the world the idea of the οἰκουμένη and an incomparable language to bind it together and make possible a precision of thought and expression essential for the further advance of civilization. We can see clearly how this paved the way for the spread of Christianity and all that that brought with it. The Book of Daniel lets us see that there was another side to what was a very thrilling chapter of human history, a point of view which should not just be condemned as short-sighted lack of appreciation of the great benefits which Alexander brought to races which had stagnated. There were other values which the world, then as now, desperately needed and which were in danger of being lost. It may well be that it was only by an extreme attitude of opposition to the dominant civilization that in that particular crisis of history these values could be conserved. But perhaps the most important lesson that can be learned from this chapter of the Book of Daniel is that those who represent a dominant and, it may be, a noble civilization should try to see themselves as others see them and to realize that there are things which, in the sight of God, may be of more value than culture.

The breaking of the great horn in the vision was followed by the springing up of four horns which undoubtedly symbolize the four main successor kingdoms of the Diadochi, *viz.* Macedonia and Greece, Asia Minor, Syria with Babylonia and the farther East, and, finally, Egypt. While there were other minor states, none of them was on a level with the four large states just mentioned and it is not surprising that this general pattern of affairs impressed itself on the popular memory. It seems less likely that the author is influenced here by some theory of numbers. The four-empire theory had to do with *successive* empires.

[9–12] The writer hurries on to what is of supreme interest to himself and his readers, *viz.* to the little horn which sprang from one of the four horns and clearly represents Antiochus Epiphanes of the Seleucid line of kings. There is general agreement about this identification even among those who refuse to see any reference to Antiochus Epiphanes in chapter 7. Antiochus will figure again very prominently in chapter 11, which will also reflect the fact that for the writer the two successor states which affected most closely the fortunes of the Jewish people were those of Syria under the Seleucid kings, of whom Antiochus IV Epiphanes was one, and of Egypt under the Ptolemies. We shall read in much greater detail in chapter 11 of the activities of Antiochus Epiphanes, as of certain of his predecessors, but in the present chapter we merely learn of his campaigns against Egypt to the south and against Parthia to the east and, if the text is correct, against Jerusalem (cf. Dan. 11.16, 41, 45; Ezek. 20.6, 15; Jer. 3.*19*; Mal. 3.12). This cryptic reference to Judaea—the expression translated 'the fairest of lands' (see note) means literally 'beauty'—seems entirely in place here, as we are just about to be told of Antiochus's interference in religious matters through which he came into conflict with those Jews who were not prepared to compromise their religious faith.

The two or three verses which follow are extremely obscure in the original and, although it is in general quite certain what the author is talking about, it is quite impossible to be sure of all the details. It is possible that the obscurity is in part deliberate—in dangerous times men have to resort to indirections of speech—but that does not account for everything and it is probable that there is a good deal of textual corruption.

In v. 10, where we are told that the little horn pitted its strength against the host of heaven and even brought down some of the stars, it is reasonably clear that the reference is to the arrogance which led Antiochus Epiphanes to interfere with the religious customs of his subjects. This is hinted at in I Macc. 1.41–42, while in Dan. 11.36 we are told of him that 'he shall exalt and magnify himself above every god'. The imagery of the stars might have been suggested by Isa. 14.13ff. where it is prophesied that the arrogance of the king of Babylon who had thought to ascend to heaven and enthrone himself above the stars of God is to be punished by his being brought down to the underworld. The contrast between this vaulting ambition and the ghastly disease which terminated Antiochus's life in misery and squalor is emphasized in II Macc. 9.10 which may be a reference to this passage.

The Prince of the host who is next challenged by the horn is God himself (v. 11) who is supreme over the host of heaven, just as these celestial beings have authority over the nations. (See Deut. 32.8. Deut. 4.19 shows how much of a temptation astral worship was. Cf. Job 31.27.) The challenge to God was made by depriving him of his due, the daily offering of the *tāmīd*, the regular sacrifice of a lamb morning and evening according to the prescription of the Torah (Ex. 29.38ff.; Num. 28.3ff.). To the pious Jew any interference with the prescribed service of God from outside or any neglect on the part of the worshippers themselves was a dreadful disaster. That the sanctuary suffered from both violence and neglect is shown by what we are told in I Macc. 4.38–39. When Judas and his followers recovered control of the temple precincts they found to their dismay 'the sanctuary desolate, the altar profaned, the gates burned up and shrubs growing in the courts as in a forest, or in one of the mountains, and the priests' chambers pulled down'. Worst of all was what had happened to the altar of burnt offering. The text in v. 12 is quite uncertain (see commentaries) but from what we are told in v. 13 and in 9.27 it may be

conjectured that something was done to the altar which made it unclean. It has been plausibly suggested (E. Bickermann, *Der Gott der
Makkabäer*, pp. 105ff.) that, for the purpose of sacrifice to Zeus
Olympius with whom the God of Israel was associated by Antiochus,
a *baetyl* consisting of stones (λίθοι ἔμψυχοι, see Philo Byblius; cf.
S. A. Cook, *The Religion of Ancient Palestine in the Light of Archaeology*,
1930, pp. 26–27) was built upon the altar of burnt offering and that
this is what was called the abomination of desolation. As we see from
I Macc. 4.42ff. the whole altar was regarded as defiled and had to be
pulled down and replaced by a new altar built in accordance with the
Law. The truth which is cast down is the revealed will of God as dis-
closed in his Law. The account in I Macc. 1.45ff. shows the extent to
which Antiochus interfered with the prescribed religious customs. We
read of the forbidding of sacrifices and the observance of the sabbath
and the festivals, of the proscription of the rite of circumcision, of the
attempt to make men break the food laws and, worst of all, of the
destruction of any copies of the Torah that were found and the putting
to death of any who were found in possession of the Scriptures or could
be convicted of obedience to the Law. In fact, as v. 12 says, the active
measures taken by Antiochus met with a large measure of success
mainly because there was a large section of the Jews (see I Macc.
1.11ff.) who had for some time past committed themselves to a policy
of hellenization and were in entire agreement with what Antiochus
was doing.

[13–14] In these verses a somewhat artificial device is used to convey to his readers the writer's conviction as to the length of time that
the desolation of the sanctuary and the cessation of its services could
continue. Daniel is represented as overhearing the conversation of two
holy ones or angels, one of them asking the question 'How long?'
which was forcing itself to the lips of the pious in Jerusalem at this
time and the other indicating the precise duration of the time of
trouble. Commentators refer especially to the parallel passage in
Zech. 1.12ff. in which it is told how the the angel standing among the
myrtle trees asks God how long he is going to withhold his mercy from
Jerusalem and the cities of Judah and receives a gracious reply. This
is the prophet's way of asserting that his conviction that God is about
to show mercy to Jerusalem is God-given. The same is true here. By
what process, however, the author arrives at his belief as to the exact
number of days that the disastrous situation will last we simply do not
know. The number as given in v. 14 almost certainly means 1,150

days, during which period of time 2,300 morning or evening offerings of the *tāmīd* would have taken place. It is improbable that we should interpret the phrase as meaning 2,300 morning-evenings, i.e. days, as has been suggested. It is clear from I Macc. 1.54, 59 and 4.52, 59 that the actual period of the profanation of the sanctuary was three years, so that the prophecy made here was not very far out. It is true that the temple had been plundered in the late summer of 169 B C but the date 25 Chislev, 167 was indelibly imprinted on men's minds and 7.25 with its prophecy of a time, times and a half almost certainly indicates three and a half years which is roughly equivalent to what we have here. This matter will come up again for discussion at the end of chapter 9 and once again at the very end of the book and need not detain us longer here.

It is sometimes argued that vv. 13 and 14 are interpolated, but it should be noticed that they stand or fall with v. 26 which refers back to them. If the question of the actual duration of the time of trouble was of burning importance to the writer and his readers, as we may well believe it was, it could obviously not be dealt with in a vision alone; there had to be an audition and that is precisely what these verses supply. The awkwardness with which the audition is introduced is merely one more example of a certain literary ineptitude which is a feature of the writer's style.

[15–27] The remainder of the chapter is taken up with an interpretation of the vision of the ram and the goat which in the foregoing discussion has already been largely anticipated and which is put into the mouth of the angel Gabriel. When angels appear they are invariably in human form and that is what is indicated here. This is the first place in Scripture where an angel is mentioned by name. We know from the Book of Enoch 9 and 20 that Gabriel was one of the four or seven archangels and he appears in Luke 1 as the angel of the Annunciation. Gabriel is instructed by a mysterious voice to explain the vision to Daniel, who reacts with an appropriate exhibition of terror (cf. 10.7ff. and frequently elsewhere). We cannot doubt that the numinous experience was known to the writer, even though he is probably influenced in his descriptions by what he read in the Book of Ezekiel.

Gabriel's interpretation of the vision is in response to the earnest desire of Daniel to understand it. Once again there is imitation of Ezekiel in the title by which Gabriel addresses Daniel. Daniel as the recipient of revelation is thought of in his creatureliness as a man.

Gabriel's announcement that the vision is for the time of the End (cf. Hab. 2.3 where the certainty of the coming of the End is emphasized) serves a double purpose, both to remind the reader that from Daniel's point of view the End was far ahead and that from the reader's point of view it is now imminent.

Daniel is represented as falling into a trance state from which he has to be roused by the angel. This becomes part of the machinery of apocalypse. As the writer of Daniel imitates Ezekiel (2.2), so the apocalyptist in the Book of Enoch (60.3–4), elaborates on Daniel. The curious phrase translated by RSV as 'set me on my feet', probably means 'made me stand up where I was'. Daniel is to keep his distance.

Gabriel explains that he is about to tell Daniel what is about to happen at the end of the indignation or wrath (v. 19), a curious expression which occurs again in 11.36 and obviously, to judge from both contexts, refers to the period during which God is angry with his people. As in the time of Isaiah God used Assyria as the rod of his anger to chastise Israel and there was then to be a limit to his indignation (10.5, 25) so now God's indignation was using for his own holy purposes the tyranny of Antiochus. But God recognized the tendency of the instrument to overstep the permissible limits (see Isa. 10.7, 12ff.; Zech. 1.15) and this is what had happened in the present instance. Antiochus had far exceeded all permissible limits and had reached a climax of wickedness which seemed to indicate that the time of God's intervention was very near (cf. v. 23). It is quite true that, as Heaton says (p. 198), 'there arose after the fall of Jerusalem in 586 BC a conviction that Israel was more sinned against than sinning'. Yet this point must not be exaggerated. Daniel's prayer in chapter 9 reveals, as we shall see, a very deep sense of guilt and there is not a trace of self-righteousness. The author, however, while recognizing that his people is under the wrath of God, is equally, if not more, certain that the time of Antiochus's doom is drawing near. The term has been fixed by God. Dreadful as is the situation in which the Jews find themselves, it has not got outside the divine control.

Gabriel's interpretation of the vision is very succinct and need not long detain us in view of what has been said above. It is quite evident that the writer has no great interest in the Persian period or even in the astonishing career of Alexander the Great. Mighty as he was, he very quickly disappeared from the scene. He does not linger over the Diadochi, whose power was inferior to Alexander's, or, in particular, over the earlier Seleucid monarchs, except to make it clear that they were all sinners whose sin cried out for judgment. He hurries on until he comes to Antiochus Epiphanes whose strangely mixed character he sketches for his readers in a few vivid words, now grim and threatening, now showing a smooth diplomacy behind which lurked cunning and deceit. In v. 23 'one who understands riddles' should probably be 'a master of intrigue'. The word we would translate 'intrigue' is the same as is used for the riddles which Samson propounded to the Philistines (Judg. 14.12, etc.) and for the questions with which the Queen of Sheba tested Solomon (I Kings 10.1). Bevan (p. 139) thinks that the reference here is to Antiochus's 'double-dealing' and compares Dan. 11.21. The power and success of Antiochus are quickly indicated, his conquests and in particular his actions directed against 'the people of the saints' (i.e. the Jews). There is an evident link here with 7.25. The Hebrew of v. 25 is difficult but may be made to yield the meaning that the king's mind is always busy hatching plots which he carries through to a great measure of success. He is full of grandiose plans—that is what this Jew felt about Antiochus's plans for unifying his kingdom in which he may well have been imitating the policy of Alexander though without his vision and genius —and in putting them into execution he catches men when off their guard. Commentators generally illustrate this by referring to the treacherous attack upon Jerusalem in the summer of 168 BC by Apollonius, who came as the royal collector of tribute and lulled the suspicions of the inhabitants to sleep before striking his blow (I Macc. 1.29ff.). The culmination of Antiochus's wickedness was his attack upon God himself and we know that that consisted in the drastic measures taken against the religion of the Jews. The point is not elaborated here, but the promise is given that his power will be broken without any human agency. The disease which terminated his career (see II Macc. 9) was regarded as a manifest judgment of God (cf. 11.45).

As has been already said the reference to the vision of the evenings and mornings (cf. v. 14) is not to be regarded as an interpolation but as an indication that the writer knew that the readers of his book were deeply concerned to know how long it would be before the end came and that he shared their concern. The assurance given to Daniel that the vision is true is intended for the readers of the book, whose faith in a desperate time the writer wishes to confirm. The fiction that the vision was prophetic and experienced by Daniel centuries before is kept up by the injunction given to him to keep it secret, since, though

D.–I

given to him, its reference is to a distant time and it has no relevance for Daniel's contemporaries. It is quite probable that the original readers were not deceived but understood that this was the writer's way of saying that the events of history are under the control of God. At all events we may be sure that ultimately we have to do here with a great affirmation of faith.

The concluding verse (v. 27) provides a link with what is to follow. We may compare 7.28 which links the two divisions of the book together. As Jeffery rightly points out (p. 483) the fact that Daniel gets up after a few days' indisposition and gets on with his work in the king's service proves that he had been in Babylon all the time and that his presence in Susa was purely visionary. Daniel's inability to understand the interpretation is a little odd. It is little more than a device on the part of the author to prepare the way for the highly detailed interpretation of chapter 11.

IX

CHAPTER NINE

9 ¹In the first year of Darius the son of Ahasuerus, by birth a Mede, who became king over the realm of the Chaldeans—²in the first year of his reign, I, Daniel, perceived in the books the number of years which, according to the word of the LORD to Jeremiah the prophet, must pass before the end of the desolations of Jerusalem, namely, seventy years.

3 Then I turned my face to the Lord God, seeking him by prayer and supplications with fasting and sackcloth and ashes. ⁴I prayed to the LORD my God and made confession, saying, 'O Lord, the great and terrible God, who keepest covenant and steadfast love with those who love him and keep his commandments, ⁵we have sinned and done wrong and acted wickedly and rebelled, turning aside from thy commandments and ordinances; ⁶we have not listened to thy servants the prophets, who spoke in thy name to our kings, our princes, and our fathers, and to all the people of the land. ⁷To thee, O Lord, belongs righteousness, but to us confusion of face, as at this day, to the men of Judah, to the inhabitants of Jerusalem, and to all Israel, those that are near and those that are far away, in all the lands to which thou hast driven them, because of the treachery which they have committed against thee. ⁸To us, O Lord, belongs confusion of face, to our kings, to our princes, and to our fathers, because we have sinned against thee. ⁹To the Lord our God belong mercy and forgiveness; because we have rebelled against him, ¹⁰and have not obeyed the voice of the LORD our God by following his laws, which he set before us by his servants the prophets. ¹¹All Israel has transgressed thy law and turned aside, refusing to obey thy voice. And the curse and oath which are written in the law of Moses the servant of God have been poured out upon us, because we have sinned against him. ¹²He has confirmed his words, which he spoke against us and against our rulers who ruled us, by bringing upon us a great calamity; for under the whole heaven there has not been done the like of what has been done against Jerusalem. ¹³As it is written in the law of Moses, all this calamity has come upon us, yet we have not entreated the favour of the LORD our God, turning from our iniquities and giving heed to thy truth. ¹⁴Therefore the LORD has kept ready the

calamity and has brought it upon us; for the LORD our God is righteous in all the works which he has done, and we have not obeyed his voice. ¹⁵And now, O Lord our God, who didst bring thy people out of the land of Egypt with a mighty hand, and has made thee a name, as at this day, we have sinned, we have done wickedly. ¹⁶O Lord, according to all thy righteous acts, let thy anger and thy wrath turn away from thy city Jerusalem, thy holy hill; because for our sins, and for the iniquities of our fathers, Jerusalem and thy people have become a by-word among all who are round about us. ¹⁷Now therefore, O our God, hearken to the prayer of thy servant and to his supplications, and for thy own sake, O Lord, cause thy face to shine upon thy sanctuary, which is desolate. ¹⁸O my God, incline thy ear and hear; open thy eyes and behold our desolations, and the city which is called by thy name; for we do not present our supplications before thee on the ground of our righteousness, but on the ground of thy great mercy. ¹⁹O LORD, hear; O LORD, forgive; O LORD, give heed and act; delay not, for thy own sake, O my God, because thy city and thy people are called by thy name.'

20 While I was speaking and praying, confessing my sin and the sin of my people Israel, and presenting my supplication before the LORD my God for the holy hill of my God; ²¹while I was speaking in prayer, the man Gabriel, whom I had seen in the vision at the first, came to me in swift flight at the time of the evening sacrifice. ²²He came* and he said to me, 'O Daniel, I have now come out to give you wisdom and understanding. ²³At the beginning of your supplications a word went forth, and I have come to tell it to you, for you are greatly beloved; therefore consider the word and understand the vision.

24 'Seventy weeks of years are decreed concerning your people and your holy city, to finish the transgression,† to put an end to sin,‡ and to atone for inquity,§ to bring in everlasting righteousness, to seal both vision and prophet, and to anoint a most holy place. ²⁵Know therefore and understand that from the going forth of the word to restore and build Jerusalem to the coming of an anointed one, a prince, there shall be seven weeks. Then for sixty-two weeks it shall be built again with squares and moat,** but in a troubled time. ²⁶And after the sixty-two weeks, an anointed one shall be cut off, and shall have nothing;†† and the people of the prince who is to come shall destroy the city and the sanctuary. Its end shall come with a flood, and to the end there shall be war; desolations are decreed. ²⁷And he shall make a strong covenant with many§§ for one week; and for half of the week he shall cause sacrifice and offering to cease; and upon the wing of abominations shall

* So Greek and Syriac. Better 'He said clearly to me'.
† 'To curb rebellion.'
‡ 'To seal sin', by a slight emendation.
§ 'To wipe out iniquity.'
** 'Conduits.'
†† 'Without trial' with Theodotion.
§§ Perhaps 'the mighty'.

come one who makes desolate,* until the decreed end is poured out on the desolator.'

UP TO THIS POINT in the book the author has among other things expressed his conviction about the immediate future, when God would intervene decisively in history, and has sketched a considerable stretch of past history leading up to this expected event in the form of a dream sent to Nebuchadnezzar king of Babylon and interpreted for him by Daniel, and further of two visions seen by Daniel himself and interpreted for him by angelic beings. Moreover, in chapter 8, Daniel is represented as having received, through the agency of the angel Gabriel, a revelation as to the exact duration of the period during which there would be intermission of the daily offering in the temple at Jerusalem and which would be brought to an end by the final crisis. As has already been said, we do not know the ground of the author's confidence, but, while we may have our reservations when he comes to give exact dates, we may well believe that it had its origin in deep religious experience and from confrontation with the word of the living God.

In the present chapter a further step is taken. The author evidently felt the need of finding scriptural authority for his reading of contemporary history and he believed that he had found it in the Book of the prophet Jeremiah in the oracle Jer. 25.11ff. and in Jeremiah's letter to the exiles (29.10), which passages both mention a period of seventy years for Babylon's dominion. As we shall see, that prediction had caused a certain amount of perplexity and our author now comes forward with a novel interpretation which would give it contemporary relevance. The fiction by which he himself is kept in the background and his own convictions are given in the guise of revelations made long before is maintained, while a long prayer of confession and supplication attributed to Daniel probably gives us a welcome clue to the piety of the author's own day. Indeed, it is this prayer, which some critics would treat as an interpolation, which gives its chief value to the chapter. In view of the tragic story of misplaced ingenuity to which the reinterpretation of Jeremiah's seventy years has given rise, leading, right up to our own day, to ever renewed attempts to pierce the mystery of the future, it should be a relief to the thoughtful reader to find that the author's original intention was, not to provide any such calculations of distant events, but merely to reinforce his own conviction that

* Perhaps 'and on a corner of the altar shall come an abomination of desolation'.

in the immediate future God's transcendent power would manifest itself on his people's behalf. The relevance of the supposed revelation made to Daniel was confined to the expected crisis in the time of Antiochus Epiphanes.

In finding, then, the relevance of this passage of Scripture to ourselves, we must allow ourselves to be guided by the witness of this man to the availability of God in every crisis in history, without following him in his mistake of supposing that one can calculate in advance exactly what God will do. All the more important is it to realize how well he understood the need for men to humble themselves beneath the judgments of God and acknowledge their justice. If this was indeed how men prayed in those days, then we are in a position to understand how the faithful among the Jews came through the storms and stresses of that terrible time.

The reinterpretation of the prophecy of Jeremiah about the seventy years is no more than an illustration of the tendency characteristic of that age to seek to make earlier prophecy contemporary in its relevance. We can study how this was done in the Dead Sea Scroll containing the *pešer* on the first two chapters of the Book of Habakkuk, and in II (4) Esdras (12.10ff.) where the fourth kingdom of the Book of Daniel is reinterpreted as referring to Rome, and we can recognize the truth that men were seeking to express in this way. We must, however, not fail to make the intellectual effort necessary to distinguish between the essential truth and the temporary nature of the way in which it was expressed. Indeed, it is most important that we should recognize and be prepared frankly to admit, that there is definite error here; the history of the interpretation of the Book of Daniel should have taught everyone long before now that an error will not turn into truth by mere repetition. Unfortunately there are some minds which seem incapable of recognizing a *reductio ad absurdum*. But what was excusable on the part of the author of the Book of Daniel, who had divine revelation to communicate to his people, however much he mixed it up with wrong-headed arithmetical calculations, is surely inexcusable today, when two thousand years have passed during which the folly of reasoning from wrong premises has been demonstrated again and again. It would not matter so much if the persistence of error did not tend to blind men to what God is really seeking to say to them through the witness of the Scriptures.

[1–2] The discovery as to the meaning of the prediction of Jeremiah which the author believes he has made is attributed by him to Daniel, who is enlightened by an angel, and the discovery is dated in the first year of Darius the Mede. It should be noted that the king is described as the son of Ahasuerus (Xerxes), while the Darius of history, Darius I Hystaspis, was actually the father of the Xerxes who was defeated at Salamis. It is possible that this particular date is given because it refers to the time immediately after the fall of Babylon, when thoughtful Jews might be supposed to be wondering whether the exile might not be about to come to an end.

Whether or not Jeremiah actually prophesied that the exile would last for seventy years we cannot be absolutely sure. But, even if he did, the number seventy should probably be regarded as a round number and so as one not intended to be taken literally. The exile was to last long enough to make the advice which Jeremiah gave in his letter to the exiles (chapter 29) very wise and practical. At the time of the fall of Babylon less than fifty years had passed since Nebuchadrezzar[1] captured Jerusalem, though it was almost sixty years since Jeremiah wrote his letter to the exiles, and it is possible that the prophecy, which rightly or wrongly it was believed Jeremiah had made, was giving rise to the hope of its literal fulfilment. The Book of Zechariah (1.12) shows that in the year 519 BC men were speaking about God's indignation against Jerusalem and the cities of Judah as having lasted for seventy years. II Chron. 36.21 implies that the seventy years were calculated, not from the date of Jehoiakin's surrender, but from the fall of Jerusalem in 587 BC, but shows further that the prophecy was exercising men's minds as early as the first year of Cyrus. Incidentally, it is possible that, during the period of its desolation during the Exile, the statement that the land kept Sabbath to fulfil seventy years (cf. Lev. 26.34ff.) may have suggested to the author of the Book of Daniel his own peculiar interpretation of the seventy years. Actually, however, the sole reference he gives is the one to Jeremiah.

[3–19] At this point in the chapter there is the insertion of a long prayer of confession and supplication which Daniel offers on behalf of his people. It has been argued that v. 21 follows naturally upon v. 2 and that vv. 3 and 20 have the appearance of having been constructed to fit the prayer into a context not originally intended for it. Furthermore, it has been said that the language of v. 3 is designed to suggest that the following prayer is one for illumination, which manifestly it is not. In reply it may be urged that the phraseology of v. 3 does not

[1] It will be observed that the incorrect spelling Nebuchadnezzar has been preserved in the fictional narratives.

necessarily imply that Daniel was asking for revelation. The expression *l^ebaqqeš t^epillā* may mean, not 'to seek in prayer', but 'to pray earnestly' (suggestion of G. R. Driver who connects *baqqeš* here with the Accadian *baqašu*, 'big'). While it is quite true, as commentators point out, that fasting is sometimes mentioned as preliminary to receiving revelation (see Ex. 34.28; Deut. 9.9 and among later writings II (4) Esd. 5.13, 20; 6.35; 9.26, 27; 12.51), it is clear from Neh. 9.1ff. that the customs mentioned here were also associated with confession of sins. Chapter 10.12 refers back to 10.1–3 rather than to 9.3. It is quite true that the revelation through the agency of Gabriel follows on immediately after the prayer. On the other hand, the author is not so inept that he could not have composed a prayer for illumination if he had felt that one was needed at this point. In fact the suggestion that the ineptness of the prayer for its presumed purpose justifies the conclusion that it is an interpolation has obscured the very good reason why the author put it here. He is not thinking primarily of the need for Daniel to be illuminated as to the meaning of a passage of scripture; rather, in the crisis of history during which he is actually writing, he desires to give in the words of this prayer expression to the piety of those for whom he himself is speaking. Without this prayer there would be something essential missing from the Book of Daniel. The book was written to announce that the God of Israel was about to perform one of his mighty acts on behalf of his people Israel, the final mighty act, as he himself mistakenly believed. The prayer also contains a reference to the acts of God in the past (the Exodus, v.15; the Covenant, v. 4; the sending of prophets, vv. 6 and 10). But it also gives very clear expression to the faith by which Israel appropriated the mercy of God. In the stories too about Daniel and his companions we are reminded of the qualities of steadfastness and loyalty which God honours when manifested by the individual, and of which there were many shining examples during the persecution of Antiochus Epiphanes. But, if it be true, as Montgomery suggests, that 'the saint prays as the Church prays, and this prayer is modelled after customary liturgical forms of the Synagogue', then we have here a precious glimpse into the way in which the spirit of loyalty to the ancestral faith was nourished among the people. It is true that many Jews apostatized (I Macc. 1.11ff.)— some, no doubt, not altogether unworthily, but attracted by the prospect of entering into a wider culture—but there were also many who did not (I Macc. 1.62ff.), and it is the voice of these *Ḥasidim*, as they were called, that we are allowed to hear in this prayer. Indeed, the author of the Book of Daniel is probably himself to be regarded as a *Ḥasid.*

Montgomery (p. 361), while recognizing that Daniel's prayer in this chapter is of the Deuteronomic type and has analogies in Solomon's prayer at the dedication of the temple (I Kings 8) and certain prayers found in the Book of Jeremiah (26, 32, 44) and in the Book of Ezra (9) and the Book of Nehemiah (1, 9), credits it with possessing positive literary qualities of its own and, indeed, describes it as 'a liturgical gem in form and expression'. He further points out (p. 362) that the long prayer of Baruch (Baruch 1.15–3.8) seems to have been modelled on Daniel's prayer, and we may remember that the Book of Baruch almost certainly throws light on the piety of the Jews at the time of the struggle with Rome which ended with the destruction of Jerusalem.

The prayer begins with a frank confession of sin, sin that was made all the more heinous by the fact that it was against a God (the personal name Yahweh is used only in this chapter of the Book of Daniel here in the prayer and in v. 2 in the phrase 'the word of the LORD [Yahweh] to the prophet Jeremiah') who, in the classic language of Deuteronomy (7.9, 12), echoed in Solomon's prayer (I Kings 8.23), had loyally kept the covenant with his people. In the original we have here the two linked words *bᵉrit* (covenant) and *ḥesed* (steadfast love), the latter designating the quality of loyalty which binds the members of the covenant people together in a close unity with each other and their God. Here the word refers to the loyalty of Yahweh towards the covenant which he had initiated and it is contrasted with the disloyalty of the people. This disloyalty was inexcusable, because the people and their rulers all down the generations had been warned by prophets sent by Yahweh.

The word translated 'fathers' in v. 6 might be translated 'fore-fathers'. If 'fathers' is correct it would then refer to the heads of the fathers' houses in Israel. Jeffery (p. 487) would then be right in speaking of 'the descending order of classes in the social scale', i.e. 'royal house, princely houses, family houses, commoners.'

The gist of the confession is summed up most expressively and succinctly in the phrase (v. 7), 'Thine is the right, ours is the shame', and it is acknowledged that this shame is shared by all the Jews in the homeland and in the lands of their exile without distinction of class. The sin has been committed against a God whose compassionate nature is known. And then, in illustration of the difficulty of dealing with the paradox of God's judgment and mercy, it is acknowledged that Israel, by its evasion of God's Law, had brought down upon itself the curse with which it had been threatened in the adjuration or solemn charge laid upon it long ago. The expression 'the curse and oath' seems to be a zeugma for 'the oath of the curse' (Num. 5.21). There is a clear reference to the two passages in the Pentateuch, Lev. 26.14–39 and Deut. 28.15–68, while the qualification of the curse and the oath to the effect that they are written in the Law of Moses echoes the passage Deut. 29.18ff., one of the grimmest passages in Scripture, in which the land of promise is pictured as a burnt-out crater in consequence of God's judgment upon a people which had been unfaithful to the covenant. In this prayer, however, we have the refusal to accept as final this unparalleled calamity which has fallen upon Jerusalem. Just as in the Book of Lamentations hope breaks forth from the depths of the disaster, as soon as the justice of God's judgment is fully admitted, so here the belated act of confession leads to renewal of hope. The calamity was threatened, no heed was paid to the threat, the blow fell and in that very faithfulness of God to his threat Israel took comfort, even though up till then it had done nothing to placate God (the Hebrew expression used here conveys the idea of smoothing the frown from the face of someone) and had failed to consider God's consistent faithfulness to what he promises. God, however, had been vigilant throughout and had seen to it that the deserved calamity had come. (The word for to 'keep ready' 'be vigilant' is the word Jeremiah uses when he tells how God was watchful over his word to perform it, see 1.12 and cf. 31.28; 44.27.) And then it is acknowledged that God has been in the right in all this (cf. especially Lam. 1.18 and Neh. 9.33, where precisely the same salutary admission is made).

In v. 15 the prayer turns definitely from confession to supplication and it does so by invoking God as the God who delivered his people from servitude in Egypt by an act of grace which had never been forgotten. That God was a God of salvation was part of his revealed character and the memory of what he had done was indelible. He had shown his righteousness both in his acts of grace and in his acts of judgment and so appeal is now made that he should show himself righteous by permitting his anger to turn away from Jerusalem. Through the calamity which had overwhelmed it, Jerusalem had become a byword among the surrounding nations. Yet it was God's holy hill and so God is asked for his own sake—in the familiar words of the Aaronic blessing (Num. 6.25)—to make his face shine upon the desolate sanctuary (the word used for desolate is possibly an allusion

to 'the abomination of desolation'), remembering that the city in
which it was situated had been dedicated to himself, and therefore was
his own peculiar property.

The final plea is based, not on anything of merit in the lives of those
who pray, but solely upon God's great mercy, and the prayer ends
with words which have been fitly described as the Old Testament
kyrie eleison (so Montgomery, Jeffery, Heaton, *ad loc.*). The appeal is
made to God to act in accordance with his revealed character. The
thought emerges in Jeremiah in the great passage (14.7–9) which
begins: 'Though our iniquities testify against us, act, O Lord, for thy
name's sake', and is carried on by both Ezekiel and the Second Isaiah
(e.g. Ezek. 20.44 and Isa. 48.9–11). The thought is not one of Yahweh's
self-centred absorption in his own glory, since it is his glory to be at the
disposal of his people.

[20–23] What follows the prayer has a touch of the grotesque about
it. As we have seen, the prayer is in its present position of its own right.
The writer, however, also uses it to form a measurement of time. The
angel Gabriel, who had already appeared to Daniel to interpret the
vision of chapter 8, approaches Daniel in swift flight. It is true, the
Hebrew original here might with an effort be interpreted as meaning
'greatly wearied', but it seems better to accept the translation of the
versions (LXX, Theod. and Vulg.) 'flying' or 'flying swiftly'. Although
it is true that the angels in Jacob's dream (Gen. 28.12) require a stair-
case (*sullām*) for their traffic between heaven and earth, the concept
of winged angels appears shortly after this passage in Daniel in Enoch
61, while in I Chron. 21.16 an angel is seen standing between heaven
and earth and presumably had to fly to get there! Gabriel explains to
Daniel that, at the moment that the latter began his prayer of confession and supplication, a revelation was given for Daniel which
Gabriel had been commissioned to bring to him as one specially
favoured by God, and that all the time Daniel had been praying
Gabriel had spent on the way. There does not appear to be any more
point in this than appears on the surface. It strikes the modern reader
as a little bit of 'theatre'. The reference to the hour of the evening
sacrifice is probably intended to suggest that the revelation came to
Daniel at one of the stated times of prayer.

[24–27] In the concluding verses of the chapter the revelation which
Gabriel had been sent to communicate is given. The solution of
Daniel's perplexity about Jeremiah's prophecy of the seventy years is
given by the explanation that the seventy years are to be understood

as seventy 'weeks of years', i.e. as a period of 490 years. There is no exact parallel in the Old Testament to this use of the word year as meaning a week of years, i.e. as seven years, though, as Montgomery says (p. 373), the usage may have been suggested by the instructions about seven-year periods in Lev. 25 and 26. It appears in later writings, e.g. Mishna Sanh. 5.1, Baba Metzia 9.10. The seventy 'weeks of years' are clearly intended to span a certain stretch of time, but, as a period of 490 years cannot be made to fit exactly the known facts of history, it may be concluded that it is a round number. This, however, need not trouble us unduly, as the purpose of the revelation is to suggest powerfully to the readers of the book that the predetermined time for God to act is imminent and that history has been leading up to this crisis.

What God has it in mind to do is expressed in six brief clauses which roughly balance each other three and three. Unfortunately the text is in several places uncertain, and so we cannot in every case be sure that we have caught the exact intention of the writer. The curbing or ending of rebellion corresponds to the bringing in of everlasting right, i.e. of the triumph of the righteousness of God which includes the idea of salvation (cf. Isa. 45.17), and doubtless implies the responsive righteousness of the people; the putting an end to (or sealing of) sin, perhaps the reaching by sin of its full measure (cf. 8.23), corresponds less obviously to the sealing of vision and prophecy (lit. prophet), which means either confirmation or ratification of vision and prophecy or the bringing of them to an end as no longer necessary; the wiping out of iniquity (the technical term employed, *viz. kapper*, means 'atone for' when used of the priest, and 'absolve' or 'forgive', when used, as here, of God) corresponds to the anointing, i.e. the consecration, of a most holy place. The expression 'most holy' of the original text, which is here interpreted as 'a most holy place' probably refers either to the altar of burnt offering, which is definitely known to have been desecrated by Antiochus Epiphanes, or to the temple as a whole. This complex term is used in the Old Testament in a wide variety of ways, of material objects particularly sacred to God and of sacred places including the *debir* or inmost shrine of the temple. In spite of I Chron. 23.13, where the term may conceivably refer to Aaron, there is no justification for the Early Church's view that there is here a reference to the Messiah, however natural at the time such an interpretation must have seemed. It is important to notice that the writer intends to imply that an end will be brought, not only to the wickedness of

Antiochus, but also to the rebellion of Israel. Daniel's prayer of confession must be taken in all seriousness.

We now come to the detail of the seventy week-years. The author must have been well aware of the ordinary view that the seventy years of the original prophecy referred to the span of time from the fall of Jerusalem in 587 B C to the completion of the rebuilding of the temple in 516 B C. He must also have been aware that the return from exile was followed by a widespread feeling of disillusionment. The glowing expectations aroused by a Second Isaiah had faded into the light of common day and a very ordinary common day it proved to be. The expected climax had not come. But now, hundreds of years later, the conviction had grown upon this Jewish writer that at long last God was about to act. Was a secondary interpretation of Jeremiah's prophecy possible that would lend support to this conviction and perhaps help others to share it with him? Interpreting the seventy years as week-years, the author analyses them into three divisions of 7, 62 and 1 week-years, i.e. 587–539, 539–170, 170–164, 539 being the date of the fall of Babylon and 170 the date of the murder of the high-priest Onias III, while the terminal date is that of the rededication of the temple by Judas Maccabaeus. It is odd that in his division of the periods the author should have ignored the terminal date of the original interpretation of the prophecy, viz. 516, but apparently he considered the date of the actual return to be more significant. It was almost exactly 49 years (7 × 7) between the fall of Jerusalem and the fall of Babylon. The third and final division, though not yet completed when the book was written, was expected to last for only one week-year, i.e. 7 years, falling into two equal parts, $3\frac{1}{2} + 3\frac{1}{2}$, and, though the climax did not prove to be the eschatological event the writer hoped for, the actual event of the recovery and rededication of the temple was sufficiently dramatic to make the prophecy a remarkable one. The middle division, however, (539–170 B C), was considerably shorter in actual fact than 62 week-years, i.e. 62 × 7 years. Whether or not the author was aware of this discrepancy it is impossible to say, but, as the historical memory which the Jews retained of the period in question was very dim as regards facts, it may well be that they were equally vague as to the actual length of time that had elapsed since the return from exile.

There is some uncertainty as to the meaning of certain of the terms used here. The difficulty about the phrase 'an anointed one, a prince' in v. 25 is that both the words in the original, viz. mašiaḥ and nagîd can be applied variously. The root meaning of the second term is 'leader' and it could be applied to a king or prince, whether native or foreign, and also to various other officials in temple or army, including the high-priest. The first term is, in one of its usages, the Messiah. The Christological interpretation of the Early Church must, however, be rejected. Unfortunately for the purpose of a clear decision, both kings and priests in Israel were anointed at their inauguration, while the heathen monarch Cyrus is once called 'my anointed' (Isa. 45.1). In view of the fact that the first division apparently ends with the fall of Babylon, some scholars propose to identify the *mašiaḥ nagīd* with Cyrus and the suggestion has not a little to commend it. Another proposed identification is with Zerubbabel, the Davidic prince who figures in Ezra 3.2 and in the Books of Haggai and Zechariah. Since, however, Onias III, the high-priest who was deposed by Antiochus, is called 'an anointed one' in v. 26 and 'the prince (*nagīd*) of the covenant' in 11.22, if the most probable interpretation of these verses is correct, there is more to be said for the view that the designation 'an anointed one, a prince' in v. 25 refers to Joshua ben Jozadak, the high-priest who is associated with Zerubbabel at the time of the Return in 539 (see Ezra 2.2; 3.2) and was active along with him at the time of the re-building of the temple.

All that is said of the events of the middle division of time is that during it Jerusalem is to remain restored and rebuilt. The word translated 'conduits' is interesting. Until recently it appeared with this meaning only here in Hebrew, though it was known both in Phoenician and Accadian with the meaning 'moat'. The word has now turned up in Hebrew with the meaning 'conduit' in the Dead Sea Copper Scroll, a welcome confirmation of the accuracy of the Massoretic Text here. Montgomery, however, prefers the translation 'moat' and argues that 'street and moat' means the whole city with its complex of streets and circumvallating moat. A crisis is to come at the end of the sixty-two week-years with the removal of an anointed one. This could refer to the supersession of Onias by Jason in 175 BC on the orders of Antiochus Epiphanes. It is more likely, however, that the tragic event of the murder of Onias at the instigation of Menelaus, the successor of Jason who supplanted him in the favour of Antiochus, is intended. That took place in 170 BC (II Macc. 4.33ff.). The translation adopted above 'without trial' is obtained by supplying a word with Theodotion, though he prefers the translation 'although there is nothing against him judicially'. Some prefer to understand the words of the Massoretic Text as meaning 'vicariously', lit. 'and not for himself', but this seems highly unlikely. The bringing of destruction upon city and sanctuary by the people of a prince who shall come is probably an allusion to the punitive expedition of Apollonius in the summer of 168 B C when Jerusalem was sacked, the walls and many houses were demolished and the Citadel (*akra*) commanding the temple area was built. All this culminated in a torrent of invasion by the troops of Antiochus and Jerusalem experienced the horrors of warfare (I Macc. 1.29ff.). The phrase which reads literally 'and its (or his) end in a flood' is sometimes taken as referring to the death of Antiochus, but that seems unlikely, since Antiochus's activities are still being described in v. 27. The war which the writer anticipates is no doubt conceived of by him as the final eschatological struggle between good and evil (cf. Ezek. 38 and 39; Rev. 16.16 and *The War of the Sons of Light and the Sons of Darkness*).

In v. 27 it is said that he (i.e. Antiochus) will form a strong covenant with the mighty (or many), by which is to be understood the fact that Antiochus made an alliance (*bᵉrīt*) with the renegade Jews, who are described here either as the aristocrats or as the majority. This is to be a feature of the final year-week or period of seven years. Half-way through that period the author placed the decree of Antiochus which caused the daily offering to be suspended—on Chislev 15 or 25, 167 B C. Though he could not yet know it, the suspension was to last for three years or a little more, i.e. until Chislev 25, 164 B C, Chislev being roughly our month of December. Still more terrible for Jewish feeling was the placing upon a corner of the altar of burnt offering of a *baetyl* for the offering of sacrifices to Zeus Olympius, with whom the God of Israel was identified by the hellenizing Jews, though actually 'Zeus Olympius' was already a title concealing the Canaanite deity *Ba'al Šāmēm*, God of heaven. This was the so-called abomination of desolation, presumably a pun on 'the God of heaven' (*Mᵉšōmēm, Ba'al Šāmēm*). The desecration of the altar was to last till a predetermined end should overwhelm the desolator (*šōmēm*), i.e. Antiochus, whose miserable end is thus foretold (cf. 11.44, 45).

Throughout this whole passage about the seventy weeks of years we get the impression that the writer of the Book of Daniel takes a predestinarian view of history. It is true that he thought of the climax, which he believed to be imminent, as something which God in his wisdom had resolved to bring about and which in consequence was inevitable. This, however, was a religious certainty and not the result of a philosophical theory. Certainly he gives the impression that the periods of history which led up to the present crisis were likewise predetermined. It should be remembered, however, that what we have here, except at the very end, is not genuine prediction but known history cast into the form of prophecy, and it may very well be that the more instructed readers of the book were quite aware of this. Heaton in a very thoughtful note (p. 215) says wisely: 'No doctrine of predestination explains anything; it only shows that we have no explanation. Faith, however, may express its own certitude in predestinarian language; in that case its validity depends entirely upon the quality and content of the conviction which it helps to display.' To recognize the distinction between religious conviction and the temporary theological form in which it may express itself liberates the mind from a perplexity about the correct use of the Bible. The harm that has been done to the cause of true religion by the absolutizing of the limitations to the outlook of the biblical writers should serve as a solemn warning against further attempts to solve the code by which God is erroneously supposed to have communicated the secret of his predetermined purposes. What blinds many to the fact that it is an error to imagine that God poses puzzles of this kind is that the error begins in the Bible itself, as in the instance before us, but this difficulty must be accepted and faced boldly in the interest of honesty and truth. Nothing whatsoever is to be gained in the last resort by prevaricating on this most important issue of biblical interpretation. That the end predicted by the author of the Book of Daniel did not come, any more than the expectation of the early Christians of the imminent return of Christ was literally fulfilled, presents us with a challenge in our interpretation of the Bible, but need not affect our faith in the power of God to save to the uttermost. The Book of Daniel continued to speak to the Jews of that great truth, and it can still witness to us in every time of testing and crisis of the presence and availability of the living God. (Cf. Heaton, pp. 88ff.)

CHAPTERS TEN, ELEVEN, TWELVE

10 ¹In the third year of Cyrus king of Persia a word was revealed to Daniel, who was named Belteshazzar. And the word was true, and it was a great conflict.* And he understood the word and had understanding of the vision.

2 In those days I, Daniel, was mourning for three weeks. ³I ate no delicacies, no meat or wine entered my mouth, nor did I anoint myself at all, for the full three weeks. ⁴On the twenty-fourth day of the first month, as I was standing on the bank of the great river, that is, the Tigris, ⁵I lifted up my eyes and looked, and behold, a man clothed in linen, whose loins were girded with gold of Uphaz. ⁶His body was like beryl, his face like the appearance of lightning, his eyes like flaming torches, his arms and legs like the gleam of burnished bronze, and the sound of his words like the noise of a multitude. ⁷And I, Daniel, alone saw the vision, for the men who were with me did not see the vision, but a great trembling fell upon them, and they fled to hide themselves. ⁸So I was left alone and saw this great vision, and no strength was left in me; my radiant appearance was fearfully changed, and I retained no strength. ⁹Then I heard the sound of his words; and when I heard the sound of his words, I fell on my face in a deep sleep with my face to the ground.

10 And behold, a hand touched me and set me trembling on my hands and knees. ¹¹And he said to me, 'O Daniel, man greatly beloved, give heed to the words that I speak to you, and stand upright, for now I have been sent to you.' While he was speaking this word to me, I stood up trembling. ¹²Then he said to me, 'Fear not, Daniel, for from the first day that you set your mind to understand and humbled yourself before your God, your words have been heard, and I have come because of your words. ¹³The prince of the kingdom of Persia withstood me twenty-one days; but Michael, one of the chief princes, came to help me, so I left him there with the prince of the kingdom of Persia† ¹⁴and came to make you understand what is to befall your

---

* 'A hard task.' (See Supplement, p. 186).

† Probably translate: 'but, as I was still left there, Michael, one of the chief

people in the latter days. For the vision is for days yet to come.'

15 When he had spoken to me according to these words, I turned my face toward the ground and was dumb. 16And behold, one in the likeness of the sons of men touched my lips; then I opened my mouth and spoke. I said to him who stood before me, 'O my lord, by reason of the vision pains have come upon me, and I retain no strength. 17How can my lord's servant talk with my lord? For now no strength remains in me, and no breath is left in me.'

18 Again one having the appearance of a man touched me and strengthened me. 19And he said, 'O man greatly beloved, fear not, peace be with you; be strong and of good courage.' And when he spoke to me, I was strengthened and said, 'Let my lord speak, for you have strengthened me.' 20*Then he said, 'Do you know why I have come to you? But now I will return to fight against the prince of Persia; and when I am through with him, lo, the prince of Greece will come. 21But I will tell you what is inscribed in the book of truth: there is none who contends by my side against these except Michael, your prince. 11 1And as for me, in the first year of Darius the Mede, I stood up to confirm and strengthen him.*

2 'And now I will show you the truth. Behold, three more kings shall arise in Persia; and a fourth shall be far richer than all of them; and when he has become strong through his riches, he shall stir up all† against the kingdom of Greece. 3Then a mighty king shall arise, who shall rule with great dominion and do according to his will. 4And when he has arisen, his kingdom shall be broken and divided toward the four winds of heaven, but not to his posterity, nor according to the dominion with which he ruled; for his kingdom shall be plucked up and go to others besides these.

5 'Then the king of the south shall be strong, but one of his princes shall be stronger than he and his dominion shall be a great dominion. 6After some years they shall make an alliance, and the daughter of the king of the south shall come to the king of the north to make peace; but she shall not retain the strength of her arm, and he and his offspring shall not endure; but she shall be given up, and her attendants, her child, and he who got possession of her.

7 'In those times a branch from her roots shall arise in his place; he shall come against the army‡ and enter the fortress of the king of the north, and he shall deal with them and shall prevail. 8He shall also carry off to Egypt their gods with their molten images and with their precious vessels of silver and of gold; and for some years he shall refrain from attacking the king of the north. 9Then the latter shall come into

---

princes, came to help me against the general of the King of the Persians (based on Theodotion) and I came . . .'

* For possible reconstruction of text see Commentary.
† 'Mobilize the whole world.'
‡ 'Pass through the outworks' by a slight emendation.

the realm of the king of the south but shall return into his own land.

10 'His sons shall wage war and assemble a multitude of great forces, which* shall come on and overflow and pass through, and again shall carry the war as far as his fortress. ¹¹Then the king of the south, moved with anger, shall come out and fight with the king of the north; and he shall raise a great multitude, but it shall be given into his hand. ¹²And when the multitude is taken, his heart shall be exalted, and he shall cast down tens of thousands, but he shall not prevail. ¹³For the king of the north shall again raise a multitude, greater than the former; and after some years he shall come on with a great army and abundant supplies.

14 'In those times many shall rise against the king of the south; and the men of violence among your own people shall lift themselves up in order to fulfil the vision; but they shall fail. ¹⁵Then the king of the north shall come and throw up siegeworks, and take a well-fortified city. And the forces of the south shall not stand, or even his picked troops, for there shall be no strength to stand. ¹⁶But he who comes against him shall do according to his own will, and none shall stand before him; and he shall stand in the glorious land, and all of it shall be in his power. ¹⁷He shall set his face to come with the strength of† his whole kingdom, and he shall bring terms of peace and perform them. He shall give him the daughter of women to destroy the kingdom; but it shall not stand or be to his advantage. ¹⁸Afterward he shall turn his face to the coastlands, and shall take many of them; but a commander shall put an end to his insolence§; indeed he shall turn his insolence§ back upon him. ¹⁹Then he shall turn his face toward the fortresses of his own land; but he shall stumble and fall, and shall not be found.

20 'Then shall arise in his place one who shall send an exactor of tribute through the glory of the kingdom; but within a few days he shall be broken, neither in anger nor in battle. ²¹In his place shall arise a contemptible person to whom royal majesty has not been given; he shall come in without warning and obtain the kingdom by flatteries. ²²Armies shall be utterly swept away before him and broken, and the prince of the covenant also. ²³And from the time that an alliance is made with him he shall act deceitfully; and he shall become strong with a small people. Without warning‡ ²⁴he shall come into the richest parts of the province; and he shall do what neither his fathers nor his fathers' fathers have done, scattering among them plunder, spoil, and goods. He shall devise plans against strongholds, but only for a time. ²⁵And he shall stir up his power and his courage against the king of the south with a great army; and the king of the south shall wage war with an exceedingly great and mighty army; but he shall not stand, for plots shall be devised against him. ²⁶Even those who eat his rich food shall be his undoing; his army shall be swept away, and many shall fall down slain. ²⁷And as for the two kings, their minds shall be bent on mischief; they shall speak lies at the same table, but to no

* 'And one of them.' † 'To gain control of.' But RSV may be correct.
§ Read 'challenge'.
‡ Perhaps 'in a time of security' at end of v. 23.

avail; for the end is yet to be at the time appointed. ²⁸And he shall return to his land with great substance, but his heart shall be set against the holy covenant. And he shall work his will, and return to his own land.

29 'At the time appointed he shall return and come into the south; but it shall not be this time as it was before. ³⁰For ships of Kittim shall come against him, and he shall be afraid and withdraw, and shall turn back and be enraged and take action against the holy covenant. He shall turn back and give heed to those who forsake the holy covenant. ³¹Forces from him shall appear and profane the temple and fortress, and shall take away the continual burnt offering. And they shall set up the abomination that makes desolate. ³²He shall seduce with flattery those who violate the covenant; but the people who know their God shall stand firm and take action. ³³And those among the people who are wise shall make many understand, though they shall fall by sword and flame, by captivity and plunder, for some days. ³⁴When they fall, they shall receive a little help. And many shall join themselves to them with flattery; ³⁵and some of those who are wise shall fall, to refine and to cleanse them, and to make them white, until the time of the end, for it is yet for the time appointed.

36 'And the king shall do according to his will; he shall exalt himself and magnify himself above every god, and shall speak astonishing things against the God of gods. He shall prosper till the indignation is accomplished; for what is determined shall be done. ³⁷He shall give no heed to the gods of his fathers, or to the one beloved by women; he shall not give heed to any other god, for he shall magnify himself above all. ³⁸He shall honour the god of fortresses instead of these; a god whom his fathers did not know he shall honour with gold and silver, with precious stones and costly gifts. ³⁹He shall deal with the strongest fortresses by the help of a foreign god;* those who acknowledge him he shall magnify with honour. He shall make them rulers over many and shall divide the land for a price.

40 'At the time of the end the king of the south shall attack him; but the king of the north shall rush upon him like a whirlwind, with chariots and horsemen, and with many ships; and he shall come into countries and shall overflow and pass through. ⁴¹He shall come into the glorious land. And tens of thousands shall fall, but these shall be delivered out of his hand: Edom and Moab and the main part of the Ammonites. ⁴²He shall stretch out his hand against the countries, and the land of Egypt shall not escape. ⁴³He shall become ruler of the treasures of gold and of silver, and all the precious things of Egypt; and the Libyans and the Ethiopians shall follow in his train. ⁴⁴But tidings from the east and the north shall alarm him, and he shall go forth with great fury to exterminate and utterly destroy many. ⁴⁵And he shall pitch his palatial tents between the sea and the glorious holy mountain; yet he shall come to his end, with none to help him.

* Possibly by slight emendation 'with people devoted to a foreign god'.

12 [1]'At that time shall arise Michael, the great prince who has charge of your people. And there shall be a time of trouble, such as never has been since there was a nation till that time; but at that time your people shall be delivered, every one whose name shall be found written in the book. [2]And many of those who sleep in the dust of the earth shall awake, some to everlasting life, and some to shame and everlasting contempt. [3]And those who are wise shall shine like the brightness of the firmament; and those who turn many to righteousness, like the stars for ever and ever. [4]But you, Daniel, shut up the words, and seal the book, until the time of the end. Many shall run to and fro, and knowledge shall increase.'

[5] Then I Daniel looked, and behold, two others stood, one on this bank of the stream and one on that bank of the stream. [6]And I said to the man clothed in linen, who was above the waters of the stream, 'How long shall it be till the end of these wonders?' [7]The man clothed in linen, who was above the waters of the stream, raised his right hand and his left hand toward heaven; and I heard him swear by him who lives for ever that it would be for a time, two times, and half a time; and that when the shattering of the power of the holy people comes to an end all these things would be accomplished. [8]I heard, but I did not understand. Then I said, 'O my lord, what shall be the issue of these things?' [9]He said, 'Go your way, Daniel, for the words are shut up and sealed until the time of the end. [10]Many shall purify themselves, and make themselves white, and be refined; but the wicked shall do wickedly; and none of the wicked shall understand; but those who are wise shall understand. [11]And from the time that the continual burnt offering is taken away, and the abomination that makes desolate is set up, there shall be a thousand two hundred and ninety days. [12]Blessed is he who waits and comes to the thousand three hundred and thirty-five days. [13]But go your way till the end; and you shall rest, and shall stand in your allotted place at the end of the days.'

IT IS GENERALLY agreed that these chapters belong together as a single whole and tell of a single revelation supposedly made to Daniel in the third year of Cyrus by a heavenly being, who sketches for him in considerable detail the history of the Seleucid period up to and including the reign of Antiochus Epiphanes, prefacing it by a very slight account of the Persian period and of the reign of Alexander the Great and following it by a prophecy of the end of Antiochus Epiphanes and of what is to come thereafter. The point at which history passes into genuine prophecy gives us the position in time of the author. The book closes with another revelation regarding the meaning of the expression 'a time, times and a half' (cf. 7.25; 9.27) and an injunction to Daniel to keep the revelation of the end secret. Chapter 12.1 is the crucial verse which tells how God brings in the great consummation through the agency of Michael the patron angel of Israel. Chapter 11 is mainly devoted to contemporary history or to the history of the fairly recent past as it appeared from the point of view of this Jewish observer who watches the course of power politics unfolding itself until, with the challenge of Antiochus Epiphanes against God himself, it seems inevitable that God should intervene. It was the circumstance that, in these desperate final years before the expected consummation, there were some who stood firm even at the cost of martyrdom, that enabled the author to rise to the daring faith that death would not exclude such from participation in the coming kingdom of God upon earth. God's rule would be an empty thing apart from those who by their loyalty show that they above all are willing to accept it. To accuse the author of being more interested here in the fate of the individual than in the kingdom of God which he believed was about to come and the expectation of the coming of which dominates much of the rest of the book would be to minimize the very essential truth that, when God acts, he acts through his children as well as on their behalf, and that, as he is the living God, the giving of life is the purpose of his activity.

[**10.1–11.2a**] [**1**] 10.21 and 11.1 are almost certainly corrupt. NEB reconstructs as follows: 'I have no ally on my side to help and support me, except Michael your prince. However I will tell you what is written in the Book of Truth', (omitting the inappropriate reference to 'the first year of Darius the Mede'). The reign of Cyrus may have been selected in the present instance because the prophecy is to start with the Persian period. 'King of Persia' would not be a contemporary title of Cyrus but is a natural description from the standpoint of a later time. In this verse Daniel is spoken of in the third person and his Babylonian name Belteshazzar serves as a link with the first part of the book. It is said in summary fashion that a word came to Daniel and that, though he came to understand it, it cost him a severe struggle. The original is somewhat ambiguous at this point (cf. Jeffery, p. 500), but the translation suggested is intended to guard against the view that there is a reference to the warfare in heaven described later in the chapter. In the verses which follow and amplify v. 1 Daniel, speaking in the first person, describes the strenuous experience through which he has passed. Apart from the appearance of the angel to Daniel there does not seem to be any suggestion of a vision in the ordinary sense of the word, but the word 'vision' can

be used in the sense of the substance of a revelation and that is probably
what we are to understand by it here.

[10.2–9] Daniel tells how he had been fasting for three weeks.
The word used here is 'mourning' which, as Matt. 9.14–15 shows,
could be used as a synonym for 'fasting'. Another synonym for 'fasting'
appears in v. 12, viz. 'humbling oneself', i.e. 'mortifying oneself', an
expression which is especially connected with the rites of the Day of
Atonement and therefore with confession of sin (see Lev. 16.29, 31;
23.27, 32; Num. 29.7; cf. Isa. 58.3–5 where the linking of the ideas of
fasting and humbling oneself is made very clear; and cf. the word
ta'ănît, Ezra 9.5, which eventually became the regular term for 'fasting'). Fasting as practised in preparation for receiving a revelation is
also mentioned (see Ezra 8.21; II (4) Esd. 5.20) and it is usually held
that this was the implied purpose of Daniel's fast. Nevertheless the
thought of confession of sin should not be excluded (cf. 9.3), and seems
quite in place in the present passage. There is a close parallel in Test.
Reuben 1.10: 'Wine and strong drink I drank not, and flesh entered
not into my mouth, and I ate no pleasant food; but I mourned over
my sin, for it was great, such as had not been in Israel.' In view of the
prayer in chapter 9, we need not assume that the fasting here was no
more than an ascetic exercise preliminary to receiving revelation. The
delicacies (lit. 'bread of pleasantnesses') from which Daniel re-
frained may be contrasted with the bread of affliction of Deut. 16.3,
i.e. the unleavened bread of passover and matzoth.

On a day which is identified by an exact dating as the twenty-
fourth day of the first month—it thus being made clear that the Passover week fell within the period of fasting—Daniel finds himself on
the banks of the great river which is identified in the Massoretic Text
with the Tigris, though one would more naturally suppose the Euphrates was intended. While there, Daniel has a vision of an angelic
being of dazzling appearance, who is not given a name, but is probably to be understood as being Gabriel in view of his manner of addressing Daniel (cf. vv. 11 and 19). The description of this being
echoes the language of Ezek. 1. Jeffery comments (p. 502): 'The
description given here seems to transcend that given of Gabriel in the
earlier chapters, and his appearance had a graver effect on the seer
than that of Gabriel had, which suggests some supernatural being
superior to Gabriel and Michael and carefully distinguished by the
writer from them. Early Christian commentators saw in this figure
the Messiah Jesus.' On the other hand, it should be noted that this

impressive figure comes merely to communicate a revelation, while in
the celestial contest which he recounts he seems to rank himself along
with Michael and is in need of his support. While it is true that the
high-priest in Israel was dressed in linen, it does not follow that the
description here implies that the angel is 'a celestial high-priest'
(Jeffery). The tarshish-stone to which the colour of his body is compared is now supposed to be the yellow jasper.

The numinous character of the experience is heightened by the
circumstance that men who were in company with Daniel, though they
did not see what he saw, were seized with panic and left him alone
(cf. Acts 9.7). The effect on Daniel himself was that he collapsed and
lay on the ground in a trance and had to be revived by the action of
a mysterious hand (cf. II (4) Esd. 5.14–15). Once again, as in 9.23,
Daniel is addressed as 'man greatly beloved'; that is to say, he is
favoured by God and chosen to be the recipient of divine revelation.
Indeed he is assured that, from the very moment when he began his
fast, mortifying or humbling himself and earnestly desiring to understand God's purpose for Israel, there had been a response from God's
side. The angel (Gabriel?) had been immediately commissioned to
take the revelation to him.

[10.10–11.2a] And now comes a curious passage, in which Daniel
tells how the angel explained to him why there had been a delay of
three weeks, the period of Daniel's fast, between the sending out of the
angel and his coming to Daniel with the revelation. It had been due to
angelic opposition in heaven. The language used does not make it
absolutely clear whether the celestial contest was of a legal nature or
took the form of actual warfare. The idea of warfare in heaven appears
picturesquely in the strange passage in II Macc. 5.1–4 and supports
(so Jeffery, p. 510) the second alternative: 'Now about this time
Antiochus made his second inroad into Egypt. And it so befell that
throughout all the city, for the space of almost forty days, there appeared in the midst of the sky horsemen in swift motion, wearing robes
inwrought with gold and carrying spears, equipped in troops for battle;
and drawing of swords; and on the other side squadrons of horse in
array; and encounters and pursuits of both armies; and shaking of
shields, and multitudes of lances, and casting of darts, and flashing of
golden trappings, and girding on of all sorts of armour. Wherefore all
men besought that the vision might have been given for good.' In
the present passage, however, the contest, of whatever nature it was,
seems to be confined to the angel who may be Gabriel and to the

patron angels of the nations, and the thought is that in some way the fortunes of the nations are dependent on what happens in the celestial sphere. There is an obvious parallel to this, of course, in the Homeric poems and in Virgil's *Aeneid*. As a way of expressing the importance of historical events and of asserting belief in the divine control of history this thought of the contest of angelic representatives is not particularly helpful today, but may be accepted as witness to the truth that men are not left to themselves in the bitter contests which seem to make up so much of the human story. History cannot simply be summed up in the words of Matthew Arnold:

> We are here as on a darkling plain
> Swept with confused alarms of struggle and flight,
> Where ignorant armies clash by night.

It is interesting that in the Middle Ages the Archangel Michael should have been believed in as the celestial champion of Christendom, against the Saracens at Roncesvalles and again when the orders of German knights were engaged in their long struggles against the barbarians on the eastern frontier. Faith assumes strange forms and so, when we read in chapter 11 of the Book of Daniel what the history of several centuries looked like to this Jewish observer, we may be glad that he saw a meaning in it which enabled him and those who accepted his message to come through one of the great crises of history, in however bizarre a way he expressed his faith.

The idea that each nation had its patron angel had its roots in Jewish tradition. Deut. 29.26 reflects the curious view that the God of Israel, as the Supreme God, had allotted to each nation its own subordinate deity. The LXX version of Deut. 32.8–9 says:

> When the Most High gave to the nations
>   their inheritance,
>   when he separated the sons of men,
> he fixed the bounds of the peoples
>   according to the number of the sons of God.
> For the Lord's portion is his people,
>   Jacob his allotted heritage.

In the Massoretic Text of this passage 'sons of God' is 'children of Israel'. The Targum of pseudo-Jonathan on these verses refers to the nations proceeding from Noah (see Gen. 10) which were reckoned as seventy and to the seventy angels who were allotted to them and adds that this number seventy was determined by the number of the seventy souls of Israel who went down into Egypt (see Ex. 1.5). It will be noticed that the passage in Deuteronomy implies that no angel was allotted to Israel, but that it was placed under the direct control of God himself (cf. Ecclus 17.17 and also Jub. 15.31–32 where the function of the angels is to lead the nations astray!). In Enoch 81.59 there is a reference to the seventy angels who were appointed to shepherd Israel with disciplinary intent when it refused obedience to its true Shepherd, the God of Israel—a curious variant of the tradition.

In this chapter of the Book of Daniel and also in 12.1 Israel itself is represented as having a patron angel, *viz*. Michael. It is particularly interesting to find that in one of the Dead Sea Scrolls, in *The War of the Sons of Light with the Sons of Darkness*, ch. XIV, Michael is definitely mentioned as the patron angel of Israel, God intending to exalt among the gods the rule of Michael, which implies the supremacy of Israel. Michael's victory will mean the triumph of righteousness in the high places. Michael's name always appears in the lists of archangels, whether they are counted as four (Enoch 9.1) or as seven (Enoch 20.5 where Michael is assigned to Israel). Michael is mentioned twice in the New Testament, *viz*. in Jude 9, where he contends with the devil for the body of Moses, and in Rev. 12.7, where we read of the war in heaven in which Michael and his angels fight against the dragon.

The angelic visitant—to continue Daniel's narrative—explained to him that he had been delayed for the three weeks of Daniel's fast by the opposition of the patron angel of Persia, who is unnamed. Then he explained how Michael, the patron angel of Israel (see 10.21; 12.1) came to his help and how he had left him to carry on the struggle (unless the usual emendation of the text is not accepted as in RSV and the meaning is taken to be that Michael had come in view of the fact that the other angel had held out alone for three weeks). Daniel was now to be told what was to happen to Israel at the end of the age. For the second time he collapsed and this time he was struck dumb. A human-like being, whether the original angel (Gabriel?) or another is not clear, touched Daniel's lips (cf. Isa. 6.6; Jer. 1.9) and he recovered the power of speech, and explained to the angel somewhat unnecessarily how overwhelmed he had been by the experience he had passed through (cf. Isa. 21.3). For the third time he received the reviving touch and was addressed in encouraging words. In this somewhat strange fashion the author is seeking to convey the awesomeness of contact with the superhuman world. It has been pointed out that the angel's words of encouragement to Daniel virtually consist of the opening and closing epistolary formulae, what Montgomery (p. 415) calls 'the Alpha and Omega of friendly greetings'. Daniel had had experience of the *tremendum* and required reassurance.

The Hebrew text of 10.20–21; 11.1–2a seems disordered and commentators have made numerous suggestions which can only be fully appreciated by study of the original. The simplest solution is perhaps to replace the 'And now I will show you the truth' of 11.2a by the similar but fuller sentence 10.21a, 'But I will tell you what is inscribed in the book of truth', which, by its removal from its present context restores the natural sequence of thought. Most commentators agree that the words 'and as for me, in the first year of Darius the Mede' are a gloss added by someone who did not realize that chapters 10 and 11 are continuous. The heading involves a quite unnatural leap back in time. A slight emendation enables the words which follow the gloss to be taken as applying to Michael, so that they would run, 'standing up for my help and support'.

A distinction should probably be drawn between 'the book of truth' here and 'the books' of 7.10, as Jeffery does (see pp. 458, 459, 510). As we saw, Heaton, probably wrongly, identifies 'the books' of chapter 10 with the Babylonian 'Tablets of Fate', associated with the Creation Epic and the New Year Festival (so also Montgomery, p. 418 but not p. 299). 'The book of truth', however, does seem to be something very like 'the Tablets of Fate'. Jeffery has a helpful note (p. 510): 'In the Talmud (Rosh-ha-Shana 16b) we read how on New Year's Day the books were opened and fates recorded. These tablets and the book are frequently mentioned in Jubilees and the Testaments of the Twelve Patriarchs; and in the prayer of Joseph preserved in Origen, *Philocalia* xxiii, 15 we read, "For I have read in the tablets of heaven all that shall befall you and your sons." ' In a note on Jub. 3.10 Charles, discussing a reference to the heavenly tables wisely remarks: 'The conception is not a hard and fixed one; in Enoch and Test. XII. Patriarch. it wavers between an absolute determinism and prediction pure and simple: whereas in our text, in addition to these significations, it implies at times little more than a contemporary heavenly record of events' (cf. also Charles, *The Book of Enoch*, 1912, pp. 91–92). The tablet of good deeds and the tablet of sins, however, to which the celestial Judge makes reference do seem to be distinct. In the present instance the Book of Truth is represented as containing an account of events to come, though it is quite likely that readers of the Book of Daniel understood the convention and realized that much of chapter 11 is really *vaticinium post eventum*. However this may be, we may believe that the author wished to suggest that these events were included within the divine providential control of history and were moving towards the divinely planned climax.

[**11.2b–12.4**] In this long section the pages of the book of truth are turned for Daniel that he may see, as it were, the show of things to come. What is actually given is a selective account of past history from the Persian period down to a certain date in the latter part of the reign of Antiochus IV Epiphanes—that being the actual viewpoint in time of the writer—with a very short section at the end in which he takes up the role of prophet and forecasts what he believes is about to happen in the immediate future.

In the historical part of this final 'vision' attention is concentrated on a number of episodes which were of particular interest to Jewish readers. To us perhaps the chief interest of this section of the Book of Daniel is just this, that, through the eyes of one who was living at a strategic point in space and time, we can see what the impact of world events on such a one felt like. It was in these historical circumstances that this faith proved possible. This is witness to which we are bidden pay heed, because through such witness God can speak to us in our day and generation.

The survey of history begins at a slightly later point than in Nebuchadnezzar's dream (ch. 2) and in Daniel's vision of the beasts (ch. 7), but at the same point as in Daniel's vision of the ram and the he-goat (ch. 8). In fact we are now given the amplification in detail of that vision, the various kings appearing *in propria persona* and no longer disguised as horns of heraldic beasts. Like Macbeth in the witches' cave Daniel is supposedly permitted to see king after king appearing on the stage of history, strutting out his part and making way for his successor. In the commentary the fiction of prophecy will be dropped and the references treated as references to past events.

First comes the Persian age (v. 2b) which was significant for the Jews since it was under the Persian kings that the Jewish ecclesiastical state came into existence. Special attention seems to be directed to the beginning of the great clash between East and West. Then in two verses (3,4) the dramatic rise to power of Alexander the Great is referred to, his swift passage from the scene and the break-up of his empire among the Diadochi. The stage is thus set for the events which were of particular interest to Jewish readers. Once again we notice how Alexander's importance is assessed merely in terms of power. Not a hint is given that this writer had any inkling of the nobler side of Alexander's character or of his dream of a unified world enjoying the blessings of Greek culture. The Jews remembered Alexander as a portent. What his dreams came to was the reality of Ptolemaic and Seleucid rule and the culture associated with these dynasties, which the Jews welcomed or rejected in accordance with their religious convictions. A passing reference is made to the two men who founded the dynasties with which the Jews chiefly had to do, particular emphasis being laid on Seleucus whose assumption of royalty in 312 BC fixed the beginning of the Seleucid (or Greek) era according to which the Jews came for certain purposes to reckon the dates of their history. Then (vv. 6–9) comes the attempt at an alliance between the Seleucid and Ptolemaic dynasties (cf. 2.43) and its disastrous issue. It is not improbable that there lingered in Judaea some memory of the brilliant cavalcade which had once passed by on its way from Egypt to Antioch escorting the ill-starred Egyptian princess, and of the hideous tale of murder and revenge, which some time later must have been the common talk of the bazaars, and especially of the story which told how the gods of Egypt at last went home.

Coming much nearer to his own time, the writer next tells of the catastrophic events of the reign of Antiochus the Great (vv. 10–19)—the battles of Raphia and Panion, the latter of which settled the fate of Palestine and set the stage for contemporary history—and of the disasters which eclipsed the hopes of Antiochus and caused the long and grim shadow of Rome to fall across the east-Mediterranean world. The ruinous policy of Antiochus the Great determined the cautious policy of his successor to which brief reference is made in v. 20. The longest and, from the point of view of the writer and his readers, much the most important section (vv. 21–45) is devoted to the reign of Antiochus Epiphanes. Against a vivid background of marching and counter-marching, of fighting and scheming, we get an impression of the strange, enigmatic character of this man, whom so many of the Jews hailed as the representative of a culture in which they were eager to share, but whom the pious regarded as the arch-enemy of their ancestral faith. A glimpse is given of the Roman galleys bringing the representative of the power which was to set a limit to Antiochus's ambitions and provoke him, in reaction to his disappointment, to his worst excesses against the faithful in Judaea. The agony of those who suffered from the persecution is well suggested, and likewise the horror of the pious at the blasphemy of the persecutor and at the many who shared his guilt by their apostasy, and so the writer passes from history to prophecy and forecasts a dramatic end for the tyrant, which, though it actually took place at about the time expected, falsified the prophecy as regarded both its place and its manner.

When the writer finds himself under the necessity of saying what the coming of the kingdom of God will be like he allows the angelic interpreter to tell Daniel merely of the triumph of Michael, the patron angel of Israel, who will vindicate those who remain faithful, and of a resurrection from the dead which will give the martyrs a share in the glory that is to be and the apostates the punishment they have deserved and so far escaped. It is made quite clear that the interest of the writer is focused on the contemporary crisis, for which he believes he has a relevant word from God, and on God's transcendent power, which is available for those who stand firm.

Montgomery (p. 421) describes the author of the Book of Daniel as 'the Jewish counterpart of Polybius' who was his contemporary and whose interest in writing his great history was to show 'how it was that almost the whole world within some fifty-three years (220–168 BC) fell under the single empire of the Romans'. The Jewish writer, however, is concerned, not merely like the Greek with the horizontal plane of events, but with the vertical relation of God's activity to what men do on earth. He stands in the succession of the great prophets of Israel who like him saw that human history had a meaning, which could not indeed be read off from the events taken by themselves, but which was given to them by God according as they served or opposed his ultimate purpose for the world.

[11.2b] The Persian period is dismissed in summary fashion. We cannot be sure exactly which Persian kings the writer had in view and it does not greatly matter. There is even some doubt as to whether we are meant to think of four after Cyrus or of four including Cyrus, the latter alternative being the more probable. Owing to the fact that the last clause of the verse is textually uncertain one cannot be confident about the identity of the king who is described as the fourth, but, if the translation adopted is approximately correct, we should probably think of Xerxes, whose mobilizing of the subject nations of the East against Greece must have made a tremendous impression on men's minds. 'Was there a nation in all Asia which Xerxes did not bring with him against Greece?' says Herodotus (VII, 21). For the rest it seems unprofitable to add to the suggested identifications (see commentaries), especially as it may be suspected that the writer was dependent on unreliable traditions. How unreliable they were is suggested by the fact that almost a century and a half of history is telescoped into nothing, that is to say, the time between Salamis and the rise of Alexander. It is difficult to believe that the fourth king is meant to be Darius III Codomannus, the feeble opponent of Alexander.

[3–4] Alexander is remembered as a great soldier whose power seemed to be irresistible, as he built up an empire the like of which the world had not yet seen. Yet, even more than his dramatic rise, what impressed a writer, who believed that human history was not a closed system, was the suddenness of his passing from the scene (cf. 8.8) and the immediate break-up of his empire. There is little doubt that the successor kingdoms which are intended are Macedonia, Thrace and Asia Minor, Egypt, and Syria and Babylon, which came under the control of certain of Alexander's marshals, his feeble descendants being brushed aside. A passing reference seems to be made to the fact that certain smaller states (e.g. Armenia, Cappadocia, etc.) emerged from the wreck of Alexander's empire. None of his successors, however, rivalled Alexander in the extent of his power. It may be permitted to follow Montgomery (p. 425) and Heaton (p. 228) in quoting the picturesque words with which Edwyn Bevan underlines the drama of Alexander's passing (*House of Seleucus*, vol. I, p. 28): 'In the spring of 323 before Christ the whole order of things from the Adriatic away to the mountains of Central Asia and the dusty plains of the Punjab rested upon a single will, a single brain, nurtured in Hellenic thought. Then the hand of God, as if trying some fantastic experiment, plucked this man away. Who could predict for a moment what the result would be?' (vv. 5–20). From the time when the Ptolemaic (or Lagid) and the Seleucid dynasties were founded Palestine was between the upper and the nether millstone.

[5] The king of the south (i.e. Egypt) who is mentioned first is Ptolemy I Soter. He had become satrap of Egypt after the death of Alexander and had consolidated his position there by the defeat of Perdiccas, though it was not for many years (305 BC) that he assumed the title of king. His general who was destined to outshine him was Seleucus, another of Alexander's marshals, of whom Arrian wrote (*Anabasis* VII.22.5), 'He had the royalest mind of them all, and, after Alexander himself, ruled over the greatest extent of territory' (quoted

by Jeffery, p. 514). Seleucus had occupied Babylon, but later had to flee from Antigonus and took refuge with Ptolemy. In 312 BC, the year recognized later as marking the beginning of the Seleucid or Greek era, Seleucus, after the Battle of Gaza in which he and Ptolemy defeated Demetrius, the brilliant son of Antigonus, recovered control of Babylon and established his power in the East. It was not till after the Battle of Ipsus (301 BC), however, that Seleucus really came into his own and was able to build a new capital city at Antioch on the Orontes. He reigned there till 280 BC and is known to history as Seleucus I Nicator.

[11.6] There is nothing in the text here to make it clear that the episode referred to had nothing to do with Seleucus and Ptolemy Soter but concerned the ill-omened alliance between their successors Antiochus II Theos and Ptolemy II Philadelphus, which was sealed by the marriage of the latter's daughter, Berenice, to the former. That was about the middle of the third century BC (250 or 249). Antiochus's former wife, Laodice, had been divorced, though later he returned to her, and her children had been excluded from the succession. Laodice took a terrible revenge. Antiochus died suddenly and it was said that he had been poisoned by Laodice, presumably to forestall any possible return by him to Berenice. Then the infant son of Berenice was murdered and finally the intrepid queen herself. A slight and attractive emendation gives: 'his progeny shall not endure', i.e. 'he and his progeny', a reference to the ill-fated child who was the grandson of Ptolemy II Philadelphus. The reference to Berenice's Egyptian escort as having shared the fate of their mistress is one of those vivid touches which enable us to see, if only for a moment, the passing of the gay company escorting the young princess to her new home.

[7–9] In v.7 a brief account is given of the so-called Laodicean War which was undertaken by Berenice's brother, Ptolemy III Euergetes, who had succeeded to the Egyptian throne, in the first instance to bring help to his sister and, in the event, to avenge her death. The statement that Ptolemy penetrated the outworks (if Montgomery's emendation is accepted) and entered the fortress of the king of the north (i.e. Seleucus II Callinicus) probably refers to the capture of Seleucia, the port of Antioch and of Antioch itself. Ptolemy is said to have overrun a large part of the Seleucid kingdom (v. the Adulian Inscription copied by Cosmas Indicopleustes), and, while it is unlikely that he made much headway in Asia Minor, he may well have marched deeply into the eastern territories of Seleucus and visited certain of the ancient centres of power. That Ptolemy returned to Egypt with vast booty, including images of the gods, is corroborated both by the Adulian Inscription and by Jerome who explains that the images were those of Egyptian gods which had been carried off by Cambyses long before. Bevan (*A History of Egypt under the Ptolemaic Dynasty*, p. 198) comments: 'Egyptian idols and other objects discovered in Babylon or Ecbatana or Susa he must have restored to the Egyptian priesthood with such pomp and circumstance on his return that it was talked about at court, that Greek courtiers and Greek historians noted the action as significant and interesting, and that Jews in Jerusalem eighty years later could remember hearing their fathers describe how the army of the king of Egypt had come home through Palestine, triumphantly escorting the idols which they had taken away from the countries of the king of the north.'

The concluding words of v. 8 seem to mean that Ptolemy remained inactive for some years, enabling Seleucus to recover northern Syria and his capital city, Antioch. When the latter marched south into Palestine, however, about 242 B C, he met with a decisive defeat at the hands of the Egyptian king.

[10–19] At the beginning of v. 10 it is said (RSV) that his (i.e. Seleucus's) sons shall wage war. If this translation is correct (the $k^e t\bar{\imath}b$ and the LXX read the singular, but the $q^e r\bar{e}$, Theod. and Vulg. probably correctly read the plural), the sons intended must be Seleucus III Keraunus (226–223) and Antiochus III the Great (226–187) and this would seem to imply that the new attack on Egypt began in Seleucus III's reign. Of this we have no confirmatory knowledge from elsewhere. Seleucus III's father, Seleucus II had been carrying on hostilities for some time against his brother Antiochus Hierax in Asia Minor and at the time of his death had been confronted by the Pergamene power under Attalus. His successor now crossed the Taurus and attacked Attalus, though with what success or failure we do not know. An early death, probably by assassination, terminated his reign. The biblical writer may have known or believed that Seleucus III began to prepare for the attack upon Egypt which his successor was to launch.

At all events the verbs very quickly become singular and a description is given of the campaigns of Antiochus (not yet 'the Great') in Syria and Palestine during the years 219 and 218 B C. The first move against Ptolemy IV Philopator had been made in 221 B C, but after that Antiochus was for some time busy in the east dealing with Molon, the rebel satrap of Media. The campaign of 219 B C was occupied with the recapture of the port of Antioch, Seleucia, which had been in Egyptian hands since it fell to Ptolemy Euergetes, and with securing the Phoenician coast as far south as Ptolemais (Acre). Part of this operation had to be repeated the following year in consequence of the surprising carelessness of Antiochus, after which he turned east and, crossing into Trans-Jordan, gained control of the region to as far south as Rabbath-Ammon. During the winter 218–217 B C the Seleucid army seems to have occupied the fortresses of Gaza and Raphia near the Egyptian border. It is all these military operations which are compared in the text to a flood. The last words of v. 10 seem to refer to the advance of Antiochus in the spring of 217 B C to Gaza or Raphia, but scarcely as far as to Pelusium.

In 11.11–12 there is a rather vague description of the astonishing battle of Raphia in which the pusillanimous Ptolemy IV Philopator for once roused himself to action and, after a desperate struggle, defeated the Seleucid army with enormous slaughter. Ptolemy, however, did not press his advantage, and eventually Antiochus surrendered Coele-Syria to him and made peace. The peace lasted for many years (fourteen or more) during which Antiochus recovered for the Seleucid house control of the essential regions of Asia Minor, though Pergamos under Attalus maintained its independence, and, by a series of brilliant campaigns which took him as far as Hyrcania, Bactria and the borders of India, reconquered the Seleucid eastern empire. These successes earned Antiochus the title 'the Great' by which he became known to history. He was more distinguished, however, by military daring than by organizing ability and statesmanship.

In v. 13 it is described how Antiochus assembled his troops and resolved on war against Egypt. Ptolemy IV Philopator had died in 205 B C and had been succeeded by a mere child who became Ptolemy V Epiphanes. A year or two later the armies of Antiochus were on the march. An Egyptian army under the capable Aetolian soldier Scopas, who, after being leader of the Aetolian league, had had to take refuge in Egypt, had overrun Coele-Syria. The clash between the two armies took place near the sources of the Jordan at Panion ('precinct of Pan'), where the city of Paneas was later built and in still later times was refounded as Caesarea Philippi. Scopas was defeated and, with what remained of his army, took refuge in the fortress of Sidon, while the control of Palestine passed definitely into the hands of the Seleucid king, an operation which was complete by 198 B C. The course of this operation, unfortunately, is somewhat obscure and it is not easy to be sure about the correct interpretation of every clause of the account given here. The end of v. 13 seems to refer to the enormous baggage train which accompanied Antiochus and would include the fresh supply of elephants which he had secured from India as a result of his eastern campaigns. In v. 14 those who resisted the king of the south may include both disaffected people in Egypt, who took advantage of the minority of the king, and Philip of Macedon, who, in the course of his struggle with Rome and with Attalus of Pergamos, had allied himself with Antiochus and so was hostile to Egypt. 'The men of violence among your own people' must have been Jews who chose at this time to take the side of Antiochus, though whether or not they were, as Schlatter suggested, the Tobiadae, who had farmed the taxes of Palestine under the Ptolemies but were now in favour of the Seleucid house and were opposed to the high-priest Onias III, it is not possible to say definitely. The phrase 'in order to fulfil the vision' is puzzling. It seems better to say that we do not really know what is referred to than to conclude with Jeffery (p. 520) that the meaning is 'that unwittingly by their action they are fulfilling a prediction in this vision of Daniel'. Surely this would apply to any of the 'prophecies' in this chapter. Whoever these violent men were, however, Jeffery is probably correct in his conjecture that their failure was due to the activities of Scopas. The interpretation of v. 15 which best suits what is known to have happened is that the fortified town which was besieged by Antiochus was Sidon, where Scopas held out until famine compelled him to surrender. Ptolemy's army had been unable to relieve him. Antiochus occupied Jerusalem and was welcomed by the Jews as a deliverer. His presence in Judaea is indicated by the words 'He shall stand in the glorious land' (cf. 8.9). What follows in the Massoretic Text would, if the text can be accepted, mean 'and destruction in his hand'. A slight emendation gives the more satisfactory sense that he gained control of the whole of Judaea (so RSV). Verse 17 tells how Antiochus contemplated the conquest of Egypt itself. Although that did not take place, it is known that Antiochus took the Philistine city of Gaza by storm, but eventually came to terms with Ptolemy and sealed the treaty by betrothing his daughter, Cleopatra, to the young Egyptian king. Cleopatra is called literally 'the daughter of women,' an expression that may mean no more than 'a woman'. Montgomery (p. 441) suggests that, 'The term may express the essence of femininity, i.e. the Woman, *par excellence*.' However that may be, Cleopatra undoubtedly played a notable part in Egyptian public life right up to the time of her death in 173 BC, and it may be that the curious expression used of her here represents some honorific title. Antiochus evidently hoped that through Cleopatra he would get the chance to interfere in Egyptian affairs. Actually it worked the other way, as she proved loyal to the country of her adoption. In spite of the treaty which had been made Antiochus continued to attack Egyptian possessions in Asia Minor and elsewhere. In v. 18 there is given a very sketchy summary of the events of the year 197–190 BC which followed the decisive defeat of Philip of Macedon by the Romans at Cynoscephalae. Antiochus first tried to secure as much of the eastern shore of the Aegean as he could, being limited by the opposition of Rhodes and Pergamos, both in alliance with Rome. He then crossed over to the Thracian Chersonese to claim the former satrapy of Lysimachus who had been defeated by Seleucus Nicator. At Lysimachia he encountered the representatives of Rome who warned him not to interfere either with the cities in Asia Minor owing allegiance to Ptolemy or with the former possessions of Philip of Macedon which Rome claimed by right of victory. The free cities were to remain free. Antiochus was indignant that Rome should interfere in affairs in Asia which he thought concerned the Romans as little as Italy concerned Antiochus. The real bone of contention, however, was Greece which Antiochus had threatened by his invasion of Europe. After a delay of several years —years marked by indecision on both sides—Antiochus in 192 BC landed in Greece which had been evacuated by the Romans. Neglecting the wise advice of Hannibal who had joined him, Antiochus proved his incompetence as a general and in 191 BC was defeated by the Romans at Thermopylae. The Romans followed up this victory by winning a naval battle over the fleet of Antiochus with the help of the Pergamene and Rhodian fleets. The following year, 190 BC, the Roman consul, Lucius Cornelius Scipio, inflicted a crushing defeat on the huge but cumbrous army of Antiochus at Magnesia near Smyrna and earned the title 'Asiaticus' to match the title 'Africanus' conceded to his more famous brother Publius after his defeat of Hannibal. This victory meant the end for Antiochus so far as his dominion west of the Halys and the Taurus was concerned.

The concluding clause of v. 18 is difficult in the original. A slight emendation would give the meaning that the consul's defeat of Antiochus at Magnesia prevented Antiochus from repeating his challenge. Bevan, however, may be right in his ingenious suggestion (pp.

184–5) based on the LXX: 'He shall requite his insults seven-fold.' It has been pointed out that the word *qaṣin* applied to Scipio is used elsewhere of both a civil and a military leader (cf. Josh. 10.24; Judg. 11.6; Isa. 3.6, 7) and is therefore singularly appropriate as the term for a Roman consul. In v. 19 it is stated ironically that Antiochus who had been trying to capture strongholds in the west had now to content himself with the strongholds of his own proper territories. The concluding words refer to his banal end (187 BC), for all that he had been Antiochus the Great, as he was attempting to plunder the treasury of a temple in the wilds of Luristan (Elymais: Elam).

[11.20] Verse 20 refers to the twelve-year reign of Seleucus IV Philopator (187–175 BC) who inherited the shattered finances of Antiochus and had therefore to refrain from foreign adventures. The obscure words of this verse seem to refer to the sending of the minister Heliodorus on a tax-gathering mission, in the course of which he made the notorious attempt on the temple treasury at Jerusalem (described in II Macc. 3) in which he was foiled by a vision and nearly lost his life. Bevan prefers (pp. 185–6) to rearrange the words slightly, making the term 'exactor' (collector of tribute) apply to Seleucus himself— 'and there shall arise in his place an exactor who shall cause the royal dignity to pass away'. The reference would thus be to the decline in royal dignity during the reign of Seleucus and only indirectly to the mission of Heliodorus. The latter eventually headed a conspiracy which brought about the murder of Seleucus—an inglorious end for a king.

[21–45] With v. 21 the author comes to contemporary history and without more ado characterizes the reigning Seleucid as a contemptible person, unworthy of the royal honour which he had seized. Antiochus, who had been sent as a hostage to Rome after the Battle of Magnesia, had been exchanged for Demetrius, the elder son of Seleucus Philopator, not long before the latter's death. During a short residence in Athens he had actually got himself elected to the chief magistracy. 'Then', as Bevan (*House of Seleucus*, vol II, p. 126) puts it, 'whilst playing at being the successor of Pericles the prospect suddenly opened before him of being the successor of Seleucus Nicator.' Demetrius was the lawful heir, but another conspiracy to seize power was on foot, that of Heliodorus, ostensibly to put Seleucus's younger son on the throne. With the help of the Pergamene power Antiochus won the contest. That trickery was involved was widely believed. Antiochus was able to bear down all opposition and almost immediately launched his hellenizing policy. One of the first victims was Onias III, the high-priest in Jerusalem (cf. Dan. 9.26), whose brother Jason, a prominent member of the hellenizing party among the Jews, by offering Antiochus an enormous bribe, procured the deposition of Onias and his own appointment to the high-priesthood. That was in 175 BC. Onias was murdered in 170 BC, but before that Jason had been out-bidden and replaced by Menelaus. The author, however, does not go into details but speaks generally of how Antiochus, starting with a small body of supporters and with the aid of the Pergamene alliance, established himself in a position of power almost before people realized what was happening. What precisely is referred to in v. 24 we do not know for certain, but the words are best interpreted, not of Antiochus's Egyptian campaigns, which came later, but of his operations in Syria and Palestine by means of which he got the better of his opponents. With a different rendering from that sug-gested above (p. 147) of a difficult word and placing, Bevan gets the translation for the first clause of v. 24: 'and by stealth he will attack the mightiest men of (each) province'. In support of this view he refers to 8.25: 'He shall destroy many at a time of security.' Cf. Jeffery (p. 526) for other possibilities. The author speaks here of one well-known characteristic of Antiochus, his lavish and indeed crazy generosity to his supporters in distributing among them booty taken on his various campaigns. But perhaps the most important words to take note of are the concluding words of v. 24, 'but only for a time'. These express the writer's quiet confidence, which he would com-municate to his readers, that, powerful and successful as this strange, enigmatic tyrant is, a limit has been set to his activities—by God.

In 11.25ff. our author makes his own important contribution to the tangled history of Antiochus's campaigns in Egypt and of his dealings with the Jews. In 173 BC the restraining influence of the queen-mother, Cleopatra, in Egypt was removed and two of the entourage of the young king Ptolemy VI Philometor began their machinations to bring on a war between Egypt and Syria with a view to recovering Palestine for Egypt. In 169 BC they invaded Palestine but suffered a crushing defeat by Antiochus, whose army captured the frontier fortress of Pelusium and presently occupied Memphis. Ptolemy Philometor had already attempted flight to Samothrace but had fallen into the hands of Antiochus, and his younger brother had been made king as Ptolemy Euergetes at Alexandria. In v. 26 it seems to be suggested that Ptolemy Philometor's collapse was due to the bad advice he had received. The two kings who planned mischief, presumably against each other, while sitting at the same table are Antiochus and Ptolemy Philometor. Of the dishonest intentions of the former who was plotting to seize the power in Egypt for himself we have no doubt, but that the boy king who was under his control was also playing a double game there is no evidence apart from this passage. Then once again comes the reminder that a limit is set to all this intrigue and, though other suggestions have been made, it is likely that the author is here also thinking of the final crisis which God is to bring about. In v. 28 we are told of Antiochus's departure from Egypt carrying off vast booty, though actually his calling off of his campaign was a confession of failure. Indeed he was in a furious rage which was increased by the news that Jason had made an attempt to recover the high-priesthood from Menelaus. If we are to believe the statement in II Macc. 4.21–22, Antiochus had paid a friendly state visit to Jerusalem in Onias's time. He now paid a second visit in anger, plundered the temple and massacred many of the inhabitants. Worse, however, was to come later.

The second invasion of Egypt was also, it is hinted, included in God's overruling providence. As soon as Antiochus had left Egypt the two young kings composed their quarrel and Antiochus found his subtle measures for controlling Egypt thwarted. Once more he invaded the country and might have captured Alexandria but for the fateful intervention of Rome, now set free from its preoccupation elsewhere by the victory over Perseus of Macedon at Pydna in June 168 B C. C. Papillius Laenas arrived in Egypt and Antiochus had the bitter experience of being ordered out of Egypt by an authority which he dared not disobey. He left the circle which the Roman ambassador drew round him on the sand a beaten man. It is clear that it is this famous incident which is alluded to in v. 30, Kittim here being a designation for the Romans, as in the Commentary on Habakkuk, whereas in I Macc. 1.1 it is a name for the Greeks. The author of the Book of Daniel seems here to be adopting the same method of interpretation as the author of the Habakkuk scroll, since the language he uses suggests that he is giving Num. 24.24 a contemporary interpretation. The Syriac version speaks of the legions coming from the land of the Kittaeans.

In what follows there is given an account of the persecution of the faithful Jews in Jerusalem which seems to have been carried out in two stages. First there was the punitive expedition of Apollonius who, in addition to massacring many of the inhabitants and destroying numerous buildings, fortified the so-called *akra* dominating the temple and garrisoned it with foreign soldiers. (The 'fortress' or citadel of v. 31 is probably not the *akra* but the temple itself regarded as a fortified area.) It is made clear that there were two parties among the Jews, those who were determined to remain faithful to the ancestral laws, and endure persecution, and the hellenizers (cf. I Macc. 1.13–15). Secondly there was the positive interference with Jewish religious practice not only in Jerusalem but throughout Judaea (cf. I Macc. 1.44ff.), and the actual desecration of the temple by the suspension of the daily offering and the setting up of the abomination of desolation (cf. on 9.27) and apparently the identification of Israel's God with Zeus Olympius. In v. 32 there is a reference to the ways in which the hellenizers were brought to open apostacy. Heaton (p. 236) gives the literal translation of the second half of the verse 'The people that know their God shall be strong, and do' and comments: 'This splendid statement draws its strength from the two verbs "know" and "do". The first means to be in a real relationship with God, that is, one which is personal and intimate; the second could almost be rendered "and get on with it".'

With reference to v. 33 an important issue of interpretation must be raised. Heaton (p. 236–7), in agreement with RSV, translates the first word as 'they that be wise among the people' and thinks that the reference is to the class of scribes and sages to which the writer of the book himself belonged and who 'equally devoted their learning to the instruction of the many in true Judaism and were no less opposed than their successors' (i.e. the *Ḥasidim*) 'to the infiltration of hellenistic culture'. It seems more probable that the words should be taken more narrowly and translated 'the wise leaders of the people', meaning those who came forward in the crisis and paid, many of them with their lives, for their courage and loyalty. The 'little help' of v. 34 is supposed to refer to the Maccabees (so Porphyry), but clearly the writer is more impressed by the action of the martyrs who proved their loyalty in the fires of persecution and contributed to the purifying of the community. It is hinted in v. 34 that not all those who joined in the movement of resistance were sincere. Once again reference is made to the limit appointed by God, this time to the period of persecution—an expression of faith from the very middle of the dark days.

In 11.36ff. the Jewish writer goes on to describe what was for him the appallingly blasphemous pretensions of Antiochus, possibly expressed in so many words. Pagan writers tend to emphasize his zeal for religion and his patronage of temples. There is doubtless some substance in the charge that he ignored the gods of his ancestors and Tammuz, i.e. 'the one beloved by women' (cf. Ezek. 8.14), and he certainly plundered temples. But what impressed the pious Jew was not so much the worship of Zeus Olympius which he introduced everywhere as the fact that he identified himself with Zeus and assumed the title Theos Epiphanes, the manifest God (cf. evidence of coins). This to a Jew was sheerest blasphemy and clearly a challenge to God which he could not ignore, but which demanded his intervention. All might go well with the blasphemer for a time, since this was the period of the Wrath. That God is indeed on the side of those who at whatever cost oppose the deification of man, whatever form it takes, is the truth in the conviction which the writer expresses here. But that period also had an end. In v. 38 there is a curious statement which is usually interpreted as a reference to the fact that Antiochus built a temple at Antioch to Jupiter Capitolinus. The Hebrew of the first clause of v. 39 is very obscure but perhaps the translation 'he shall man his strongest fortresses with the people of a foreign god' hits the meaning, a possible reference to the foreign garrisons in Jerusalem and other Jewish towns. That Antiochus distributed favours to those who took his side in the quarrel is understandable (cf. I Macc. 3.36).

It should be said at this point that vv. 36–39 so clearly are applicable to what is known of the career of Antiochus Epiphanes that we may confidently reject the view that these verses are a prophecy of Antichrist. Such a view is based on *a priori* reasoning and does not arise out of sober exposition of the text. Indeed it is theologically valueless.

At v. 40 the writer passes from pseudo-prophecy to genuine prediction as is shown by the fact that he is speaking of the eschatological event or at least of events immediately preceding it. He forecasts a whirlwind invasion of Egypt by land and sea for which there is no reliable evidence elsewhere. He also speaks of an invasion of Palestine in the course of which large numbers will be slaughtered. Why Edom, Moab and Ammon are thought of as escaping it is impossible to say with certainty. The writer may merely mean that the invasion will pass to the west of the Jordan and Dead Sea. A conquest

of Egypt to its farthest limits is predicted and the securing by Antiochus of the fabulous wealth of that land. And then the writer, possibly
inspired by the prophecy of Isaiah (10.32–34), as Bentzen (p. 83)
suggests, or by the incident of Sennacherib's retreat from Jerusalem
(Isa. 37.36ff.; II Kings 19.35ff.), describes the departure of Antiochus
as the result of rumours from east and north where in those days the
Parthian threat loomed large. It is not surprising that the death of
Antiochus is forecast as about to take place somewhere between
Jerusalem and the sea in the area where prophecy had been wont to
stage the final climax (see Ezek. 38.14–16; 39.2–4; Joel 3.2). In
actual fact Antiochus did shortly come to a miserable end through
a mysterious disease at Tabae in Persia after an abortive plundering
expedition in Luristan where his father Antiochus the Great had
perished. Attempts to reconcile this passage in Daniel with the well-
attested facts of history are a waste of time. The critic, however, is
grateful for this only in part fulfilled prophecy of Antiochus's death,
inasmuch as it has made possible the accurate dating of the Book of
Daniel. It must have been written shortly before the death of Antiochus and the rededication of the temple by Judas Maccabaeus (*circa*
165–164 BC).

The first four verses of chapter 12 are the completion of the long
section which began with chapter 10. They give in remarkably brief
compass and restrained language the writer's expectation of what the
divinely appointed end would be like. It would be a climax of which
Israel would be the centre, as is shown by the fact that Michael, the
patron angel of Israel, is to play the decisive part on God's behalf.
The great tribulation will come to a head but Israel will escape, all
those in Israel, that is to say, whose names are written in the book of
life (see Ex. 32.32; Isa. 4.3; Ps. 69.29; cf. also Phil. 4.3; Rev. 3.5).
God already knows his own. And then comes the remarkable prediction of a resurrection, of which the only real parallel in the Old
Testament is to be found in another late passage (Isa. 26.19). It
depends on the interpretation of the word 'many' whether we are to
think of a general or a limited resurrection as having been in the
writer's mind. It seems wisest to suppose that he is not primarily
concerned here with the whole problem of life after death and certainly not with the fate of the individual as opposed to that of the
righteous community, since it is undoubtedly the coming kingdom
of God which he has in view. But, in the stress of a persecution believed to be the prelude to the final consummation, he seems to have

felt that God must do justice on the one hand to the martyrs for the faith and on the other to the apostates. He has a word of promise too for the wise leaders who contributed so much to the resistance of the faithful. (Cf. Isa. 53.11 which may have influenced the wording here.) It is a flash of inspired insight like that which called forth the great utterance 'Shall not the Judge of all the earth do right?' (Gen. 18.25). To read into it a doctrine of heaven and hell is probably to go too far, though undoubtedly our author prepared the way for the doctrine of a Final Judgment and the irrevocable separation of the good from the evil. But primarily what we have here is witness to the springing up of a great hope rather than statements which we must accept just as they stand and endeavour to build into a system of dogmatic truth. Heaton shows real wisdom when he writes (p. 247): 'If we owe a debt of gratitude to the writer for breaking the silence of the grave and affirming the communion of saints as part of the purpose of God, we must at the same time regret that he did not rise above the crude demand for strict retribution, which runs through the OT like an acrid stream.'

In accordance with the fiction Daniel is bidden seal the book, since its contents are to be kept secret until the time of final crisis to which it refers draws near, i.e. till the time when the book was actually written. Montgomery (p. 473) helpfully compares Rev. 22.10 where the command is given not to seal the book since the time of fulfilment was near at hand when it was written. Sealing and concealing are necessary parts of the fiction of attributing a prophecy pseudonymously to some figure of the past. The concluding words of the verse are uncertain in meaning. Montgomery (pp. 473–4) detects an allusion to Amos 8.12 which speaks of the famine of the Word of the Lord and translates 'many shall run to and fro that knowledge may increase', the search being a vain one. A slight emendation of the last word would give, instead of 'and knowledge shall increase' the translation 'and disasters shall increase', and this is to some extent supported by I Macc. 1.9 which may have this verse in mind.

[12.5–13] These verses form an epilogue to the book rather than a late addition to it. We are recalled to the situation of Daniel near the banks of the Ulai. Two more angelic figures appear, possibly, as Bevan (p. 204) suggests, to witness the oath which the man dressed in linen is about to take in reply to the question which either Daniel

or one of the newcomers is about to put as to the time when these
portentous events which have been recounted will come to an end.
The angel gives the answer of 7.25, i.e. 'a time, two times, and half a
time', and confirms it with a mighty oath. A slight emendation (given
by Bevan, pp. 205–6) would give the translation 'when the power of
the oppressor of the holy people comes to an end', and this would
probably refer to the passing of Antiochus as the sign that will be
given of the coming of the end. Daniel asks for further information
and the request is refused. Yet he is told that the distinction between
the saints who are purified and the wicked who continue in wickedness will be maintained right up to the end. But the faithful will be
able to look to their wise leaders for guidance.

As an alternative to the view taken above in the comment on 7.25
it may be suggested that the periods of 1,290 days and 1,335 days,
which are usually interpreted as successive corrections of the 1,150
days of 8.14, when the end did not come at the time originally expected but faith rose above disappointment (so Gunkel and others),
might be regarded as marking successive stages in the events leading
up to the final climax. There is, it must be confessed, some difficulty
in seeing how urgent corrections, such as these would be, could have
been added to a book that had just been issued, even though in a
limited number of copies. This would apply even to the broadsheet
theory suggested above. Of course it remains possible, though in the
present writer's view improbable, that vv. 11 and 12 are not from
the pen of the author of the Book of Daniel at all but are glosses of
some later scribe who wished to adjust the number of days to the
known facts of history. We do not have enough data to check up on
this. It seems preferable to believe that behind these mysterious
calculations an unquenchable faith was active which kindled and maintained a like faith in many who were living through dark and calamit-
ous days. This reflection may lead us to be more charitable towards
those who foolishly misuse the Book of Daniel today by employing it
as a key to future events, but proclaim thereby their conviction that
God is indeed at work in the events of our time. At the same time they
would be wiser to recognize that it was just because the author of the
Book of Daniel was primarily speaking to his own day that he can
with profit be read in ours.

At the end of his commentary (p. 87) Bentzen finely says, 'While
the Maccabees strengthened political messianism, Daniel worked for
an attitude which prepared the way for the Christian attitude as it

was embodied in Jesus when he, following Isaiah 53, saw confronting him the task of the Son of Man in the atoning death of the Redeemer. . . .' The faith which inspired the Book of Daniel is still essentially the faith of the Church. But the witness of the book is important, not in spite of, but precisely because of, its limitation in time and circumstance. It can still inspire and instruct us, because it mirrors the faith of men who believed and endured in a definite situation which determined their limited perspective.

The Book of Daniel finishes on a peaceful note. Daniel is bidden go now to meet the end which awaits him in the grave. Yet that will not be a final end for him, for he too will have a share in the great consummation of the age. And so the past as well as the present will have its share in the glorious future.

SUPPLEMENT
TO THE SECOND EDITION

SINCE THIS COMMENTARY was originally written a number of new ones have appeared, in particular three of outstanding quality, namely those of Plöger, Delcor and Lacocque. The author has learned a great deal from the study of all three and in this revised edition wishes to acknowledge his indebtedness to them. After a period of years one can stand back from one's own work and take a more objective view of it, recognizing that, with fuller knowledge and upon maturer reflection, one might have said certain things differently or with a change of emphasis. *Dies diem docet!* Of the many merits of the commentaries mentioned above one might single out Plöger's detailed documentation of the Aramaic forms, with references to Bauer-Leander's Aramaic Grammar which students must find invaluable, the same scholar's careful and penetrating study of the interrelationship of the various chapters of Daniel (e.g. the links between chs. 2 and 7, 3 and 6, 4 and 5 and the interlocking of 1–6 and 7–12), Lacocque's wide knowledge of all the relevant ancient literature, in particular the Rabbinic parallels, and the service rendered by both Delcor and Lacocque in introducing readers to important French discussions. This shorter commentary, which, as Klaus Koch remarks, appeared at a time when in Germany at least apocalyptic was not a very popular subject, had to conform to the general pattern of the ATD series. Although it was based on a careful study of the original text, Aramaic and Hebrew, the 'working' could only be exhibited minimally in the eventual publication. As it is, the book is about fifty per cent longer than it was originally supposed to be. The elaborate philological and textual apparatus which is to be expected in the larger commentaries had to be excluded, attention being concentrated on the religious and theological significance of the Book of Daniel, on the basis, to be sure, of a scientific treatment calculated to reassure discriminating readers and to warn certain others against the misuse to which this part of Scripture has been especially liable.

In this new edition a number of necessary corrections and brief additions have been introduced into the translation and the body of the commentary without involving serious dislocation. It has seemed desirable, however, to take some account of more recent publications, not to speak of the wider studies of the author. As an alternative to a complete rewriting of the commentary it has been judged preferable to add this supplement, which will have the merit of underlining rather than concealing changes of view and will serve to set certain matters in a wider context. Of particular importance in the latter connection have been the massive volumes of Martin Hengel's *Judaism and Hellenism*, which have opened up new lines of enquiry and have shed a flood of light on the history of the period to which the Book of Daniel belongs. In addition a great many other articles and books have had to be perused. Special attention must be drawn to a new number of the Harvard Semitic Monographs by John J. Collins entitled *The Apocalyptic Vision of the Book of Daniel*, a book which is undoubtedly one of the most impressive recent contributions to a perplexing subject. There have been moreover the discoveries at Qumran which have made abundantly clear the importance of the Book of Daniel for the Essene community and which help to some extent in the relative dating of the other apocalyptic books. It is now beyond doubt that there must be some connection between the tradition about Nebuchadnezzar's madness in chapter 4 and the tradition about Nabonidus, though what exactly the connection was remains obscure.

It is a commonly held view that what one ought to aim at in a commentary is to expound as clearly as possible the meaning of the text commented upon, leaving the reader free to make his own reaction. The result can be that, especially in the case of an ancient text, the thought being expounded can be made to seem so alien that the modern reader feels that he is being asked to interest himself in a piece of antiquarianism. This kind of treatment differs from the way in which a philosopher proceeds in dealing with a text; he tries, if at all possible, to get inside the mind of the writer and see things from his point of view and so make the argument come alive. He assumes that it is by way of seeking to enter into what may at first sight seem to be an alien process of thought that one can carry on and help others to carry on the job of thinking philosophically. Similarly, in literary criticism, the critic seeks himself and would help his readers so to enter by imagination into pieces of literature emanating from experience of life which may be very different from their own that their own experience is enlarged and deepened. It might be maintained too that the historian, as distinguished from the mere chronicler, should strive to enable his readers to share his own vital relationship with the past.

If the above argument is not completely wrong, then should it not be accepted as possible that, when we turn to the Old Testament, for all that it comes to us from a far distant time and out of a very different culture from our own, we should hope to enter into a living relationship with many parts of it? There will inevitably be many exceptions, where we encounter closed doors that we may not open. But that there is much in this book that we can use in our own lives without misuse is surely borne out by experience. We become persons in relationship to others and we must not limit unduly the possibilities of such creative relationships. At the close of his book *Inspiration and Revelation in the Old Testament* (1946) H. Wheeler Robinson wrote about 'the once-living, vibrating, and dynamic religion of Israel': 'Let us constantly remind ourselves that this religion, like any other, can be understood only from within, or through a sympathy that makes us its "resident aliens" (*gerim*).' Eichrodt too declares that there must be a certain congeniality between the interpreter of an ancient religion and his subject.

It may be admitted, of course, that the relevance of Scripture is not a constant quantity; a portion of Scripture may become meaningful with a change in circumstances, or, on the other hand, may cease to speak to us today. This happens to be particularly true of the Book of Daniel, which presents us with peculiar difficulties because of the outlook on history characteristic of it. In this connection the author has found himself drawn back to a book originally published in 1922 which was the first to set him thinking about the problem of apocalyptic. This was A. C. Welch's *Visions of the End*, a study of the Books of Daniel and Revelation. In writing this book Welch had especially in mind the needs of the generation which had been through the cataclysm of the first world war. He recognized fully moreover the difficulty which apocalyptic writings presented to minds conditioned by the assumptions of modern science, so that religious men, however much they might long for a renewal of faith, felt that there was something wrong about expecting on God's part 'an intervention which was to force goodness on a forgetful world'. 'Spiritual ends', Welch added, 'must only be reached in a spiritual way.'

Those were the days when the optimistic belief in progress no longer carried conviction with thinking men and questions were being asked about the method of God's control of history and what he planned to bring about, if one could still believe in divine providence at all. Welch argued that the two biblical apocalyptic books 'spring from two generations which were called to undergo a real travail of soul. . . . They are not the casual product of the human mind, or even the outcome of its effort to think sincerely about the universe in which it finds itself. They are the product of the definitely religious spirit, struggling to assert itself in an untoward universe, and seeking to express for its comfort and strength the hopes and the faith which enabled it to maintain itself above the flux and the change of a world which was even more indifferent than usual to the summons of spiritual realities. The human soul, in conflict with a difficult time, was declaring how it found its nurture and its victory in the certainty of the eternal world'.

Is it surprising that, in the aftermath of a second world war, when confusion and perplexity after the lapse of many years are still worldwide, much of what Welch wrote more than half a century ago might well have been written today? It is significant that in 1970 there appeared Klaus Koch's challenging, if inconclusive, book *Ratlos vor der Apokalyptik*, which is misleadingly entitled in English *The Rediscovery of Apocalyptic*. Koch drew attention to Käsemann's essay, 'The Beginnings of Christian Theology',[1] which had appeared ten years earlier, and contained the thought-provoking assertion that 'Apocalyptic was the mother of all Christian theology'. He further referred to the movement in theology associated with the names of theologians like Moltmann and Pannenberg, who, turning away from existential preoccupation with the timeless present, have sought to direct attention to the future with its divine possibilities and so to move apocalyptic from a marginal to a central position in the theological debate.

This is not the place to enter into the intricacies of that debate or to speculate on its probable outcome. Suffice it to have indicated that interest in a book like Daniel is probably not unrelated to some felt analogy between the time when it was originally written and the

[1] 'Die Anfänge christlicher Theologie', *Zeitschrift für Theologie und Kirche* 57, 1960, pp. 162–85; Engl. trans. in E. Käsemann, *New Testament Questions of Today*, 1969, pp. 82–107; citation on p. 102.

present time when it seems to speak once more a relevant word. It is true that there is a real danger here. In the past the Book of Daniel has suffered from misunderstanding and consequent gross misuse, and the history of its interpretation has often unduly reflected the political interests and prejudices of those who have appealed to its supposed authority. There were indeed times when approval was transferred from the Maccabees to Antiochus. In Bickermann's *Der Gott der Makkabäer* there is a very interesting account of the centuries-long history of the book's interpretation. Yet when one comes to the book today with a controlled imagination and seeks to determine the conflicting motives and concerns of the original contestants in the struggle which the book reflects, one may perhaps hear it speaking a word which will stimulate the kind of thinking which God can use to further his purposes. It is to those engaged in mental and spiritual conflict for its guidance that Scripture may yield that guidance: one has to commit oneself to the consequences of decision. It would be foolish to underrate the difficulty of achieving this kind of biblical interpretation. The commentary betrays very tentative moves in this direction in the hope that the gap between then and now may in some measure be bridged and some vital commerce of mind with mind be achieved.

It is obvious that to enter into the meaning of the Book of Daniel in such a way as to make its thought and spiritual struggle come alive, the more one can learn about its context the better. Acknowledgement has already been made of the debt owed to Martin Hengel, who in his book *Judaism and Hellenism* has brought together a tremendous wealth of evidence to illuminate the Hellenistic world which encompassed Judaea in the third and second centries BC and the influence of which must have been pervasive in one way or another on the various levels of the Jewish population. Much of that influence, as it affected the humble peasantry, the artisans and petty traders, must have been mainly of a materialistic kind, but, wherever men's minds were open to new ideas or sufficiently aware of them to react positively for them or against them, the total climate of opinion must have been inescapable. Even those who reacted against it must have been influenced by it. In his commentary the author made some allowance for this and avoided the mistake of assuming a complete polarization between the so-called Hellenizers, who make their appearance at the very beginning of the First Book of Maccabees and are regarded as renegades, and those who cling faithfully to their

ancestral religion with its strict regulations and rally to the resistance
movement headed by Mattathias and his sons. Hengel has made it
clearer than ever that the very book, which has come down to us out
of the heart of the crisis and favours the anti-Hellenistic resistance, at
the same time shows an awareness of, and a certain absence of
hostility to, the bigger world to which Judaea belonged, and refrains
from condemning outright all the claims that the world was making,
especially upon younger men who felt the call to serve it. The book,
moreover, shows, in part at least, signs of belonging to the general
type of Hellenistic literature with its mixture of prose and poetry (see
chs. 2 and 7), though the same phenomenon is to be found in some
other parts of the Old Testament. Again the views about the media
of revelation are by no means peculiar to Jewish literature. Hengel
has shown it to be highly probable that Phoenicia with its international trade, and especially with its close links with the Greek
world, must have been one of the main channels by which Greek
ideas flowed into Judaea.

In his exposition of chapters 1–6, while recognizing that the
so-called court stories contained therein were similar to the Joseph-
Novelle in Genesis and a number of stories in the Apocrypha and in
the Haggada or in eastern tales like that of Aḥikar, the author was at
pains to distinguish them from the typical haggadic story by the fact
that, by being linked with the second half of the Book of Daniel, they
had communicated to them something of its atmosphere of crisis.
While the author would still hold to this opinion, he was perhaps
unduly influenced by the view of H. H. Rowley, who saw in each of
the first six chapters signs of their having been composed *ad hoc* with
recognizable references to the persecution under Antiochus Epiphanes. While it is still probably true that the Book of Daniel taken
as a whole was designed as a tract for a certain time, more weight
should perhaps have been given to the arguments of those who
favoured an earlier, independent authorship for the stories of events
at the heathen court, because they were impressed by the more
tolerant view of the non-Jewish world conveyed by them than is
reflected, let us say, in chapter 7 with its condemnation of the heathen
empires and in the picture of the Seleucid monarch with which we
are presented in the following chapters.

Hengel has made it abundantly clear that the Jews in the
Hellenistic period were aware of the intellectual movements of their
time and were influenced by them even when seeking to voice their

opposition. The somewhat austere figure of Daniel, which has been described as essentially Israel in exile, suggests how a gifted and enterprising Jew could, in the still wider world which succeeded the Babylonian and Persian, serve it to the very best of his ability and indeed exhibit his superiority, and yet would feel compelled to draw the line decisively as soon as any demand was made that would compromise his faith. The Tobiads were not the only representatives of Judaism out in the big world of opportunity. Inevitably one is inclined to concentrate on the corrupt side of Hellenism as illustrated in the half-Oriental Seleucid court and as aped by those in Jerusalem who resented the restrictions imposed by their ancestral faith and customs. One cannot but regret that the superficial side of Greek culture brought about a division among the Jewish people and led to what was virtually a civil war with one party seeking and obtaining the support of the suzerain state. It might conceivably have been otherwise if Greek culture had been represented by its better elements, which long afterwards played such an important part in the development of Christianity. While we should recognize the courage of the Maccabees and those who followed them, who dared everything to ensure the survival of the Jewish faith, we should not forget that Judaism in its resistance was compelled to take one more step towards an eventual isolation from the main stream of life.

For some time to come, however, we have to allow for the pervasive influence of Hellenism in producing a climate of opinion which made inevitable the circulation of new ideas. The emergence, for example, in Daniel of the belief in the possibility of a future life may have owed something to a movement of thought in the Hellenistic world, even though undoubtedly the main source of the hope was in Israel's own religion and experience. From the beginning too, as a result of influences from Egypt and Babylon, Israel's wisdom literature had an international flavour, but later contacts with both Ptolemaic and Seleucid culture, imbued with Greek ideas as both were, must have had far-reaching consequences in developing Jewish thought. As always, however, what was of most importance was not what was borrowed but the use that was made of it. It may be that ideas came from further east, from Babylonia and Persia for example, but these ideas were probably for the most part filtered through Hellenistic thought instead of being taken over direct, in a similar way to that in which Babylonian mythology in early days may well have reached Israel via Ugarit. Phoenicia, as we have seen, may have been the great clearing-house of ideas. All this is important for the interpretation of the Book of Daniel.

One of the most confusing debates in connection with the Book of Daniel, with which we have had to come to terms, concerns the affinities of the book. It was only to be expected that, after a large number of apocalyptic books were rescued from obscurity and edited and so made available for scholarly study, the obvious resemblances between them and the Book of Daniel should lead to their being regarded as a class. This influenced discussion as to the origin of the Book of Daniel. More attention was paid to what the Book of Daniel had in common with the other apocalypses than to what constituted its uniqueness. Moreover, the presence, as for example in the Book of Enoch, of an accumulation of varied learning gave an impression of the milieu from which apocalyptic emerged which was apt to lead to a misjudgment of the Book of Daniel. In his volume *Visions of the End*, already referred to, Welch suggested that 'it may be wiser . . . to interpret Daniel from his predecessors rather than from his successors'. In his commentary E. A. Heaton quotes this dictum of Welch with approval, and the author of this commentary was also persuaded by it to concentrate on the links between prophecy and Daniel.

The difference between his commentary and Heaton's is twofold. They differ somewhat in their view of the mythological colourings of the Book of Daniel, a matter which will be considered presently. On the question of the relation of Daniel to prophecy Heaton argues with some justification that certain of the features of late prophecy, which appear, for example, in Ezek. 38–39, in Joel and in Isa. 24–27, are absent from Daniel, and he instances the battle scenes and the elaborate pictures of the final kingdom. At the same time he recognizes that there is a link between the author of Daniel and his prophetic predecessors and admits the close connection the book has with the crisis out of which it arose. He lays particular emphasis, however, upon the ordinary beliefs in second-century Judaism upon which the author was drawing. Following possibly the lead of Aage Bentzen, he seeks to place Daniel in the wider context of Hebrew Wisdom, pointing out how, in the first main section of the book, Daniel is described as a sage whose God-given wisdom surpasses the wisdom of the court magicians of Babylon, just as Joseph showed a like superiority in Egypt. He claims that the author of Daniel stands in the main stream of normal Judaism, and illustrates this with reference to the Psalter and the Wisdom books, including Ecclesiasticus or the Wisdom of Ben Sira. It would be wrong to underestimate the value of Heaton's contribution to the debate about the affinities of the Book of Daniel. It may be that, in criticizing his position, the author of this commentary reacted too sharply against Heaton's point of view. Certainly the latter was to receive in due course a notable ally in Gerhard von Rad when that great scholar turned his attention to the Wisdom literature and claimed apocalyptic as a branch of Wisdom. Heaton states succinctly the view he shares with von Rad when he writes: 'It is evident that by the time of Ben Sira (c.180 BC), the sages had become the students, guardians and teachers of the *whole* Jewish tradition and that *all* Hebrew literature was now by adoption and interpretation the wisdom of the scribe'.

It may still be maintained, however, that, with full recognition of the way in which in the late period the different types of Hebrew literature must have interpenetrated each other, something is in danger of being lost sight of if we simply class Daniel with the Wisdom literature. Heaton certainly recognizes that there is a difference between the outlook on life of Ben Sira and that of the author of Daniel, but he is more impressed by the things that are common to them, and indeed much that he says is perfectly true and well worth saying. At the same time there may be justification for continuing to insist on the difference between the ethos of books like Proverbs and Ecclesiasticus on the one hand and the urgent concern of the author of Daniel with what he believes to be the imminent crisis of history on the other. It may be that the issue between Heaton and the author of this commentary is partly one of words, but one might be excused for thinking that it is possible to stretch the meaning of Wisdom so widely that important distinctions are in danger of being minimized.

The author was reinforced in his belief in the importance of the link between prophecy and Daniel by the appearance in 1965 of Plöger's commentary, which followed upon his earlier book *Theocracy and Eschatology*. Plöger was concerned to demonstrate that the Book of Daniel did not represent a sudden break with the past, as it had to a considerable extent been anticipated by the thought of Ezekiel and II Isaiah and late prophetic developments such as we find in III Isaiah, Joel and the so-called Isaiah-apocalypse (Isa. 24–27). One of the most interesting and persuasive features of Plöger's work is the way in which he develops his theory of a tension between the orthodox, theocratic outlook which he believes to be represented in the writings of the Chronicler, an essentially static view, and the dynamic view of those who cherished an eschatological hope and looked for an eventual establishment by God of his kingdom. This dynamic, eschatological trend Plöger associates with those among the Jews who in due course came to be known as the *Hasidim* and it is among them that he invites us to find the author of Daniel. There is a certain difficulty in accepting this view in that in I Maccabees (2.42 and 7.13–14) the *Hasidim* are represented either as being scribes or as associated closely with them, and that would suggest a pre-occupation with the Law. There is a very clear statement of the evidence about the *Hasidim* in Delcor's commentary. Indeed we are told very little about the *Hasidim* except that they threw in their lot with the Maccabees until in Alcimus the Aaronic high-priesthood was restored, whereupon they withdrew their support. Plöger, how-ever, may well be right and one may agree with him in linking Daniel with a developing line of thought which, as he has plausibly demonstrated, had already appeared in Hebrew prophecy.

At this point reference may be made to a useful distinction drawn by J. J. Collins in his recently published book entitled *The Apocalyptic Vision of the Book of Daniel*. He joins issue with von Rad in the latter's use of the word wisdom without qualification to cover very different things which ought to be distinguished. He proposes a distinction between proverbial wisdom and mantic wisdom. We can attribute mantic wisdom to Daniel as he is described in chapters 1–6 and in the later chapters as well, while there is not a trace of proverbial wisdom. Further he goes on to say that there is a closer connection between mantic wisdom and prophecy than between proverbial wisdom and mantic wisdom. One may be happy to accept what is a meaningful distinction.

A further plea for associating apocalyptic with prophecy, especially as it is represented in the Book of Daniel, is to be found in a mono-graph by Peter von der Osten-Sacken entitled *Die Apokalyptik in ihrem Verhältnis zu Prophetie und Weisheit* (1969) in which he investigates the origin of the strain of determinism which appears in Daniel. He traces it back to the Old Testament prophets with their certainty that Yahweh was the Lord of history and that his will would prevail. It was especially with II Isaiah that fresh emphasis was laid on Yahweh as Creator, though he remains as the One who is about to intervene decisively on the stage of history. The concept of deter-minism in nature appears in one book in the Old Testament, namely in Ecclesiastes or Qoheleth, and one might have expected that apocalyptic thought would have seized upon this new development. This, however did not happen. It is certainly true that, as apocalyptic developed, it drew to itself a great deal of miscellaneous learning— astronomical, astrological, geographical, meteorological, etc.—as is very obvious in a compilation like the Book of Enoch. But this is not true of the Book of Daniel, which is primarily concerned with a historical crisis. Certainly there is a development of angelology beyond what is found in the rest of the Old Testament, but this too is linked with history. Von der Osten-Sacken sums up his illuminating discussion in these words: 'Apocalyptic is a legitimate, even if late and peculiar, child of prophecy, which, although already in youth not without learning, has only with increasing age accepted the influence of Wisdom' (p. 63).

In fairness to von Rad's view of the connection between prophecy and Wisdom, a quotation may be permitted from Hengel, who is speaking of the late period (*Judaism and Hellenism* I, pp. 206–7): 'Prophetic consciousness and the learning acquired by wisdom were now inseparably intertwined. *The wise men acquired prophetic features, and the prophets became inspired wise men.* It should be noted here that for this late period "wisdom" is no less vague, general and therefore disputable than the word "apocalyptic". Essentially it could mean the most different forms of learning practised in schools, from the "Greek Wisdom" of the Hellenists to the casuistic distinctions of the *soperim* entrusted with the custody of the law, who laid the foundations of the Mishnaic law. "Apocalyptic wisdom" was marked off from other forms of wisdom by the fact that it rested on special revelations of God and therefore was granted only to a few elect. . . . The modern approach which wants to derive apocalyptic one-sidedly from wisdom or prophecy would have been almost incomprehensible to Ben Sira or to the Hasidic apocalyptists.' Well, there is no point in quarrelling about the use of the word 'wisdom', certainly not with a scholar with the tremendous range of knowledge possessed by Hengel. What really matters is that the author of Daniel, wise man or not, reveals a mind dominated by the imminence of crisis, a crisis in which God will vindicate himself. This conviction is related to what he believes to be a divinely-communicated interpretation of Jeremiah's prophecy about the seventy years of the exile, now to be understood as seventy weeks of years.

This brings us to a subject which, though mentioned in the com-

mentary, has not had sufficient justice done to it. Ginsberg's somewhat arbitrary handling of the question of the unity of chapter 7
probably resulted in less than justice being done to his discussion of
the appearance of the *pesher* method of interpretation in the Book of
Daniel. The *pesharim* found at Qumran ought to have prompted
more sensitivity to similar methods found elsewhere. The author of
Daniel betrays by the language he uses the fact that he saw in the
events of his time the fulfilment of scriptural texts of long ago,
Dan. 11.30 pointing back to Num. 24.24 (the Kittim actualized as
the Romans); Dan. 11.10 and 14 to Isa. 8.7 and Jer. 47.2; Dan. 11.36
to Isa. 10.23. This is in line with the crucial interpretation of Jer.
25.11ff. and 29.10 which is communicated by the angel in chapter 9
and is so central in the Book of Daniel. Perhaps most important of all
is Ginsberg's thesis put forward in his article 'The Oldest Interpretation of the Suffering Servant' (*VT* III/4, 1953, pp. 400-4), in which
he suggests that there is a definite echo in Dan. 12.3 of the famous
poem in Isa. 52.13-53.12. This is not to say that the author of
Daniel correctly interprets the song, if that is indeed his intention,
any more than he correctly interprets, let us say, the statement about
the ships of the Kittim in Numbers (see above). But it is indeed possible that Ginsberg is right in detecting a *pesher* here. Lacocque, who
lends his support to Ginsberg, in his commentary (pp. 150 and 152)
translates Dan. 10.1 as 'This word is true: there will be a great
servitude', and supposes an allusion in *pesher* style to Isa. 40.2. This
is a possible way of dealing with an obscure text. Note that NEB
translates the second part of 10.1, emending slightly: 'Though this
word was true, it cost him much toil to understand it; nevertheless
understanding came to him in the course of the vision.'

    This suggestion of Ginsberg links up with the contribution of
Collins to the question of the authorship of the Book of Daniel. He
notes that the word *maskilim*, skilful, is applied to the Hebrew pages
(including Daniel) in 1.4 and that in 11.35 and 12.3 there is mention
of the *maskilim*, wise teachers, of whom it is said that in the consummation 'those who are wise shall shine like the brightness of the
firmament; and those who turn many to righteousness, like the stars
for ever and ever.' Collins, following Ginsberg, argues that this
echoes Isa. 53.11 and possibly implies an interpretation of *yaskil* in
Isa. 52.13 as a noun, being the proper name of the servant, namely
'the wise one'. Incidentally, C. C. Torrey (*The Second Isaiah*, 1928,
p. 415) regarded this interpretation of *yaskil* as probable and sug-

gested that we need not blame the apocalyptist for taking a similar view. At all events Collins supposes that the *maskilim* or enlighteners, as he translates the word, formed a special group (to be distinguished from the *Ḥasidim*) to which he thinks the author of Daniel may have belonged. The *maskilim* would instruct the many (the ordinary Jews who in the crisis remained faithful) and they, with those who accepted their instruction and so became righteous, would inherit the kingdom, the *maskilim* themselves being raised to dwell with the angelic host. Whether this view does justice to all the evidence will come up in a different connection.

At this point it may be suggested that the above-mentioned examples of the *pesher* method of interpretation should be valued as possible illustrations of the way in which a Jewish seer believed that revelation was conveyed. In trying to understand what God was about to do in present history, he searched the scriptures for possible clues, on the assumption that the past was in some sense contemporaneous with the present. As C. H. Dodd demonstrates in his book *According to the Scriptures* (1952), the early Church adopted the *pesher* method in seeking to explain to itself the new thing which had happened in Christ. The modern biblical critic may frown upon this way of using Scripture and may rightly say that one must not ignore what passages of Scripture originally meant to those who wrote them. But we should not overlook the fact that Scripture was used in this strange way to express truth about the mysterious present in which men found themselves involved. We must at least recognize that they were employing the categories of thought available to them. That the problem of Scripture was a very real one to the author of Daniel is indicated very well by Delcor (p. 217) where he says: 'At all events it is the non-fulfilment of the prophecies which seems to have troubled our author.'

Reference should perhaps be made to the article entitled 'Das Buch Daniel, ein kanonisierter Pescher?' (*VTS* 15, 1966, pp. 278-94), by A. Szörényi, in which he suggests that the Book of Daniel represents a *pesher* from the Maccabaean period of an earlier prophetic book, which is actualized so as to make it apply to contemporary events. For example, he supposes that the four parts of the statue (ch. 2) and the four beasts (ch. 7) were originally contemporary parts of the Persian empire which the author of the *pesher* reinterprets as successive kingdoms culminating in the tyranny of Antiochus Epiphanes. Szörényi agrees with Jepsen ('Bemerkungen zum

Danielbuch', *VT* XI/4, 1961, pp. 386–91) and with Coppens and Dequeker (see below) in a radical handling of chapter 7, which the present author has found unconvincing. However that may be, it is certainly worth considering whether the recognition of the *pesher* method of interpretation may not furnish the key to some of the problems with which Scripture presents us.

It is with a certain degree of trepidation that one returns to reconsider the problems raised by chapter 7, which is rightly regarded as being at the heart of the Book of Daniel. The debate about these problems still goes on, and there seems to be something about the evidence contained in chapter 7 which makes it extremely difficult to reach agreement. Whatever view is adopted, there always seems to be something left over which does not quite fit in!

As regards the question of the unity of the chapter, there is something unsatisfactory about assuming the presence of interpolations in the text to account for the slightest illogicalities. Especially in an imaginative piece of literature like the one being considered it would be surprising not to find discrepancies. In a careful and friendly article published in 1963 J. Coppens (*Analecta Lovaniensia Biblica et Orientalia* XXVIII, Ser. iv. Fasc. 8) subjects the author's treatment of chapter 7 to a detailed treatment and criticism. In this he is developing previous studies by L. Dequeker and himself published in 1961 (*op. cit.* VII, Ser. iii. Fasc. 23). Without trying to answer every point, it may be permissible to draw attention to one of the main arguments. Coppens points out that in v. 26 the eleventh horn, namely Antiochus, is condemned, whereas one would suppose that the whole fourth beast had been destroyed already (see 7.11). The explanation surely is that the biblical writer is especially interested in the eleventh horn and singles it out in this rather awkward way for fuller treatment in the interpretation. The eleventh horn sums up, as it were, the iniquity of the whole fourth beast which is destroyed with it. The author's view of the substantial unity of chapter 7 is reinforced by the reply made by Collins (*op. cit.*, pp. 129–30) to both Noth and Dequeker, which concludes with these words: 'In short, despite the persistent efforts of critics to drive wedges between the sentences of Daniel 7, there is no reason to posit that this vision existed in any form before Maccabean times or that it includes any later editorial insertions.' Certainly the mixture of prose and verse (or rhythmical prose) in chapter 7 does not justify doubt as to its unity: such changes of style are not only found elsewhere in the Old

Testament but, as pointed out already, are characteristic of contemporary Hellenistic writing.

Of much greater importance for the understanding of chapter 7 is the problem of the mythological language used by the writer, and indeed of the mythological background of the later chapters. It may be thought that in his commentary the author has been unduly critical of those who have laid great emphasis on the probable links with Babylon and especially with Ugarit. The parallels in thought are numerous. More weight should perhaps have been allowed to the suggestion that the four monsters emerging from the great deep must have been felt to represent the powers of Chaos rising up against the Creator, the explicit identification of them with four historical kingdoms not exhausting the meaning of the language used. It is quite true, as Collins maintains, that allegory is not to be treated as merely equivalent to plain historical statement, but adds a dimension which should not be explained away by the unimaginative interpreter. It should also, however, be insisted that mythological language can detach itself from the original myths which produced it and can be used to symbolize a whole complex of ideas which is essentially different. To say this is not to depreciate the value of tracking mythological language back to its origins. Collins sees this and writes (*op. cit.*, p. 105): 'Like all apocalyptic writings, Daniel draws imagery from various sources. He does not simply take over an ancient myth, but he uses old images to construct his new vision. . . . Daniel uses the fragments of older mythology to build his own mythological world.' Admittedly it is extremely difficult, if not impossible, to determine exactly what associations of ideas imaginative language calls up, but there is surely wisdom in looking hard at the primary meaning, especially when, as in Daniel 7, the writer specifically indicates that meaning.

We must now give further consideration to the problem concerning 'the one like a son of man' or perhaps simply 'the one like a man'— as G. Vermes maintains in his Appendix to M. Black's *An Aramaic Approach to the Gospels and Acts*—and to the nature of the kingdom which he was to receive at the hands of the 'One old in years'.

The meaning of 'the one like a man' cannot be separated from the meaning of the holy ones of the Most High, who replace the mysterious figure in the interpretation. Let us look again at Noth's contention (following N. Schmidt, Procksch, Volz and others) that the holy ones of the Most High are angels and not to be identified with the faithful among the Jews or the Remnant. The argument is impressive and formulated with Noth's characteristic clarity of thought. Moreover we should not fail to put it to his credit that he frankly admits the negative instance in Ps. 34.10 which he regards as outweighed by the large number of positive instances. It should further be conceded that C. H. W. Brekelman's article (*Oudtestamentische Studiën*, Deel XIV, 1965, pp. 305ff.) does not completely dispose of Noth's view, even though it provides a considerable amount of contrary evidence. On the other hand, the contention that the clouds which, we are told, accompany the one like a man, as he is brought near to the One old in years, are evidence that some kind of theophany is intended and that this lends support to Noth's theory, is by no means conclusive. Delcor (*op. cit.*, p. 155) adduces a passage in Enoch 14.8 in which a son of man ascends from earth to heaven accompanied by a cloud. T. W. Manson (*BJRL* 32, 1950, pp. 174–5) takes the same view. He writes: 'The clouds are a means of transportation *from earth to heaven*. The Danielic Son of Man is not a member of the heavenly court; he appears before it. . . . It cannot be too strongly emphasised . . . that this figure is a symbol as the preceding monsters were. What the symbol stands for is made crystal clear in verses 18 and 27 of the same chapter. . . . Just as the beasts stood for the pagan empires, so the Son of Man stands for Israel or for the godly Remnant within Israel.' The qualification, which must be made, however—and Coppens (*op. cit.*, p. 92) recognizes that the author makes it on p. 96 of this commentary and, therefore, is so far in agreement with himself—is that the saints of the Most High, that is to say the faithful in Israel, are controlled by the heavenly powers or are thought of as having celestial warriors mingled with them. This is certainly the view expressed in *The War of the Sons of Light and the Sons of Darkness* (QM). It may be insisted that we are dealing essentially with a symbol like that of the four monsters, but that we should go a little beyond what Manson says. In both cases the historical reality, namely the pagan kingdoms and the faithful Jews, are linked with the supernatural. It is worth while to repeat for the sake of clarity what is said on p. 110 above: 'It seems clear that what the author intends is a contrast between the one like a son of man and the beasts which issued from the abyss. As the kingdoms that are to pass away are symbolized by supernatural beasts, it seems appropriate that the symbol of what is to replace the bestial kingdoms should be both human and supernatural.' Once again, on p. 112 it is argued 'that the symbol which interests us so much because of its subsequent history was understood by the writer as signifying the saints of the Most High, who are the faithful among the Jews, with emphasis upon the power of God which was to operate through them when they would represent his triumphant rule'.

It may be maintained, therefore, that it is right to recognize a certain ambivalence in the symbol of one like a (son of) man. Valuable as is the book by Collins with all its interesting suggestions, one may be justified in making reservations regarding his view that the author of Daniel believes that the decisive contest, military or judicial, is being fought out entirely on the angelic level. There is undoubtedly the thought of the encounter of Michael, the guardian angel of Israel (ch. 10) with the prince of the kingdom of Persia and later with the prince of the kingdom of Greece, but that all human participation on the level of history can be ignored is improbable. We cannot have the Olympians without the Trojans! The crucial struggle in the time of Antiochus Epiphanes took place on two levels. However critical the author of Daniel may have been of the Maccabees, there is something unsatisfactory about Collins's contention that he was merely interested in a small group of wise teachers, the *maskilim*, to which the author of Daniel supposedly belonged, and the many, the *rabbim*, whom they were instructing. This fails to take full account of Daniel 7.27, which states that 'the greatness of the kingdoms under the whole heaven is to be given to the people of the saints of the Most High' and that 'all dominions shall serve and obey them'.

The first four verses of chapter 12 are not at all clear about the nature of the end which the author of Daniel expects. It may be suggested that the obscurity of the passage is due to the fact that it represents a period of transition in thought. The author of Daniel has not completely made up his mind as to whether the kingdom is to be this-worldly or other-worldly and as to what is meant by resurrection. Collins can make out a case for his view that the wise teachers, the *maskilim*, are to be translated to the sphere of the angels, this, he believes, being the implication of the reference to the stars. It is difficult to believe, however, that the author of Daniel is indifferent to the future for Israel in this world. It is surely not in some heavenly sphere that all dominions are to serve and obey the people of the saints of the Most High. There is still a very clear trace of the old prophetic view of Israel's future dominance in the new state of affairs that God would bring about. In a transition period of thought it is not surprising that there should be inconsistencies and ambiguities.

To return once more to the problem of the identity of the one like a (son of) man in chapter 7, we may agree with Delcor (*op. cit.*, p. 155), that 'Here the Son of Man is a symbol, like the four beasts, and not a member of the celestial court, whatever that means'. It would also be mistaken, it may be suggested, to identify this symbol with any of the angelic figures who appear in the latter chapters, including Michael. It is true that they are described as having a human appearance. Yet they are certainly not symbols but individuals who appear for a specific purpose. The part of Lacocque's commentary in which he ventures upon these identifications may be adjudged the least satisfactory of a brilliant and most illuminating book. It seems probable that, if the author of Daniel had intended the identification of the mysterious figure of chapter 7 with Michael, he would have said so explicitly. To sum up what has been said, the symbolic figure he introduced is surely very much more suited than an individual angel such as Michael would have been to balance the four monsters symbolizing the heathen kingdoms. What the writer wanted to symbolize was that the faithful among the Jews were on the side of the angels or, better still, that the angels were on their side. Yet the present writer may be unreasonably cautious and even blind to what certain others find so obviously suggested by the text. In such a case as this it is only wise to speak under correction and certainly to avoid, if possible, misrepresentation of other people's opinions. Lacocque's views are presented with a wealth of scholarship which merits respect.

On the question of the bearing of any of the other apocalyptic books on the interpretation of the Book of Daniel a most significant contribution has recently been made by the highly authoritative work edited by J. T. Milik in 1976, entitled *The Books of Enoch: Aramaic Fragments of Qumran Cave 4*. It is not necessary to enter in detail into the evidence now made available. Suffice it to say that Milik has made it abundantly clear that, while parts of the Book of Enoch, in particular the so-called Book of the Watchers (Enoch 1–36), may be dated in the period which saw the appearance of Daniel, the Book of the Parables or Similitudes (Enoch 37–71), which is usually dated in the pre-Christian era, must be brought down into the Christian era. Using the argument from silence, Milik would judge that it comes from the third century AD or later (p. 74). Even if one is not prepared to draw such an extreme conclusion from the absence of explicit evidence for the existence of the Similitudes earlier, the view of those who insist that in the Book of Daniel we are only at the source of certain ideas, which were later to have a remarkable and significant development, must be maintained. At most one might say that in the Book of Daniel we are on the brink of new creative ideas, which would lead presently to the emergence of the expectation of a heavenly Messiah or of a supernatural Son of Man. Such a development was almost inevitable. To what extent early Christian thought was indebted to any of the later apocalyptic books need not be considered here.

It will be remembered that von der Osten-Sacken, in his monograph devoted to discussing the relation between prophecy and apocalyptic, lays great emphasis on the deterministic strain of thought which apocalyptic inherited from prophecy, from the prophetic conviction, that is to say, that Yahweh was the Lord of history and that he had determined an end for it which would most certainly come to pass. Von Rad distinguished prophecy and apocalyptic by asserting that, while the prophets recognized a *Heilsgeschichte*, which was moving towards a goal, apocalyptic as represented by the Book of Daniel showed no interest in the past history of Israel, but concentrated attention rather on the succession of heathen empires, namely Babylon to Greece, regarded possibly, on the principle of *pars pro toto*, as representing the whole of history, and thought of it as about to be broken off by the predetermined act of God. Von Rad, as we saw, drew attention also to the belief that natural events were likewise determined, and illustrated this from the Book of Ecclesiastes. Hebrew thinkers, however, do not seem to have been over-consistent in holding deterministic beliefs. Within a framework of history, in which events were moving towards an end determined by God, individual men were not thought of as automata acting without the exercise of free-will. In particular, the possibility of repentance on the part of men is illustrated by the Book of Jonah. Lacocque, in his commentary (pp. 69–70), allows for this and makes the penetrating remark: 'In the Scriptures liberty is not a static notion. Man *becomes* free.' That this is so is not underlined in the Book of Daniel, but the stories in chapters 1–6 show how much was thought to depend on the decisive acts of free men confronted by tyranny. Moreover, while, on the one hand, Nebuchadnezzar is told by Daniel that the end of the heathen kingdoms is predetermined,

since the dream which the king had had was certain and its interpretation sure, on the other hand, in 4.24 Nebuchadnezzar is called
upon to repent, so that at least there may be a lengthening of his
tranquillity. Moreover, in chapter 5, Belshazzar is told by Daniel
that he ought to have humbled his heart like his father and so presumably avoided the doom which Daniel must now announce. It is
important to notice how this paradox of free-will and determinism
emerges in biblical thought, not in consequence of philosophical
speculation but in the strenuous conflicts of life. No solution to the
problem is dictated to men that they must simply accept. And so, as
we seek to enter into the experience of the men who gave us the
Bible and to think with them, we may come to hear the word addressed to us: '*Tua res agitur*'—or, in modern phrase, 'This means
you!'

Klaus Koch, in his challenging book *The Rediscovery of Apocalyptic*,
speaks of the universalism which appears in apocalyptic. It is perfectly true that in apocalyptic and in particular in the Book of
Daniel we get something which can be called a philosophy of history.
Two things, however, should be said about this. In the Old Testament there is a universalist strain going right back to the Yahwist
and on to II Isaiah, even though the thought that God might have a
purpose of good for mankind becomes submerged at times. In the
Book of Daniel, however, on Collins's interpretation of the teaching
of the book, the kingdom which God will bring in is to be strictly
limited. What he apparently overlooks is that in 7.14 and 27 a place
is to be found for all peoples, nations and languages. All dominions
are to serve and obey the people of the saints of the Most High.
This surely is in line with certain prophetic expectations and should
be taken into account when we are trying to determine the outlook
of the author of Daniel. The nations certainly are to be subordinate
to faithful Israel, but they are not ignored. As we study the Book of
Daniel in its context in the Hellenistic world, we cannot help regret-
ting that what was evil and corrupt in the Hellenism with which the
Jews were confronted, and with which they had to come to terms,
prevented what might have been a creative synthesis between
Judaism at its best and Hellenism at its best, a synthesis which
eventually was brought about by Christianity and from which
Rabbinic Judaism excluded itself. Good, however, can often be preserved only by extreme measures, as, for example, in the impasse
between Luther and Erasmus. In the Book of Daniel we see reflected

the nobility of the Jew standing for his principles *contra mundum*, and that was how it had to be, if the treasure of Israel's life and belief was to be preserved. But something was lost, and this too we should remember, as we study this precious part of the Old Testament.

Bickermann, in his book *Der Gott der Makkabäer*, has put in a plea for Antiochus Epiphanes and argued that less than justice has been done to him, since the main blame should be laid at the door of the Hellenizers, the Jews who wished to assimilate to the way of the wider world. The evidence Bickermann adduces should certainly be taken into consideration, but perhaps he protests a little too much; there must have been something to account for the abhorrence with which the author of Daniel regards the Seleucid monarch. Bickermann, however, did a real service in reminding us that the Book of Daniel provides us with one perspective in which to view the great crisis in Israel's history, but not the only one.

One more topic has been reserved for the end of this Supplement, namely the question of the prayer in chapter 9. At the time when this commentary was written the authenticity of the prayer was defended and was welcomed as giving a clue to the piety of those Jews who remained faithful in the crisis of the struggle against Hellenism. It was gratifying to find that Plöger too accepted the authenticity of the prayer, as indeed Jeffery and Heaton had done earlier. Support came too from B. W. Jones in America ('The Prayer in Daniel IX', *VT* XVIII/4, 1968, pp. 488–93), who suggested that the author of Daniel intended to imply that the Deuteronomistic outlook of Daniel's prayer was opposed by Gabriel's announcement of the irrevocable end; repentance was irrelevant. Collins rejects the prayer on the ground that it is out of character. Gabriel certainly does not rebuke Daniel for praying as he is represented as doing. One should be open to conviction, but it may simply be asked whether the author of Daniel is not being forced into too rigid a consistency. The prayer is by no means a mere cento of liturgical phrases, but it does represent a familiar liturgical tradition, which the author may well have felt to be appropriate in the mouth of the exile in Babylon, who in chapter 6 is depicted as a man of prayer. This was how a pious Jew would pray in the sixth century BC or in the second. Our author may well have felt that Daniel, in praying thus, was representative of an Israel which might hope to survive the cataclysm which he believed was coming on the earth. The *maskilim* were those who were turning the many to righteousness, and their teaching would surely have included instruction in the way of repentance. The end, he believed, was upon them, but men had to prepare to meet the end. It may have been the author's prayer put into Daniel's mouth. There is more in the book than the 'gospel' of determinism. Surely in chapters 3 and 6 the emphasis is on loyalty to God and on the way of life that Israel, even Israel in exile, stood for in the world. Israel is being reminded of the unchangeable purpose of God, but also of what it was itself committed to, and that is reflected, not only in Daniel's prayer, but perhaps most appropriately there.